GLUCK

Diana Souhami is the author of many widely acclaimed books, including *Gluck: Her Biography, Gertrude & Alice, Mrs Keppel and her Daughter, The Trials of Radclyffe Hall* (short-listed for the James Tait Black Prize for Biography), and, most recently, *Selkirk's Island*.

Also by Diana Souhami

Selkirk's Island
Gertrude and Alice (*Phoenix Press*)
Greta and Cecil (*Phoenix Press*)
Mrs Keppel and her Daughter
The Trials of Radclyffe Hall

GLUCK

1895–1978

Her Biography

Diana Souhami

PHOENIX
PRESS

5 UPPER SAINT MARTIN'S LANE
LONDON WC2H 9EA

A PHOENIX PAPERBACK

First published in Great Britain
by Unwin Hyman Ltd in 1988
First published in paperback by Pandora Press in 1989
Revised hardback edition first published by Weidenfeld & Nicolson in 2000
This paperback edition published in 2001
by Phoenix Press,
a division of The Orion Publishing Group Ltd,
Orion House, 5 Upper St Martin's Lane,
London WC2H 9EA

Jacket design © Peter Campbell

Copyright © 1988 by Diana Souhami

A CIP catalogue record for this book is available
from the British Library.

Printed and bound in Great Britain by
Butler & Tanner Ltd, Frome and London

ISBN 1 84212 196 0

CONTENTS

'I really do want to do some good and lovely work before I die'

Gluck in a letter to Nesta Obermer, 1936.

ACKNOWLEDGEMENTS

The kindness and assistance of many people made this biography possible. I acknowledge my gratitude and indebtedness to them, though I am responsible for all opinions expressed.

My special thanks go to Gluck's nephew, Roy Gluckstein. I would not have got far without his help. He allowed me to have sight of Gluck's manuscripts and other family papers and responded to my requests with fairness and promptness. His mother Lady Gluckstein, his brother David, and sister Jean Jaffa, provided me with candid and humorous accounts of Gluck. Geoffrey Salmon told me the story of the family's history and the rise in the fortunes of J. Lyons & Co., the family business. Julia Samson, Gluck's cousin, gave me her affectionate insights into Gluck's character.

Gluck had a long and distinguished association with The Fine Art Society in London and I am particularly grateful to the Society's directors, Tony Carroll and Andrew McIntosh Patrick. They did all they could to make this book a success. They commented on the manuscript, gave permission to reproduce photographs of her paintings, opened their records to me and supplied me with many useful contacts.

From Hermia Priestley, a close friend of Gluck's since the 1940s, I gained a special understanding of Gluck and her aspirations. Equally memorable and useful were my meetings with Valerie Spry. She vividly evoked London of the 1930s and Gluck's social milieu at that time. Keith Lichtenstein, who collected Gluck's paintings and believed in her talent when the world had forgotten her, helped me to understand her worth as a painter. Susan Loppert, who had planned to write a biography of Gluck in 1974, generously made her notes available to me. David Tonkinson and Vernon Blackburn, Gluck's accountants and *hommes d'affaires*, gave me their memories of Gluck and access to files of correspondence relating to her campaign to improve the quality of artists' materials. Christine Leback Sitwell allowed me sight of the first draft of her thesis, now published, which she wrote on this campaign.

I am indebted, too, to June and Raul Casares and to Dr Ivan Heald, who supplied me with information about the professional achievements and way of life of the sisters Nora and Edith Shackleton Heald; to Nesta Macdonald who loaned me letters, and cuttings from the *Evening Standard* and the *Sunday Express* of Edith Shackleton's leading articles in the 1920s; to David Yorke for his frank assessment of Gluck's psychological make-up; to those who worked for Gluck at the Chantry House and told me much about her later life: Clare Griffin, her personal assistant, Mr Lovett the gardener, Winifred Vye, the housekeeper and Mrs Guy who did the housework.

I am most grateful, also, for the help and information given to me by Chloë Blackburn, Dr Richard Boger, Meggie Bowman, the Duke and Dowager Duchess of Buccleuch, Betsan Coates, Georgina Cookson, William Davenport, Liz Drury, Peter Giffard, Robert Harris, Lady Lancaster, Marjorie-Anne Lowenstein, Julia Lowenthal, Diana Menuhin, Ralph Merton, George Morton, Gilbert Odd, Tom Parrington, Anne Pemberton, Dr and Mrs Konrad Rodan, Lt-Col. Nelson Sawyer, Edward Staysack, Marjorie Watts and Adrianne Whitney.

My thanks, too, to Jane Hawksley and to Tessa Sayle, to Peter Campbell for designing the book and for his comments on the manuscript, to Philippa Brewster, to Rebecca Wilson and Catherine Hill at Weidenfeld & Nicolson, and to Georgina Capel and Robert Caskie at Simpson Fox Associates. Acknowledgement is due to the Houghton Library, Harvard, who own the letters of W. B. Yeats to Edith Shackleton Heald paraphrased on pages 216 and 217; to the Huntingdon Library, California, for the photograph on page 216 and to the Hulton Picture Library for the photograph on page 233.

ONE

'GLUCK: NO
PREFIX,
NO QUOTES'

On the backs of photographic prints of her paintings, sent out for publicity purposes, she always wrote in her elegant handwriting: 'Please return in good condition to Gluck, no prefix, suffix, or quotes.' She pronounced her chosen name with a short vowel sound to rhyme with, say, cluck, or duck. She was born Hannah Gluckstein in 1895, into the family that founded the J. Lyons & Co. catering empire, but seldom wanted her wealthy family connections or hated patronymic known.

To Nesta Obermer, her blonde alter ego in 'Medallion', a painting of their merged profiles, she was 'Darling Tim', or 'My bestest darling Timothy Alf', or 'My Black Brat'. Romaine Brooks, twenty years her senior, did a portrait of her in 1924 called 'Peter – a Young English Girl'. To one at least of her admirers she was 'Dearest Rabbitskinsnootchbunsnoo'. To Edith Shackleton Heald, the journalist with whom she lived for close on forty years, she was 'Dearest Grub'. To her family she was 'Hig'. To her servants and the tradespeople she was Miss Gluck and to the art world and in her heart she was simply Gluck.

The reason she gave for choosing to be known by this austere monosyllable was that the paintings mattered, not the sex of the painter. She said she thought it sensible to follow the example of artists like Whistler and use a symbol by way of identification. More fundamentally, she had no inclination to conform to society's expectations of womanly behaviour and she wanted to sever herself, but not entirely, from her family.

Gluck she was, and could and did become high-handed and litigious in so being. Many were confused and bewildered as to how to address her with courtesy. She had an irritated exchange with her bank when an unwitting clerk fed her name into the computer as Miss H. Gluck. A graphic designer, faced with the uncomfortable visual dilemma of trying to make GLUCK look comprehensible on the letterhead of stationery for an art society which featured her, along with the Bishop of Chichester and Duncan Grant as its Vice Presidents, stuck in an ameliorating Miss. Gluck resigned and insisted on the inking out of her name. When Weidenfeld & Nicolson published a minor novel which featured an eccentric fictional vagabond called Glück with an umlaut, who lived in a lodging house and painted pictures of defunct clocks and bus tickets, they found themselves besieged with solicitor's letters.[1] Gluck regarded any encroachment on her chosen name as trespass liable for prosecution.

Throughout her adult life she dressed in men's clothes, pulled the wine corks, and held the door for true ladies to pass first. An acquaintance, seeing her dining alone, remarked that she looked like the ninth Earl, a description which she liked. She had a last for her shoes at John Lobb's the Royal bootmakers, got her shirts from Jermyn Street, had her hair cut at Truefitt gentlemen's hairdressers in Old Bond Street, and blew her nose on large linen handkerchiefs monogrammed with a G. In the early decades of this century, when men alone wore the trousers, her appearance made heads turn. Her father, a conservative and conventional man, was utterly dismayed by her 'outré clobber', her mother referred to a 'kink in the brain' which she hoped would pass, and both were uneasy at going to the theatre in 1918 with Gluck wearing a wide Homburg hat and long blue coat, her hair cut short and a dagger hanging at her belt.

In 1916 when Gluck was breaking from her family home and staying with the Newlyn School of painters in Lamorna, Cornwall, Alfred Munnings sketched her smoking her pipe and dressed as a gypsy. The society photographer E. O. Hoppé, who encouraged her to stage her first exhibition in 1924, featured a series of photographs of her, along with Mussolini, Ellen Terry and Bernard Shaw, in *The Royal Magazine* in December 1926:

I am often asked what I see in the face of my sitters. My answer is: 'I see what I

seek – beauty.' Gluck's facial contour indicates the qualities expressed in her
paintings, combining force and decision with the sensitiveness of the visionary.
To look at her face is to understand both her success as an artist and the fact that
she dresses as a man. Originality, determination, strength of character and
artistic insight are expressed in every line.

He seemed to imply that such qualities are quintessentially masculine. And
Gluck regarded peacefulness and mystery as female attributes and strength and
genius as male.

In company her appearance and manner were riveting. She was authoritative,
had a quality of stillness, a clear voice and no social embarrassment. She liked
the discomfort her cross-dressing caused and enjoyed recounting examples of it,
like the occasion in the 1930s when she arrived with a theatre party at the
Trocadero Restaurant, owned by J. Lyons & Co., to be told no table was free.
She pulled rank and gave her family name. ' 'Ere,' the doorman said, ' 'e say's
she's Miss Gluckstein.' Influenced by Constance Spry, with whom she had a
close relationship from 1932–6, she for a time turned androgyny into high
fashion. Constance took her to the couturiers Elsa Schiaparelli, Victor Stiebel
and Madame Karinska in Paris. They dressed her in pleated culottes, long velvet
tunics and Edwardian suits. On holidays with Constance in Tunisia Gluck
dressed in a burnous with a geranium behind her ear. In later years, when
disappointed in love and at odds with the world, she lost her sartorial flair,
bought her pyjamas and jumpers at Marks & Spencer and wore a duffel coat.
She was always fastidious though. If she found a crease in her laundered linen
painting-smock she sent it back to the kitchen for a maid to iron again.

She did several self-portraits, all of them mannish. There was a jaunty and
defiant one in beret and braces – stolen in 1981 – and another, now in the
National Portrait Gallery, which shows her as arrogant and disdainful. She
painted it when suffering acutely from the tribulations of love. A couple of
others she destroyed when depressed about her life.

She dressed as she did not simply to make her sexual orientation public,
though that of course she achieved. By her appearance she set herself apart from
society, alone with what she called the 'ghost' of her artistic ambition. And at a
stroke she distanced herself from her family's expectations, which were that she
should be educated and cultured but pledged to hearth and home. They would
have liked her to marry well, which meant a man from a similar Jewish
background to hers – preferably one of her cousins – and to live, as wife and
mother, a normal, happy life. By her 'outré clobber' Gluck said 'no' to all that,

for who in his right mind would court a woman in a man's suit? Her rebelliousness cut her father to the quick and he thought it a pose. But however provocative her behaviour there was no way he would cease to provide for her, his concept of family loyalty and obligation was too strong.

Courtesy of her private income, she lived in style with staff – a housekeeper, cook and maids – to look after her. She always kept a studio in Cornwall. In the 1920s and 30s she lived in Bolton House, a large Georgian house in Hampstead village. After the war she settled in Sussex in the Chantry House, Steyning, with Edith Shackleton Heald, journalist, essayist and lover of the poet W. B. Yeats in his twilight years. Both residences had elegantly designed detached studios.

In her painting, as in her name, appearance and manner of life, Gluck was unique. She was scornful of art school teaching and of trends and fashions in art, but appreciative of all talent she thought true. 'I cannot' she wrote, 'imagine enjoying life at all unless one's responses were catholic, embracing the first primitives of all races to the latest genuinely spiritually motivated creation.'[2] She resolved early on to show her work only in solo exhibitions, for she felt unallied to any movement, group or school. 'It used to annoy me when I was younger to be told continually how "original" I was. What is there so original in just being oneself and speaking one's mind?'[3]

The 'heart' of her paintings is an intense and private response to her subject. Though they seem like straightforward versions of reality they have a strong inward meaning. In what she called her Credo she referred to the true artist as

. . . a conduit open to any unexpected experience, a lightning conductor. . . . The Vision dictates everything in the flash of reception. The entire composition is received as a whole in scale and in content. . . . The Vision once received remains a tyrant. The process of distillation is arduous, the temptations numerous and the discipline needed sometimes hard to endure . . .[4]

Gluck held five exhibitions of her work: in 1924, 1926, 1932, 1937 and then, after a gap of thirty-six years, in 1973. All of them were met with excitement and praise. 'The private view to see the "Diverse Paintings" by Gluck', wrote *The Star Man's Diary*, 3 November 1932, in a review typical of all she received:

attracted a crowd of celebrities all day. One need not be surprised, for Gluck, as this Eton-cropped artist, who is a delightful law unto herself, insists on being called, is a remarkable genius and her pictures and their setting are arresting in the extreme.

Queen Mary, Lady Mount Temple – stepmother to Edwina, who married Lord

Mountbatten, Sir Francis Oppenheimer the owner of South African diamond mines, Cecil Beaton, Syrie Maugham and the theatre impresario C. B. Cochran were among the famous and rich who called at 'The Gluck Room' of The Fine Art Society to see her paintings and acquire them for their walls.

At the time of the Second World War and at the height of her career she faded from sight. A conflation of troubles, the acutest of which was disappointment in love, made her wilt as a person and painter. But though buried she was not dead. When nearing eighty she unearthed herself and held a final exhibition which generated as much buzz and enthusiasm as when she had been young. 'What is the link?' she asked in a letter to The Fine Art Society (14 August 1976) two years before she died. 'By what content would one recognise a picture was mine? I, of course, am the last person to be able to answer such a question. So? It will be too late for me when posterity decides.'

Gluck regarded herself as an essentially British painter and chose subjects intrinsic to her life: bleached, spare, light-filled landscapes done when she was in Cornwall, formal flower groups when with Constance Spry, genre pieces of events of the day, portraits of her family, friends and lovers and of the elegant society women with whom she socialized. She used the visual vocabulary of the decades through which she lived in an unselfconscious and personal way: like the 'Odeon' style of her painting, done in the twenties, of 'The Three Nifty Nats' doing a song and dance routine; or the thirties craze for all-white interiors reflected in her flower paintings 'Chromatic' and 'Lilies'. Her paintings linked to her inner feelings and to events, people and places in her life. In a sense she painted her life, from which her work was indivisible. But she was also rooted to the spirit of her time and in the best of her work to all time.

She had exacting standards of form and technique. Her musicality – she wavered between singing or painting as a career – is reflected in her strong visual sense of harmony and composition. She was literary which shows in her sense of implication of meaning – of more than meets the eye. And she was a perfectionist who took extraordinary care in matching colour and texture; she would spend days painting the underside of a petal of a flower with a brush with one or two hairs in it, until she got it right.

Her portraits of women are among her best work. The national art galleries house an abundance of reclining nudes but not many portraits of women by women. Gluck's women wear their hats, jewellery and clothes, to show their self-assurance, assertiveness, status and style. Her portrait of Molly Mount Temple, at one of whose glittering party weekends at Broadlands Gluck met the love of her life, is a study in arrogance and disdain: arms akimbo, wearing clothes by

Schiaparelli, her hat and aquamarines badges of status and power, her lips and nails bright red and an M for Molly and Mount Temple engraved on the buckle of her belt.

In the 1920s when the world was dancing mad, when every restaurant in town had a floorshow and C. B. Cochran's reviews were a showcase for theatrical talent, Gluck went again and again to the London Pavilion, advertised as 'The Centre of the World', to paint scenes from the most popular of his shows, *On with the Dance*. In the thirties, much influenced by Constance Spry, she painted formal arrangements of flowers in ornate vases. Fashionable interior designers, Oliver Hill, Syrie Maugham, Norman Wilkinson, hung her paintings in rooms they designed. In the war years Gluck captured the spirit of the home front in pictures of soldiers playing snooker, or the firewarden's office at one in the morning. In her last years, when she was beached, lost and lonely, that was what her painting showed: a lone bird flying into the sunset, waves washing in on a deserted shore, an iridescent fish head washed up by the tide.

Like Mondrian she tried to see paintings as part of an architectural setting. She designed and patented a frame which bears her name. It consisted of three symmetrically-stepped panels painted the same colour as the wall on which it was hung, or covered in the same paper. The effect was to incorporate the picture into the wall. She patented it in 1932 and used it in all subsequent exhibitions to create what became known as 'The Gluck Room'.

Her private income meant she was not driven to earn her living from work. She painted only what she chose. She disliked commercialism, easy production and the second-rate in art: 'I made a vow that I would never prostitute my work and I never have. . . . Never, never, have I attempted to earn my bread at the cost of my work.'[5] She had, too, grand ideas of Time and Vision and her own genius. She was capable of spending three years on a picture then destroying it if she felt it to be no good:

Your thoughts span the heavens and the earth, why should your achievements be limited to the days. Think of each day as a part of Time and the 'waste' of this day will have no more meaning for you. You cannot waste time unless what you do is unworthy of your spirit. How surely will your tortoise run to someone else's hare.[6]

She admitted to a sense of timelessness which in later life cost her dear:

As life went on I spent it prodigally, unwisely. The sense of timelessness deceived me into thinking my time was limitless for creation. Only within the

*last tormented years have I seen how ambivalent this sense of timelessness has
been. It gave eternal qualities to my work, perhaps, but it also limited its
output.*[7]

When young she felt her life was charmed. Aged forty-one she fell in love and
thought it would last for ever. In essence she was a romantic optimist and when
Love 'to all Eternity' failed her, as in the 1940s Love did because it had no
pragmatic base, she locked into sorrow with the tenacity she brought to work or
pleasure. The failure of love crippled her self-regard, made her deny herself the
consolation of work and behave in a destructive way toward those who sought to
help her.

Obsession was her Aristotelian fatal flaw of character. At its best it supported
her perfectionism – an absolute dedication and commitment to each of her
paintings. At its most wasteful it caused her to 'campaign' on issues which she
always regarded as important, but which consumed her time, energy and focus.

The great battle which kept her from her easel, was over the quality of artists'
materials. It became known as her 'paint war'. She fought it with the paint
manufacturers, the British Standards Institution and, it seemed, the world at
large, for more than a decade – from 1953 to 1967. It began because she ran into
difficulties when painting. Her materials started to behave unpredictably:

*All industrially made oil paints throughout the world exhibit a greasy turbidity
which I have named 'the suede effect' manifested by a change of tone and colour
according to the direction taken by the brush. This disgusting effect is caused by
pigments being too finely ground, linseed oil being hot pressed instead of cold
pressed, as also by lead soaps and other deleterious additives.*[8]

She eventually got the British Standards Institution to formulate a standard
for artists' oils which provided a recognized specification, and she got the
manufacturers, Rowneys, to produce specialist paints, made with hand-ground
pigments and cold-pressed linseed oil that were perfect for her. But she wasted
years of creative time in her paint war. She fought it because she wanted her
work to last for ever; yet she seemed unconscious of the irony that not to
produce paintings is the surest way to artistic oblivion.

Gluck's life divided into three parts. The first part, her rebellious years, was up
until 1936. During that period she broke from her family, lived first with an art
student called Craig, then a journalist, Sybil Cookson; divided her time between
Cornwall and London and produced the work for her four major exhibitions. In

1936 she fell in love and with the intention of starting life afresh destroyed references to her past – diaries, letters and photos. So her life up to the age of forty is chronicled more through her paintings than her words. A friend called De La Condamine (Robert Farquhason) visited her studio in 1936 on one of her days of burning. Watching,

he said very solemnly 'You know why, don't you?' and I said 'Oh yes, of course I do.' He gave me a beady look and said, 'the reason is a sexual one.' I said, 'I suppose so, the reason for creation is the same as for destruction.' I like him despite the 'camp' of it all'.[9]

Into the flames went details of her attachments to and relationships with Craig, Sybil Cookson, Constance Spry. She burned several portraits of women whom she wanted to forget and most references to her childhood. 'Anything even vaguely smelling of the past stinks in my nostrils', she told her new, her true love.

After 1936 her thoughts, feelings and daily affairs are more fully recorded. The years when she was consumed by Love, the 'YouWe' years, from 1936 until 1945, form the second part of her life. For the sake of Love she let go of her own career.

The last period of her life was from 1945 until her death in 1978. She lived in the Chantry House, Steyning, with the journalist Edith Shackleton Heald, painted in a sporadic way, suffered from frustration about her work and her life – and made others suffer too – fought her grand campaign against the paint manufacturers and then mercifully pushed her way back to the limelight for one last bow when she was seventy-eight: 'This will after all be my last one-man show and I would like to go out with a bang!'[10]

In each phase a woman was central to her life. In the first it was her mother, whom she called 'The Meteor', a woman of talent, formidable energy, great kindness, moral strength and unsettling personality. 'Everything the Meteor touches', Gluck said of her, 'always seems to lead to confusion – Even her kind acts. That's what it is to have a disturbed and unbalanced aura or base – It communicates itself to everything.'[11] In the second part it was Nesta Obermer, glittering, rich, adored by society and as elusive as the elegant women Gluck sought to capture in paint. And in the third it was Edith Shackleton Heald, clever, trustworthy, fairminded and loyal, who by her virtues seemed to create more problems for Gluck than she solved. Nor were the three women particularly separate in Gluck's psyche. They merged, with other women, more peripheral to her life, in some unresolved desire for love and home.

Gluck wanted to be remembered for her paintings, the investigation she instigated into the quality of artists' materials and the setting of a British Standard for oil pigments, and the stepped frame she designed. She also wanted her life remembered, problematic though it was. She was, more than most, full of paradoxes and contradictions. 'You couldn't', said Winifred Vye, her housekeeper in old age, 'say anything absolutely bad about her because then she'd confound you and be nice. ... She was just extremely difficult to live with.'

She was proud, authoritative, obsessive and egotistical, yet dependent in every domestic sense and humble about her work. She was a romantic and yet spent years in an arid campaign about the quality of paint. She felt herself to be a visionary painter and yet some of the best of her work was done to commission for the walls of the sophisticated and rich. She claimed that she ran away from her family, but she kept half their name and was always dependent on them financially. She was a rebel, and a misfit, but staunchly patriotic, politically conservative and good friends with several high court judges including the Master of the Rolls. She was a Jew but wanted to paint the crucifixion of Christ. She was a woman but she dressed as a man. She would call the kitchen staff to account if the housekeeping was a halfpenny out, then give a mere acquaintance £500 to buy a new typewriter. She wanted for nothing in a material sense, and yet allowed herself to be consumed by material concerns. She was unafraid of death and yet hypochondriacal.

Mercurial, maddening, conspicuous and rebellious, she inspired great love and profound dislike. Perhaps what she most feared was indifference. Her dedication to work was total, even through her fallow years. Her severance from gender, family and religion, her resistance to influence from any particular artist or school of painting, her refusal to exhibit her work except in 'one-man' shows were all ways of protecting her artistic integrity. She desired to earn her death through the quality of her work: 'I do want to reach that haven having a prize in my hand.... Something worthy of the trust that was reposed in me when I was sent out ...'[12] In reaching her destination with her paintings as her prize, she took a circuitous path – unmapped, thorny and entirely her own.

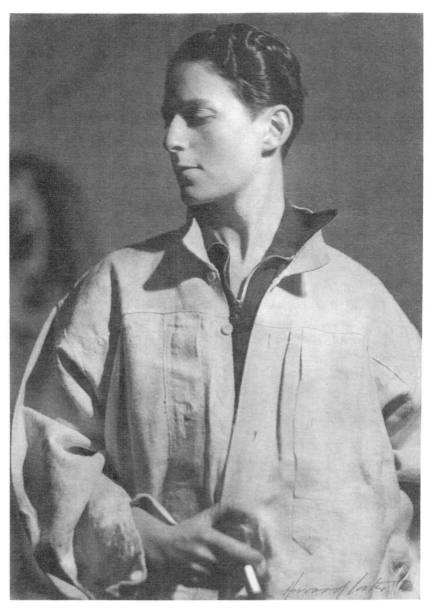

Photograph of Gluck by Howard Coster, 'Photographer of Men', *circa* 1924

PART ONE
REBELLION
1895–1936

TWO

'THE FAMILY'

No family could have been less attuned to rebellious displays of individualism than the Glucksteins. Patriarchal, dynastic, conformist, insular and proud, they took as their family motto the epigram 'L'Union Fait La Force' and featured in their family crest, as a metaphor for unity, a bundle of sticks – taken from a cautionary tract by Aesop on the perils of abandoning the group:

A husbandman who had a quarrelsome family, after having tried in vain to reconcile them by words, thought he might more readily prevail by example. So he called his sons and bade them lay a bundle of sticks before him. Then having tied them up into a fagot, he told the lads, one after another, to take it up and break it. They all tried, but tried in vain. Then untying the fagot, he gave them sticks to break one by one. This they did with the greatest ease. Then said the father: 'Thus, my sons, as long as you remain united, you are a match for all your enemies; but differ and separate and you are undone.'

The Gluckstein family strength was based on shared business and financial interests and a profound belief in the family ideal. They clawed their way up from the East End of London by enterprise and hard work. They began in the tobacco trade and then, in the partnership of Salmon & Gluckstein, created J. Lyons & Company – the vast complex of teashops, Corner House restaurants, the Trocadero in Piccadilly Circus, 'The Strand', 'Regent Palace' and 'Cumberland' hotels and then later the huge food manufacturing and distributing business – Lyons ice-cream, cup-cakes and the rest. They married their cousins and second cousins the Salmons, the Josephs, the Abrahams, out of trust, loyalty and business acumen and because they hardly knew anyone else. They talked of The Family in its extended sense with a big F, the family in its nuclear sense with a little f and of the 'outside world', which was viewed with suspicion. Male members of The Family met daily in business, socially all dined together, worshipped together, played bridge, attended each other's bar mitzvahs, weddings and funerals. They lived in the same neighbourhood, often in the same street and even, in Canfield Gardens in West Hampstead, in adjacent houses with inter-connecting doors. They named sons and daughters in honour of their grandparents, which led to a bewildering plethora of Isidores, Montagues, Samuels, Josephs, Hannahs and Helenas.

From the 1880s on, they pooled their money in an entity they called The Fund, administered for the benefit of all The Family. It paid for everything houses, health-care, education, holidays, carriages and cars. Wives and brothers-in-law put in their capital too. No one who participated in The Fund kept private wealth. Individual family members owned little but had all that money can buy. When they, their sons or unmarried daughters died, their capital and houses reverted to The Fund.

Underpinning this orderly distribution of wealth was a stern moral code. Hard work, educational achievement, parental respect, obedience, family loyalty and above all conformity to the precepts laid down by their elders and learned in childhood – those were the guiding lights. Their civic, military and academic honours, and ever-growing family trees, were recorded in bound volumes and sent to each household. They earned knighthoods, CBEs, OBEs, MBEs, mayoralties and medals. They were QCs, MPs and Councillors. There was no gambling, drinking or philandering. Pleasure was to be found in family affairs, in the honourable wooing of a suitable partner, usually a cousin, or a family week in the Majestic Hotel Vichy, or the Metropole Brighton, or in a game of bridge. There was no place for gender bending, or the quest for self-expression, or doomed and startling romantic love, or the company of raffish artists, or the wearing of outlandish clothes. Such turbulent desires for self-expression, if felt, were no doubt promptly repressed.

The pioneer of The Family fortunes was Gluck's grandfather, Samuel Gluckstein. Born in Rheinberg, Prussia, he came to England when he was nineteen in 1840 and lodged with his aunt in Whitechapel in the East End, the ghetto for Jewish immigrants for a hundred years. He married her daughter, his cousin – Hannah Joseph, who had nursed him through a bad illness. She was illiterate and signed her marriage certificate with a mark. In the manner of the time children were born with predictable frequency. They had twelve of whom ten survived.

To provide for them all he worked first as a cigar salesman then as a cigar manufacturer. When machine-made cigarettes became popular, he set up in partnership with his brother and cousin as general tobacconists. The partnership did not last. He was reputed to be 'violent and overbearing'. There were rows and, when he wished to withdraw the £2000 capital he claimed to have invested in the business, these rows escalated into a Chancery Division suit for the dissolution of the partnership. The lawsuit lasted a year, involved sixty-nine sworn affidavits, lacerated family unity, broke his health and took them all to the brink of bankruptcy. The partnership was dissolved in 1870 and all the stock – tons of tobacco, cigars, utensils and effects – sold by auction and the assets divided between them.

Though ill (he died three years later in 1873), he started up in the tobacco business once more, this time in partnership with his trusted son-in-law, Barnett Salmon, and with three of his sons, Isidore, Montague and Gluck's father, Joseph. They traded under the name of Salmon & Gluckstein. The old man died without seeing the rise in the family fortunes. His sons, aged twenty-two, nineteen and seventeen at the time of his death, built the firm he had founded into an Empire.

They had seen the internecine effect of family feuds and resolved to avoid them. Which was why they started The Fund. It was not intended primarily as a recipe for wealth, though that was what it became. It was a contract of mutual support, trust and interdependency. 'L'Union Fait La Force'; 'Differ and separate and you are undone.' It was a declaration of responsibility. No member of The Family need struggle alone. In a microcosm they created a kind of socialist economy, a pooling of assets and a distribution of benefits according to what was deemed to be need. But there was nothing widely egalitarian about it. The tie was blood. Membership was through blood, thicker than water or anything else.

The Fund, which continues in modified form to this day, defied legal definition. It was not a company, not a partnership, or a trust. Rather it was a contractual understanding, based on precedent and what was accepted as fair. Its precepts were not written down in a Constitution, but members took weekly drawings and shares of the profits according to a scale based on age, responsibilities, number of children. Unused drawings went back to The Fund and were divided up between the various capital accounts. Most of life's contingencies were accounted for in a detailed way: widows were to have the same standard of living as provided by their husbands, boys who won scholarships to Oxford or Cambridge (and only those universities) would have their studies financed. No clause was included for daughters who ran away with their lesbian lovers to paint, smoke pipes and wear men's clothes.

Membership of The Fund was voluntary, but few in The Family contracted out, for the advantages were many. And only those in it could become directors of the business. Lineage dictated status when members came to appoint directors, or the Steward of the Fund – the key administrator. Eldest sons had the highest status. Wives and daughters belonged to a world elsewhere. They did no paid work, nor was business discussed in front of them. In the early days, when the going was hard, they rolled cigars in Whitechapel. With wealth, they were expected to supervise their children's education and the running of the household, play bridge, do a little charitable work, wear elegant clothes and support their husbands at appropriate functions. None of which was very different from middle-class practice of the time.

What was different was the bonding effect of The Fund. The actress Yvonne Mitchell was born a Joseph and so descended from Samuel Gluckstein's wife Hannah. Like Gluck she shed the family name, made a bid for individual expression and took a career. She wrote a *roman-à-clef*, *The Family*, satirical, critical, affectionate, thinly-veiled in its reference to individuals and in its account of the extraordinary dynasty from which she came.

their business cars though large and expensive were unostentatiously black or darkest green, and though the women at a certain age were bound to wear mink, it was always of a sober colour and cut and their pearls, though exquisitely matching were discreetly small . . .[1]

Gluck figures in the novel as Frances

who had run away from home to put on trousers and paint . . . signing her paintings 'Frank'. She had always been a difficult daughter, but then her mother was never the most tactful of women and must in some measure have deserved what she got.

Gluck, who extolled individualism, saw The Fund and The Family from which it was inseparable as stifling and claiming. In later years she was bitter and critical and at pains to dissociate herself from everything to do with the Gluckstein name – without ever freeing herself from economic dependency on it – a dependency she resented, for it made her feel powerless and beholden. 'How I hate them with their money and general bloodiness!' she wrote to her lover in 1936. And she implored her mother not to call her by the 'dreaded name' of Hannah.

For those who conformed, as the firm's business fortunes rose, The Fund acted like cement, underpinning The Family's way of life. They moved from the East End to West Hampstead and then on to St John's Wood. There were houses for the young men who married, dowries for the daughters, allowances for each newborn baby, the best specialists, the best hotels, the best wines for the table and tickets for the theatre. All became 'carriage folk' at precisely the same time – out of the meticulous sense of fairness that regulated The Fund's dealings. A brand new carriage, with coachman and groom, was delivered to each family house at eleven a.m. on the same day. The carriages were green and black, the horses black and each coachman wore a black silk hat with a green cockade, long black boots, a black coat and a green-edged cape.

Gluck was born in 1895 when The Family's fortunes were rising. Salmon & Gluckstein Ltd advertised at that time as 'The Largest Tobacconist in the World' with over 120 branches. They ran subsidiary trades as goldsmiths and silversmiths, snuff-grinders, pipe-makers, importers of meerschaum and amber, and makers and mounters of walking sticks. Their declared capital was £400,000. But if tobacco made them rich, cups of tea made them richer. The Lyons business came about through several coincidental factors, not least The Family's respectability. They had a horror of strong drink and its pernicious social effects and in England in the 1880s there was almost nowhere for 'decent' people, particularly women on their own or with children, to get a cup of tea and something to eat in safe, clean, predictable surroundings. There was the Ritz for the rich and for the rest, drinking dens, coffee houses and 'slapbangs', where waitresses served a variety of unreliable beverages with a slap and a bang.

In the late 1880s, to celebrate Queen Victoria's Golden Jubilee, trade exhibitions were held in various capital cities. At one, in Newcastle, Salmon & Gluckstein had a window display of young women hand-rolling cigars and cigarettes. Gluck's uncle – one of the eponymous Montagues – thought it would be a lucrative service to sell foot-weary visitors to the exhibition a cup of tea. He opened the first of the teashops. Others followed in various major cities, all

Gluck's mother,
'The Meteor', in 1894

allied to exhibition catering. They proved popular and successful. The brothers opened their first London teashop, the Popular Café, an expensively built place, at 213 Piccadilly, near the Circus. The chain developed. They had a great reputation for their cup of tea — only the two top leaves of the Darjeeling crop were used. The shops were painted white and gold and served all manner of refreshments, but no alcohol. The fare was clean and cheap, any mother could take her children there and the waitresses were as pristine as their surroundings.

None of the brothers wanted the family name above a teashop. Nor did they want this new enterprise confused with their tobacco business. They needed another name. Joe Lyons was the extrovert cousin of Gluck's Uncle Isidore's wife, Rose. He painted, (he gave Gluck, when she was little, a miniature silver-gilt paintbox of watercolours, hung on a silver chain), gave demonstrations at scientific exhibitions on the workings of the microscope, and was something of an entrepreneur and rolling stone. The brothers — with his approval – took his name to go above their shops.

Expansion followed fast and J. Lyons & Co. opened a chain of teashops; there was one in every urban district. They always bought freehold shops, or very long leases and so had a farsighted hedge against inflation and an investment in property that itself proved lucrative. The Trocadero, adapted from a music hall, opened as a restaurant with a floorshow in 1896. The first of the Corner Houses, renowned for their good food and live orchestras, opened on the corner of Coventry Street, in 1908. Oliver P. Bernard, who worked for Covent Garden and the Boston Opera House, designed the interior. The walls had views of mountain scenery with pine forests and waterfalls carved in different coloured marbles. That same year the brothers built their first hotel, the Strand Palace, on the site of the Exeter Hall. The entrance staircase with its illuminated glass balustrades glittered like a set for the Folies Bergère or the Casino de Paris. There was running water in every room instead of a jug and basin and the rooms cost five shillings and sixpence a night – and no tips. Then followed the Regent Palace Hotel, the biggest hotel in London, and, in about 1930, the Cumberland, the first moderately priced London hotel, with a bathroom in every room. It cost eleven shillings and sixpence a night with full breakfast.

This was the business and family ethos into which Gluck was born. Her father, Joseph, with his two elder brothers Isidore and Montague, were the backbone of the business, The Family and The Fund. 'We pride ourselves on being the most united family in the whole world', Joseph wrote to his prospective in-laws in August 1894, when asking permission to marry their daughter. He conformed entirely to the values of hard work, family unity, loyalty and correct social behaviour. He was a good-looking fellow with dark, bright eyes and a dimple in his chin. He was serious-minded, mild-tempered for the most part, and conservative in dress, politics and outlook. He allowed himself a number of fanciful flights: when eighteen, he wrote a drama in four acts called *Leila*, an extravagant Old Testament saga of filial piety, privately printed. (A copy is lodged in the British Library.) As director of the firm's advertising campaigns, he indulged in a few theatrical flings: he once hired four horse-buses, had them painted silver, filled them with actors dressed in different national costumes, all smoking cigars or pipes, or chewing tobacco; they went round and round Piccadilly Circus puffing smoke and holding up the traffic until the police intervened. And, as his perhaps most impulsive move, he married Gluck's mother, Francesca Hallé, who was not of the Gluckstein mould.

Gluck's father,
Joseph Gluckstein, in 1894

She was his second wife. His first, Kate Joseph, was, predictably, his cousin, his mother's brother's child. (Five of the seven

Joseph children married their Gluckstein cousins.) She was nearly thirty when she married him, perilously close in the *mores* of the day to old-maid status. She died, childless, after seven years of marriage.

During my married life I was the happiest man in the world and thought I was a favoured mortal in having been blessed with such a treasure. I decided never to marry again, thinking I could not settle down, but my dear Family have for years urged me to remarry as they pointed out that my life was not a correct one, being the only unmarried one of the elder members. I believed them, but could not afford to risk being badly mated.[2]

The Family rather expected him to settle for another cousin. However, when nearly forty, at a ball given by Joe Lyons in March 1894, he met Francesca Hallé. Though an indifferent dancer, and consigned to being a spectator, it seems he suffered the *coup de foudre* when he saw her and said to himself, 'That's the girl I'm going to marry.'[3] According to Francesca's account of events she took little notice of him. She was nineteen, tall, extrovert, with copper-red hair and blue eyes and thought to be beautiful, vivacious and talented. She was American. Her family lived first in St Louis, then moved to Chicago. Her father was a whisky salesman with a strong sense of moral rectitude, a love of travel and adventure, six daughters, a frail son and no particular wealth. Francesca had a fine soprano voice and was training to be a professional singer. She was in Europe principally to study music in Berlin and had gone to London to visit cousins.

In August 1894 she and Joseph met again. Both were holidaying with their respective relatives in Margate:

Joseph was with us a lot, but I did not think very much about it. One day he asked me to walk with him on the cliffs. I suggested that the others came with us, but he said he did not want them. . . . He was very quiet and out of the blue he proposed. I was amazed and said 'I thought you were in love with Miriam!'. . . . I protested that I was too young to get married and had my career to think of. . . . The sudden proposal and his determination not to be refused overwhelmed me as I was very young and had no thoughts of marriage but only of my career . . . I capitulated, but only on the condition that my parents consented.[4]

That same afternoon he wired to her parents in Chicago: 'Will you consent to my engagement to your daughter Frances? Can offer her good home and will be true yiddisher husband, at any rate will try. My family are well known and respected in England . . .' The same night, in the middle of the night, without stopping to look through it for correction and in an excited state of mind, he wrote them a six-page letter about himself, his business situation, finances, his family, a referee on his behalf they might consult in New York and his confidence that he and Francesca would be very happy together. 'I am only at present able to picture you in my mind's eye as the Parents of a most charming, darling and good Jewish girl,' he told them and explained, 'I am not given to what is known as gush, having been trained simply as a commercial man.' He finished the letter with an exhortation to them to answer promptly, and a hint at the new status their daughter, if married to him, would acquire: 'I have explained to Frances that it will be necessary for her to give up all ideas of musical study as I could not allow my wife to work for her living . . .' 5

Six weeks later the couple married. On her own admission Francesca had not, prior to those six weeks, even considered Joseph Gluckstein in an amorous light. But she did not hesitate, and her parents were keen. For the Gluckstein family, after so much intermarrying, the arrival of this nineteen-year-old, red-headed American singer, of unknown family and with no dowry, was something of a shock. But it was not viewed as so perilous an aberration as if one of their daughters were to have taken a shine to an unknown artist of modest means. Such a romance would have been strongly opposed. And when Gluck followed her own unorthodox heart, her behaviour, unsurprisingly, was thought to be beyond the pale. But Joseph Gluckstein was old enough, senior enough and man enough to be allowed to know his mind. In adult life Gluck saw her mother's truncated career and marriage into The Family as the sacrifice of Art to Money and the coercion of woman to a subordinate status. She thought of her mother as a beautiful opera singer and saw her as a captive spirit. Gluck defined honesty and truth as the following of desire and the fulfilment of talent. When her mother was widowed and in her sixties, she urged her to recapture her adolescent self, 'the real you, what you were before you married'.

The Gluckstein wedding reception was a grand affair at Olympia where J. Lyons & Co. had the catering rights. The Hallés, who still had small children to look after, could not be there, but the bride wore her mother's wedding veil of Brussels lace handed down, mother to daughter, for generations. The married pair sailed to the States to honeymoon and for the new relatives to get acquainted. Meanwhile a house in West Hampstead, with two bathrooms on the insistence of Francesca, was built for the couple to live in on their return.

In this house Gluck was born, eleven months after the marriage, on

13 August 1895. Her father would have preferred a boy – firstborn sons were highly valued for their potential as directors of the business – but her father's hopes for her were that she should grow up as beautiful as his wife, as devoted as his mother and as conscious of family loyalties and responsibilities as them all. She was given the name Hannah, like her grandmother and not a few of her cousins and aunts. His son and heir, Louis Hallé, was born, to his great joy, eighteen months later. Gluck was a small baby, her brother, large. At birth, the doctor remarked that he was the size of a three-month child. He grew to two metres, or six foot seven-and-a-half inches. Gluck reached five foot six. At no

Gluck in 1899,
aged four

point in her childhood was she taller than her younger brother, a provoking state of affairs for a small girl. And she was to learn through The Family's patriarchal focus that being born a girl was a handicap when it came to questions of power, work, and control of money.

The children had everything money could buy and everything their ancestors had been denied. They wore fine clothes, had seaside holidays and on Sundays went for drives to Hyde Park in the family carriage. They had singing lessons and piano lessons. The Lyons caterers created for them birthday cakes of extravagance and ingenuity – trains with chocolate engines and carriages. From their nursery window they saw a performing bear, pavement artists, and barrel organs playing 'Dolly Gray' and 'Soldiers of the Queen'. There were outings and treats galore. In their parents' box at the Royal Opera House they saw Melba in *Rigoletto*, and Caruso and Tettrazzini in *La Bohème*, which made them giggle. They went to the Hippodrome and the Theatre Royal, Drury Lane. They saw *The Waltz Dream*, *The Merry Widow*, *The Dollar Princess*, *The Arcadians*, Pelissier's Follies, the Gilbert and Sullivan operettas and Alexander's Ragtime Band. But pleasure had its place. There was a strong emphasis on education, virtue and correct behaviour. They were made aware that they had not only The Family's traditions to live up to, but the added responsibilities of opportunity and wealth. Louis fulfilled all that was expected of him and more. In adult life he became a formidable public figure and was knighted for his services to the community. Gluck went another way.

In their early years they were educated at home in the schoolroom. The only other children they mixed with were their multitudinous cousins. Gluck and her brother were extremely close, and remained so until their father's death, but they were strong rivals and, according to their mother, quarrelsome and naughty. A Swiss governess taught them French and a Sarah Solomons indoctrinated them in the tenets of the Jewish faith from a red-bound book by Mrs Philip Cohen called *Bible Readings with My Children*, inscribed with the epigraph 'Even a child is known by his doings, whether his work be pure, whether it be right.'

Gluck described the family home as full of blue ornaments, diarrhoea-coloured oak, endless games of bridge and her father cheating at patience. She did, though, regard her childhood as happy. As for her latent taste for cross-dressing, her brother remembered her intense annoyance at being given a Red Cross nurse's outfit at the time of the Boer War, when he got a City Imperial Volunteers uniform with slouch hat, bandolier, leather leggings and gun. She freely admitted to a preference for games where she was Napoleon, and in her teens was commended in the *Hampstead and St John's Wood Advertiser* for her 'dignified and impressive' performance as Cardinal Wolsey in scenes from *Henry VIII* at Miss Mathilde Ellis's Pupils' Recital at the Hampstead Conservatoire. As that same evening Ruby Greenop played Romeo, and Beatrice Cohen was William III, gender crossing probably reflects more on the surfeit of girls at Miss Ellis's dramatic society, than as a reliable indicator of androgyny. Two years later, a play Gluck wrote called *King and Pope* was produced at the same Conservatoire. It ran to three mercifully short acts and a prologue and was set in eleventh-century Germany. She played Henry IV, her brother played the Prince, her cousins, Isidore and Barnett, were the Pope and the Bishop, and Sadie Cohen was the lady-in-waiting.

The role of lady of the house was not enough for Francesca Gluckstein. She was an ambitious, energetic woman with little interest in home crafts, fashion, or the restricting demands of infant nurture. Anyway there were domestic staff in abundance: parlour maids, cooks, a nanny, a governess, a butler, a coachman, a groom. In adult life Gluck's relationship with her servants was frequently terrible. She hired and fired legions of them, with repeated emotional showdowns, until she found a few, prepared out of loyalty and affection to go beyond any job description and cater to her demands.

Because Mrs Gluckstein, The Meteor, could not, given the status of her marriage, do paid work, she channelled her formidable energy into 'the service of the poor'. An article about her in a Belgian paper in 1930 called her 'La Reine des Mendiants' – the Queen of the Beggars. 'My husband and family lectured me on the subject of overwork continually. They said I was never to be found when wanted as I worked in the East End and slept in the West.'6 Her persistence in the art of extracting money for charitable causes became a family joke. The rich were said to reach for their cheque books with a sigh when they saw her coming.

Her main activity was fund-raising. She worked for the Jewish Board of Guardians, The Home for the Deaf, The Home for Incurables, The National Council for the Unmarried Mother and Her Child, the Young Women's Christian Association, the Jewish Society for the Protection of Women and Girls, the City of London Maternity Hospital, the Deaf and Dumb Home, Wandsworth, the Roseneath Home for Women and Girls at Broadstairs. During the First World War, while her son was serving as an officer in Italy and Gluck was causing utter consternation, particularly to her father, by dressing in men's clothes, living with her lesbian lover and painting portraits in a damp studio in Earl's Court, The Meteor worked tirelessly for Belgian refugees. She arranged the furnishing of houses for them and the buying and distribution of clothing. She was awarded both an MBE and the Order of Queen Elizabeth of Belgium for this work. After the war she became a Justice of the Peace and was one of the first women magistrates. Yvonne Mitchell, in *The Family*, suggested that in later life she became so garrulous that a full day's business could not be got through when she was in court. Perhaps that was fiction. Certainly she was talkative. And both of her children inherited her daunting energy and quality of persistence for the sake of a cause.

She had little interest in spending the money her husband's family so energetically accumulated – except for the benefit of the poor. The Family code dictated with rigid fairness that all wives, after twenty-five years of marriage, should receive a necklace of pearls. The Meteor thought the extravagance needless and wanted the money diverted to something nobler. As flouting family convention was frowned on, she agreed to wear a string of imitation pearls. These broke at a casino in Monte Carlo and, as staff grovelled the floor and asked how many there were, she said she did not know and that anyway they were false – a statement which was not believed. She gave the money meant for the real pearls, a thousand pounds, to Queen Mary's Maternity Home and earned herself Royal gratitude that was beyond price:

After I had the pleasure of seeing you this morning I at once handed to The Queen the magnificent donation. . . . Her Majesty desires me to tell you how keenly she appreciates the great interest you have taken in the welfare of her Maternity Home. . . . I need not assure you what great pleasure this large donation to her Home has given to The Queen.[7]

After five years of marriage The Meteor endured the first of a series of what were diagnosed as nervous breakdowns.

I never believed that I should actually break down. Suddenly I found that everything was too much for me and my doctors ordered me to a nursing home which was not a very usual thing in those days. People were usually ill in their own homes, but the doctors thought I would be tempted to work and worry if I was at home.[8]

After three weeks' treatment she had made no progress. Moreover she was homesick for America and her own family in Chicago. So with her husband and children she sailed to the States for the best part of a year in the hope this would restore her health:

being ill, I thought that the maid I engaged would be able to cope with everything on the journey, but she was seasick all the time and could do nothing for the children. They got completely out of hand. . . . They used to climb every ladder they could see, climb on the Bridge and bother the captain. Then they would overeat and be sick all over me.[9]

In Chicago, the children were looked after by their grandmother while their parents toured America. The trip helped The Meteor and when she returned to London she resumed her charitable works. 'I did much more than before,' she ominously recorded.

She suffered a more serious and protracted breakdown in 1903, when Gluck was eight and her brother seven. Of this attack Gluck's brother wrote:

Of the nature of the illness which struck my mother when I was seven I was never given any details, but I think it must have been some kind of nervous breakdown. It necessitated her entry into a nursing home and that was followed by a very long convalescence abroad and our removal from the house in Compayne Gardens, to which we never returned. The pilgrimage in search of her recovery involved much travelling in France, Germany, Switzerland and Italy

Joseph Gluckstein (back row, second left) with the Hallé family in Chicago, 1899

*and of course it precluded the possibility of my sister and me having any early
education in England.*[10]

The 'pilgrimage' for health, which lasted some years, took them to
Heidelberg, where The Meteor was nursed in a convent. The children lived in a
villa in the grounds of the Europäischerhof Hotel, were cared for by their
maternal grandparents and went to school in the town. Already fluent in
French, from having been taught by a Swiss governess in London, there they
learned German too. But it must have been disconcerting for small children,
coming from a close-knit Jewish family, to have their home closed up, be
separated from their father, see their mother languishing in a convent with
some strange affliction of the spirit and have a new language and customs to
learn.

When they returned to London the family moved to a large house in Avenue
Road, in St John's Wood, on the edge of Regent's Park. This was to become
their settled family home. The years from 1908 saw the consolidation of The
Family's business success. Gluck went to a Dame School in Swiss Cottage and in
1910, when she was fifteen, to St Paul's Girls' School, in Hammersmith. She
maintained that she learned nothing worthwhile and that her only education

Gluck, her parents and her brother Louis

came from 'omnivorous reading'. None the less she got form prizes and special prizes for drawing and painting each year she was there. She was described as 'a most energetic member' of the Drawing Club. Her work was included in a Royal Drawing Society exhibition in 1913 – she was awarded a silver star – and in a Congress on the Teaching of Drawing at Dresden. She was commended by her form mistress Miss Volkhovsky for her 'extremely good work in all subjects', and described as 'a responsible and very reliable member of her Form'.

Five years later, in 1918, when she was calling herself 'Peter', smoking a pipe given to her by her brother who was serving as an army officer in Italy, living with the first of her lady loves and wearing outlandish clothes, the Paulinas had their eyes opened as to whom she more truthfully felt herself to be. She wrote to Louis:

Tonight I got into the train with about a million St Paul's girls. One or two knew me by sight. . . . Those who didn't know were not long left in doubt and the result was such a babble that I was glad to leave the train . . .

I am flourishing in a new garb. Intensely exciting. Everybody likes it. It is all black though I can wear a coloured tie if I like and consists of a long black coat, like a bluecoat boy's with a narrow dark leather belt. It was designed by yours

Heidelberg 1904.
Gluck and Louis with their maternal grandparents

*truly and carried out by a mad dressmaker. Utterly loony. She thought I was
mad and I was damn certain that she* was *mad – Still she was very clever and
very cheap and as it was an experiment I am glad it turned out so well. It is most
old masterish in effect and very dignified and distinguished looking. Rather
like a Catholic priest. I hope you will like it because I intend to wear that sort of
thing always.*[11]

While at school Gluck oscillated between art and music as a career. She had a
fine contralto voice and 'cared greatly for music, especially Lieder and early
Italian and French songs'. Her singing teacher was impressed enough to offer to
continue teaching her free of charge, rather than see her give up singing – and
the musical training at St Paul's was good. Gustav Holst was director of music
there. In her extravagant manner Gluck liked to tell of the inspirational flash
that determined her choice of future:

*I was very torn between the two arts, but my fate was settled in a dramatic way
at the first pupils' concert at the Wigmore Hall. After receiving most*

encouraging applause I determined to choose a singer's life. While waiting for my next appearance I looked at the rows of photographs of famous musicians lining the walls of the artists' room. Suddenly I faced the only photograph of a painting in the room – Sargent's portrait of Joachim. There was a great swirl of paint in this and it hit me plumb in the solar plexus. All thought of being a singer vanished. That sensuous swirl of paint told me what I cared for most.[12]

She resolved to attend Art School. Her parents and the 'High Mistress' at St Paul's, Miss Frances Gray, wanted her to go to university, despite her total disinclination for this. The head of the Art Department, Miss Flood-Jones, spoke up on Gluck's behalf:

June 21st, 1912

Dear Mrs Gluckstein

I had a talk with Miss Flood Jones before I saw Hannah the other day, and I find that Miss Flood Jones who is a very capable judge thinks so highly of Hannah's prospects in the region of art that I am quite inclined to abandon the plan of her going to University. Miss Flood Jones thinks that Hannah has the root of the matter in her and it would be a great pity if she were not allowed to pursue her art studies as far as possible. I shall therefore, unless I hear from you

to the contrary, arrange for her to enter the French Seventh next term, to have a good deal of work in the studio and in history of art from Miss Flood Jones and lessons in design from Miss Moore . . .

Believe me

Yours sincerely

F.R.Gray

The Artist's Grandfather, 1915
Painted in an hour

Gluck saw the extra year at school as a punishment. Nor was she then allowed to go to some hotbed of liberty like the Slade. St John's Wood Art School, just round the corner from the family home, was chosen. Her father hoped her artistic yearnings would quickly evaporate and that, like her mother, she would meet a worthy man through whom she might more sensibly define her life and channel her energy. And the principals of the Art School took scant notice of her on the understanding that rich girls dabbled with Art before they became rich wives. Gluck was frustrated: 'As far as I was concerned there was nothing taught that could be considered "training".'[13]

Her frustrations tipped over into rebelliousness. She paired up with another art student who used only her surname, Craig. Together they would sneak off 'up west', with Gluck wearing a cloak. Gluck forbade her family to address her as Hannah. Their nickname for her was Hig, which she allowed. At home she painted in a room above the garage wearing an old jacket of her father's. In an hour, and with a facility that taunted her in later years when painting became a torture to her and it took her months or years to finish anything, she did a bravura portrait of 'Grandpa Hallé' looking jaunty with mutton-chop whiskers and in a nautical cap. For a time Gordon Selfridge gave her a room in his department store for her to do more of these 'instant' portraits, but she soon abandoned them, fearing she would become slick.

The climate of war added to her feelings of restlessness. Her brother volunteered for active service in 1915 and was called up the following year. The Meteor, organizing shelter and clothes for refugees, was seldom at home. Gluck, though she wanted no part in the war effort, felt herself to be trapped at home, her career stifled. Then, by what she described as 'an incredible stroke of luck', her parents allowed her to go with Craig and two other art students to Lamorna in Cornwall. They stayed with the son of the painter Benjamin Leader. 'It was a wonderful month. My first meeting with genuine artists.'[15] Alfred Munnings, Laura and Harold Knight and Lamorna Birch were all living in the village and beginning to make their reputations. Ernest and Dod Procter lived in Newlyn. It was the caucus of what became known as the Newlyn School, painting pastoral, literal scenes of Cornish life. They painted the pools and rocks, picnics and beach parties, the fair at Penzance, the races, each other's portraits, the sun reflected on the sea. A thread of sensual pleasure and delight went through their work – a deferential nod to the spell of French Impressionism. Students gathered at the School of Painting founded by Stanhope and Elizabeth Forbes in Newlyn. '. . . the very bright of life beamed on us' wrote Laura Knight of her early days in Lamorna. 'We danced, played games and lived half the night as well as working hard all day.'[15] There was room for a talented, exotic-looking, rebellious girl like Gluck. And anyway she could sing like a lark: 'I was very

spoiled by them all because they liked my singing, and we used to have a lot of
music in the Knights' huge studio. Little did I think then that this studio would
one day be mine.'[16]

She determined to run away from home. Munnings liked her work, was
sympathetic to her aspirations and offered to help her financially if her parents
refused to give her money. He did two drawings of her at this time. When Gluck
returned to Avenue Road she found the atmosphere restricting and inimical.
Her father offered to build her a studio in the house, but she wanted other
company and a world elsewhere. There were rows and recriminations too deep
to heal. She left in the middle of a war, with half a crown in her pocket, no ration
card and her father's curse. There followed before long a rapprochement,
material and financial help and an effort to find some common ground. But the
split was too drastic and outrageous ever to be truly mended. It wounded her
father to the core. The unhappiness it made him feel was, he said, 'sometimes
too strong for philosophy'. He wrote of his pain to his son (3 July 1918) whom
he felt to be fighting a more honourable war:

I don't think she will ever return permanently *and that will always remain a
cancer to me and however I try to forget, I really shall never be able to. Your dear
mother is very brave and I believe she suffers in silence to save me pain. She says
her temperament is different to mine, but when she talks of you, her
temperament is mine. I certainly do admire her bravery in the other case.
Perhaps she is wiser than me. Anyhow we can never tell and I shall always hope
for the best because one cannot live without hope.*

'Differ and separate and you are undone.' 'L'Union Fait La Force.' All that
he, his father, his brothers and The Family had worked for, his daughter had
thrown in his face, for the sake of something he could not understand and which
seemed to him scandalous. He did not forgive her for it.

THREE

STAGE AND

COUNTRY

In Lamorna Gluck felt as free as air, her spirits high. The simplicity of the place delighted her. It was a hamlet of houses in a wooded valley with a stream flowing into the sea at Lamorna Cove. All around were moorlands, standing stones and a rugged coast. 'If ever a country was "pixielated" and primitive it is Cornwall,' she wrote.[1] She developed a deep love for south-west Cornwall and all her life kept a studio there. 'My landscapes were the first that truthfully showed the immediate impression one gets there – that of very little land and great expanses of sky.'[2] She regarded herself as an English painter, 'I never want to *paint* really in any other country, though I might enjoy them to look at . . .'[3]

Lamorna Birch lived in the old coastguard's house, Laura Knight worked in the 'Letter Studio', Munnings lived at 'The Wink', the local inn, and painted at the mill nearby. They gave critical appraisal to her work: 'Laura Knight is coming this morning to have a private view of the work I have done down here,' Gluck wrote to her brother (29 August 1918). 'A very harrowing moment mon cher! Pity me.'

Her flight to Lamorna was the making of her, as a painter and a rebel. She

'I am flourishing in a new garb. Intensely exciting.
Everybody likes it.' Gluck aged 24

could be who and how she wanted. It was a bonus to wear chappish clothes and to smoke a pipe. 'My dear my pipe is a boon and a blessing to me,' she told Louis. 'I have had some gorgeous moments with it. It is going a perfectly lovely colour and is the envy of Lamorna. Our sketching permits [needed for working out of doors in wartime] came last night, so work begins. Hurrah!'[4] Her brother also gave her a man's swimming costume, large Italian handkerchiefs and a cloak.

She painted in a twelve by eight foot hut and rented a primitive cottage to live in with Craig.

The only drawbacks which have appeared at present are a few woodlice which parade our bedroom and the Auntie. Oh Luigi the Auntie is appalling! It is in the yard not in the house at all. It looks ordinary enough when you approach it but is really an ordinary seat just over ordinary ground and the smell! Lor blimey lor! Otherwise the place is stunning. We have a very comfortable sitting room and bedroom.[5]

They spent summers in Lamorna and winters in a flat in north London, in the Finchley Road. Gluck set her sights on producing enough for a 'one-man show' at a London gallery. She painted the Lamorna valley and cove, the quarry, the cliffs, the path into the hills and the incoming tide, the sun breaking through rain clouds on fields and a hamlet. She painted white clouds 'in full sail' scudding across a windswept sky and the evening star in a moonlit sky. Expanses of ever-changing sky featured again and again in her landscapes, many of which seem like skyscapes with few details of earthly life:

The sky is a bowl, not a flat backcloth and its colour and light reflect in every blade of grass, every twig . . . the colour of the sky permeates the landscape under that sky and for your grass or trees to look as if that colour was the last ever to reach them would mean you had been insensitive to their relationship with the sky and seen them by themselves, isolated in their uncompromising green or brown. Some of the sky must have caressed their leaves or twigs, or be dancing between the grasses, or lying mirrored on the waters, however shyly . . .

Wind and weather change continuously, a landscape is chameleon to the light. Are you so truly sensitive to the one you have chosen as your subject that you have caught just the inflections in the voices of the trees and fields when singing to the sky above them? Will this note have reached you so clearly that no matter what changes and interruptions occur you will, like a good tuning fork, continue to vibrate to that note unerringly?[6]

She drew Phyllis Crocker who lived with her three daughters in a bungalow near Penzance. Mr Crocker, a dentist and dipsomaniac with a passion for sailing and fishing, would go to the Scilly Isles in his boat, fish there, then arrive home drunk. Phyllis Crocker left him to marry an antiquarian bookseller, who stayed in Lamorna with his Italian business partner, Guiseppe 'Pino' Orioli, whom Gluck painted too. He wrote an anecdotal book *Adventures of a Bookseller* about his travels, and meetings with writers like D. H. Lawrence, D'Annunzio and the poet John Ellingham Brooks, who married Romaine Brooks.

Gluck stayed with the painter Ella Naper in a primitive hut on the Bodmin Moors by Dozmare Pool

'The pernicious influence...' *Portrait of Miss E. M. Craig, 1920*

where the landscape was at its wildest. Laura Knight described Ella as 'an adorably lovely creature' who, when she chose, wore workmen's corduroy trousers, smoked a clay pipe and bathed naked off the rocks.[7] Gluck did several pictures of herself and Ella. While Ella washes clothes in the pool, rakes leaves for a bonfire and stands in a meadow in a clinging dress, with her dog Minchi Fu, Gluck watches. They seem like a couple with Gluck the romantic, reflective man.

Penzance had a makeshift cinema by 1921 and Gluck's picture 'All the World's Darling' shows Mary Pickford on its screen, ringletted and grinning, in one of her little girl parts, *Rebecca of Sunnybrook Farm* or *Daddy Long Legs*, 'with her anonymous audience gazing up'. A few years later, Mary Pickford and Douglas Fairbanks came, amid huge publicity, to London. Their on- and off-screen lives were everyone's affair. They had founded United Artists and lived in 'Pickfair', a Hollywood fantasy house. Gluck wrote to offer Mary Pickford her painting. She was summoned to the Dorchester. The World's Darling hardly gave the picture or its creator a glance but, said Gluck, 'white talons with blood red nails came out to seize it'. Gluck snatched it back and left.

Paintings from Cornwall: *The Jockey*

They're Off! Another scene from the Buryan Races

Paintings from Cornwall: *Phoebus Triumphant*
'A landscape is chameleon to the light.'

Bonfire, Gluck with the artist Ella Naper in Lamorna. Gluck later destroyed the painting, but kept the fragment of herself

A Lamorna woman paid half-a-crown a go to hear her sing and Gluck did a caricature of herself, striding off with hurricane lamp and back-pack for this assignment. She did a commissioned portrait of a Lady Egmont, a family friend who lived in Exmouth and was also keen on music:

Oh Ludovici! [Gluck wrote to her brother] *Imagine what happens when I attempt to sing. The parrot screeches and whistles, the canary trills on one note for hours, Lady E sings snatches of opera and rum tiddle tum songs in a high nasal flat soprano, Gracie hums or sings through her tightly shut lips, her baby gurgles and crows, we are like a mad futurist orchestra.*[8]

They were happy days. Days of work, of bathing in the sea or walking on the moors, nights of parties with like-minded people, and plenty of encouragement to egg her ambitions on. She went with Craig to the horse races at St Buryan and painted scenes of spectators in cold weather watching the races, crowding the jockey, or playing 'toss halfpenny'. She got as brown as a berry, cooked her own food and lived 'a completely savage existence' until she missed the Russian Ballet too much, the spectacle of Nijinsky and Pavlova, the concerts, theatre and 'civilization'. Then she went back to London.

Despite his pain, her father made her freedom possible. In October 1918 he opened a bank account in her name, paid in £100, introduced her to the manager of the St James's Street branch, and

told her we would like her to let us know on the first of each month how much she had spent and we would at once pay in that amount to her credit. I said we don't want details of how you spend the money, but only the monthly totals. She was very pleased with the suggestion . . .[9]

He also opened the first of a series of trust accounts on her behalf. She could not touch the capital, of £6,500, but would get the investment income – an assured six pounds ten shillings a week. 'I am only doing this', he wrote to his son (6 November 1918),

to protect her even against herself and also against me, as I won't take the risk of her suffering financially, in case I feel inclined, through passion or otherwise, to stop her allowance. I won't trust myself and therefore intend to get it all settled . . . I told her I would allow her that amount and even more if she wanted it as my and mother's sole idea was to make her happy.

The terms of this, and revised trusts in her name, precluded her from ever having access to the capital. 'I want to avoid the risk of her marrying some

A. J. Munnings, Drawing of Gluck dressed as a gypsy, 1916.
'The caravan did not exist, but I did smoke a tiny pipe as shown'

scoundrel who might marry her for her money and then lead her a bad life.'[10] In later years, Gluck resented the financial restrictions of these trusts, but at the time she was more than pleased.

Some of the senior business partners, particularly her uncle Isidore, thought the arrangement over-generous and likely to inspire future individualists in The Family to believe rebellion paid. Gluck's father had to be diplomatic to get it approved. He met Isidore in Eastbourne for a private talk: '. . . I shall of course be very guarded and impress him, not wicked or bad but just the trend of the times, of a new womankind, I don't propose to cry stinking fish to anyone.'[11]

By the end of the First World War Gluck was well off by the standards of the time. She had a guaranteed income of £6.10s a week and a guaranteed monthly balance in her account of £100. Her father, mother, brother and uncles Samuel Gluckstein and John Joseph were her trustees. She had run away from home but had not, in terms of financial dependency, got further than any of the other members of The Family. With the exception of her brother, The Family thought her behaviour and dress outrageous and the company she kept disreputable. Her father was cut to the quick, her mother simply waited for the phase to pass, but there was no way they would be provoked into denying support to their own daughter.

The Meteor blamed Craig for Gluck's errant ways:

Hig showed me her work from Cornwall and it was very fine, but she was in trousers and that velvet coat and when I see her dressed like that I am sure she has a kink in the brain and I go heartsick. I am sure when she leaves the pernicious influence of Craig all will be well.[12]

Even suffragettes wore long dresses and respectable hats – as for that matter did Craig. But still they asked Gluck not to bring her to their home in Avenue Road and complained she could eat any elephant out of house and home and always went to bed too late. When Gluck wrote from Cornwall that Craig had sprained her leg, or had the flu, Gluck's parents tacitly ignored all mention of her. They hoped that she, and Gluck's kink in the brain would 'Please God', pass. 'It certainly is nothing but a silly mania' wrote her father to Louis (12 October 1918),

for her to practically cut herself off from her own flesh and blood and all who should be dear to her for only one person and that a perfect stranger. What sort of a position will she be in in the future if she falls out with C or if C was to die? She would be alone in the world and must then be very unhappy. It is all so unintelligent and silly for a person who is presumed to have normal common sense. We have decided not to do anything to upset her and I personally have decided to wait til you PG return, as I feel there will be then a chance for your influence and logical arguments to have some effect.

He did not comprehend that when Gluck was to drift apart from C., there were plenty of other women to fill the gap in the transference chain. Strong hopes were pinned on Louis and his power to persuade his sister to follow a straighter path. He and Gluck were very close at that time, though in later years they quarrelled. She wrote to him often – to 'Dearest darling Ludovici', 'Dearest, dearest Luigini', 'Dearest, dearest, darling old thing' – confided news of Craig, work and adventure, told him the books she was reading, the Lamorna gossip, the shows she was seeing in town and joked with him about their parents' foibles and fussy ways. 'Of course my Ludo,' she wrote to him when she was twenty-three and he twenty-one, 'you know I shall always stick by you and I hope we shall always understand or *try* to understand one another and be the very closest of pals.' She even suggested that they go away together to live the artistic life – he was to be a writer: 'My dear there is nothing I should like better than to go with you and live *of* and *with* a place. We two alone . . .'[13] But there was no way that he could persuade or dissuade her on any issue and nor did he try. Given, though, his unwavering loyalty to his parents, his strong conservatism and conformity, he was surprisingly tolerant of her outrageous garb, artistic ambitions and sexual leanings. When, years later, there was a rift between them, it was because of clashes over Gluck's business affairs, rather than how she lived.

Gluck wanted, too, to get on well with her mother and father. She was, they conceded, very affectionate. She was fond of them both and particularly so of her mother. But she regarded compromise as self-betrayal and was of a totally determined disposition. If she felt she must paint, wear plus fours and woo the ladies, nothing in the world would stop her. Her passions, desires and whims were imperative and paramount. In later years they hardened into obsessions, and caused her, and all close to her, considerable damage.

She saw her parents when in town, dined with them at the Trocadero and appreciated the 'excellent Burgundy', but embarrassed her father by her appearance. They saw, with Louis' best friend, Peter Layard, later killed in the war, a 'priceless spy play called "Pigeon Post"', by Seymour Obermer, at the Garrick Theatre, sat in the front row of the dress circle and ate chocolates the size of hens' eggs. 'It was a thorough spy drama', Peter wrote to Louis (25 May 1918), 'and Hannah and I screamed silently all the time at the most tragic parts and your Papa was fearfully thrilled as were your Mama, myself and also Hannah I think, but the latter too blasé to admit it.' Eighteen years later Gluck was to fall totally in love with Seymour Obermer's wife.

The 'kink in the brain' was there to stay and common ground with her parents was hard to find. 'I hear that her work is very good but it gives me no pleasure under all the circumstances,' her father remarked. With Craig as her ally Gluck entered another world. She visited Craig's parental home, as she told Louis:

I went into the bathroom, locked the door, put a penny in the meter lit the geyser in the approved fashion and a thin stream of water gradually growing hotter weakly fell from the tap. When it had covered the bottom of the bath with a thin layer I stepped in jauntily and it rose majestically to my ankle. Naturally I then reclined luxuriously and pretended it was a beautiful hot bath. Just as I was getting comfortable the damn thing backfired or something and flames began to dash about. I leapt at it like a wild beast and shut off all the taps at once with teeth-hair-hands-feet, anything that came handy. I took no risks as to which tap was turned off first. The vision of me leaping like a catherine wheel waving arms and legs frantically must appeal to you. And that was the end of a perfect bath.[14]

In 1918 she and Craig went, with four thousand others, to the Victory Ball at the Albert Hall. They dressed as Pierrot and Columbine, danced from ten at night until five in the morning, then commandeered a private car to take them home. They made their costumes and Craig's got a special mention in *The Sketch*. It was black and silver with a head-dress of clustered pearls lent by her landlady. They went to the Russian Ballet at the Coliseum with Gluck wearing a cossack hat, plus fours and black boots. Those were the days of the great Diaghilev productions, with costumes by Léon Bakst and dancing by Pavlova, Nijinsky and Léonid Massine. 'It is a real treat', Gluck said – and rued its passing:

It is terrible to think that there will not be any more Imperial Russian Ballet. The present and future generations will have to work very hard indeed to replace a tenth of the beautiful things that have become obsolete or been destroyed by this war.[15]

They went to Promenade Concerts, shopped from barrows in Soho and found an Italian restaurant where they could eat spaghetti. 'She is an enigma to me,' said the Meteor. 'I live in the hope of an awakening some day, but till then must suffer in silence. . . . I don't worry any more. It is useless.'[16]

The income accorded Gluck by her father meant she could do as she pleased. Living in Lamorna was cheap. Few of the artists there had any money. She subsidized the small income Craig earned from illustrating. As well as their Finchley Road flat Gluck rented two rooms in Earls Court as her London studio. She decorated the place herself. One room she painted black, with a white ceiling:

black plain walls, black board floor and ivory coloured woodwork – the chairs and tables are black . . . the effect is topping and not at all funereal. In fact it is a most cheery little room . . . I got smothered in black paint and enamel and looked a sketch.[17]

This was to be her workplace, and in it she kept only the picture she was working on. The other room she painted white, used for 'entertaining' and storing pictures and hung a 'beautiful, old rare Japanese print' on the wall.

With this freedom of town and country living, of parental support if not

Raindrops, c. 1924. The view from Gluck's studio in Earls Court

approval, of declared ambition and sexual preference, she proceeded to work hard and well. Within a few years she had enough good work for two 'one-man shows' at London galleries. The first at the Dorien Leigh Gallery in South Kensington in 1924, the second, in 1926, at The Fine Art Society in Bond Street, where all her subsequent exhibitions were held.

The first picture she did in her all-black studio was of the view from the window – a huddle of roof tops and chimneys, a leaden sky and a scattering of raindrops on the window. It was reproduced in *The Studio* in 1924. Commissions came in for portraits. One of her earliest and best portraits was of 'Bettina', a South American model who was to marry the sculptor Eric Schilksy. After a tragic love affair she killed herself in 1944. In a glancing moment, in Gluck's picture of her, Bettina adjusts her hat, but the vase-like beauty of her profile is permanent.

Similar to 'Bettina' but more stylized and provocative, was 'Lady in Mask' in silvers and greys, with textures of chiffon, velvet and silk and flesh like pale pink marble. It caused a stir when reproduced on the cover of *Drawing and Design* in October 1924. It embodied the sophisticated gaiety of the 1920s – the party days which Evelyn Waugh mocked in *Vile Bodies*:

Masked parties, savage parties, Victorian parties, Greek parties, Wild West parties, Russian parties, Circus parties, parties where one had to dress as someone else and almost naked parties in St John's Wood, parties in flats and studios and houses and ships and hotels and night-clubs, in windmills and swimming baths.[18]

And it showed Gluck's fascination with sophisticated women who were glamorous and remote.

She did a small, finely-detailed portrait of Craig, in cool colours, sad-eyed and huddled into her fur collar and a bright portrait of Nancy Morris, sister of the artist Cedric Morris, swathed in an orange scarf, her hair bobbed short, smoking a cigarette in an amber holder. She painted the actress Teddie Gerrard – notorious for her fast living, backless dresses and high-born lovers – looking demure and girlish in a white-collared frock. She did an exuberant picture, 'Flora's Cloak', of a naked girl jumping astride the world with hair flying and wings of flowers. She painted a friend with feverish eyes dying of tuberculosis; a girl in a hat of shimmering green feathers and the artistic young men she met at the Café Royal.

She dashed off these portraits with virtuoso freshness, confident that she was revealing the quintessential self of her sitters:

All men's gestures are self-revealing. . . . In some lightning split second you will see the complete revelation of the person in their pose. . . . You should be aware of this as the spiritually dominating factor from which nothing in your subsequent handling should distract. . . . This vision must pass through the crucible of your spirit. . . . This emotion is on a wave length that you must be able to tune in to at will . . . essential characteristics must be assimilated to such a concentrated degree that no accidental change of light or mood can shake you. . . . This Divine Blindness is your holy of holies which nothing else must enter, however seductive. Do not try and see everything, only put down that which is essential to the realisation of the essence of your sitter.

Once you have placed all this in a large way on your canvas, you can then attend to all the superimposed details which enhance your original vision and give it more depth of characterisation. For instance you might feel that the hands of your sitter were a complement to point the head or a contradiction to give the depth of duality . . .[19]

Gluck's exhibition at the Dorien Leigh Gallery opened on 14 October 1924.

Four portraits of women. Top left, *Beatrice*, ill with tuberculosis. Top right, *Teddie Gerrard*, actress. Below left, *Girl in Green Hat*. Below right, *Flora*

London in the twenties: *Lady in a Mask*, 1924 and
On and Off, Teddie Gerrard at the Duke of York's theatre, c. 1924

London in the twenties: *The Saxophone Player* (Emmett Baker). Top right, *The Tumbler* from the C. B. Cochran revue 'On with the Dance'.
Below right, *Danse Eccentrique*, Florence Desmond doing the cake walk in 'On with the Dance'

George Reeves, pianist

Portrait of the Son of Sir Reginald Blomfield, R. A.

There were fifty-seven pictures in it. 'The new and much-discussed artist, Gluck,' wrote *The Sketch*,

wears her hair brushed back from her forehead just like a boy and when in Cornwall goes about in shorts. At her show at the Dorien Leigh Galleries she had a long black cloak covering a masculine attire and was busy shaking hands with her left hand, for she had hurt one of her fingers on the other and wore her arm in a sling . . .

Drawing and Design ran two consecutive features on her, declared '. . . we believe Gluck has a great future' and wrote of the exceptional originality of her work. High praise came in a letter (30 October 1924) from her friend, Prudence Maufe, an interior designer married to the architect Edward Maufe

Romaine Brooks by Gluck: *Mrs Romaine Brooks* (unfinished) 1926

who designed Gluck's studio when later she moved to Hampstead:

. . . here at last is serious and beautiful painting with so many qualities of rightness about it as to fill me with a supreme sense of beauty and happiness. My dear, thank you for having painted. The first and last point to my mind is the quality of your paint. It has a texture and depth which I consider masterly. Then I like your decorative quality. Then I like your composition. I think your portraits are the best. I think the landscapes a little exaggerated and the group of the jockey quite wonderful. I was a little disappointed in 'Flora' – her hair seemed to me to dominate too much. The rest was exquisite and we were horribly tempted to buy.

All Gluck's pictures were sold and by 1926 she had enough material for a new show. At the time of her first exhibition she moved from her black and white rooms in Earls Court to a large studio in Tite Street, Chelsea, formerly used by Whistler. Craig was still with her, though more tenuously as Gluck began to mix in smart society. The same year, Romaine Brooks and Gluck arranged to do portraits of each other. Romaine called her work, which was about three feet by two feet, 'Peter, a young English girl', and exhibited it in her 1925 exhibition along with pictures of the poet Gabriele d'Annunzio, with whom she was having a tortuous relationship, and 'Una, Lady Troubridge', who lived with Radclyffe Hall. Romaine was twenty years older than Gluck and already notorious for her wealth, lesbian affairs with Ida Rubinstein and Natalie Barney and unorthodox life in the Paris salons.

Gluck by Romaine Brooks,
Peter, a Young English Girl, 1926

She went to Gluck's Tite Street studio for the reciprocal portrait. 'The elephant has come to the temple,' Gluck remarked of the visit. She thought Romaine's work technically and psychologically inferior to her own and scorned the 'lesbian haute-monde' as she called Romaine's social circle. 'All those people were very boring,' she said of them.[20] Gluck wanted to do a life-size picture and primed a six foot canvas. 'Romaine Brooks was a big woman', she said in defence of her choice of size. The encounter was not happy:

Romaine wasted so much sitting time in making a row that at last I was only left an hour in which to do what I did – but my rage and tension gave me almost superhuman powers . . . she insisted I should do one of my 'little pictures'. I refused so she left me with the unfinished portrait. However, I had to give away many photographs of it to her friends![21]

Eventually she used the canvas for something else.

Gluck called her 1926 exhibition at The Fine Art Society 'Stage and Country'. It was a reflection of her two worlds – the parochialism and peace of Cornwall and the theatre, sophistication and fun of London. Those were the dancing years, and almost every London hotel or restaurant had a band or floor show. Many of the smart eating places were owned by Gluck's family, so she had easy access to café life. Lyons Corner House in Coventry Street had an orchestra on each floor. Jack Hylton's band, of 'Bye Bye Blackbird' fame, played at the Piccadilly Hotel. In 1924 Gluck's uncle Montague asked C. B. Cochran to stage a cabaret in the grill room of the Trocadero in Shaftesbury Avenue. 'In my career as a showman there is no association which has given me greater pleasure than that with Messrs Lyons,' Cochran wrote in his memoirs.[22]

For the next fifteen years, up to the outbreak of war, his cabarets, called *Champagne Time, Supper Time, Going to Town* and the like, ran continuously. They were a show-case for talent. There was music by Richard Rogers, Cole Porter, Roger Quilter; sketches by Noel Coward; choreography by Léonid Massine, Frederick Ashton and Balanchine; sets and costumes by Gladys Calthrop, Chrétien Berard, Rex Whistler, Edmund Dulac and Norman Wilkinson; 'girls' like Anna Neagle and Alice Delysia singing 'Poor Little Rich Girl' and 'All Alone'. The cabarets featured singers, dancers, acrobatists, contortionists, clowns and comic turns. And Cochran's guests at his first-night table were the focus of the society columnists:

Among my guests at my first-night table have been Elisabeth Bergner, Tallulah Bankhead, Ivor Novello, Douglas Fairbanks, father and son, Mary Pickford Roma June ... Diaghileff and his stars ...[23]

The London correspondent of the *Manchester Guardian* described the Trocadero in 1926 as 'the meeting place of those who wore evening clothes and those who did not ... a real institution recalling the position of Evans's Supper Rooms of Thackeray's days.'[24] Thirteen of the pictures in Gluck's 'Stage and Country' exhibition were of the Cochran reviews: the dancers, musicians and audience. Through these pictures her work connects to the gaiety of the twenties.

Opposite the Trocadero was the London Pavilion, advertised in neon as 'The Centre of the World'. There, in 1925, Cochran staged 'On with the Dance', London's first great dancing show. 'For variety of terpsichorean effect and speed, I doubt if it has ever been excelled' wrote Cochran of it. 'Mr Cochran's Young Ladies' had to be neat steppers. Laurie Devine, one of the first acrobatic dancers, stood on her elbows, Terri Storri did smart contortionist work, Florence Desmond, 'Dessy', in a costume designed by Doris Zinkeisen, with a top hat, waistcoat and cheeky gloves and duotone boots did a stylized cake-walk which always got a tremendous round of applause. And they all did the can-can.

Gluck saw 'On with the Dance' again and again and sketched behind the scenes. Her paintings record the show.

The stage at the Pavilion was the size of a large dining table, there was one narrow entrance and flats, props and large hoop dresses had to be suspended from the flies. She painted 'Dessy' doing her cake-walk in a beam of light, Massine, waiting for his cue, Ernest Thesiger, described as 'London's most versatile actor,' waiting to go on stage – with Douglas Byng he did a transvestite act – the saxophonist Emmett Baker, 'The Three Nifty Nats' doing a song and dance routine. Gluck later described this as one of the true art deco paintings. The stage set was by Gladys Calthrop who often worked with Noel Coward.

'Stage and Country' opened in April 1926. 'Plus fours, hell', Gluck wrote on the envelope in which she kept its reviews. They drew attention of course to her Eton crop, breeches, man's soft hat, name and pipe and there were photographs of her looking like a squire in many of the papers. 'I addressed him naturally as "Mr Gluck"', wrote 'Onlooker' in the *Daily Graphic* (9 April 1926).

It was with a considerable shock that I found myself being answered in a soft voice, essentially feminine. I do not know that I should altogether like my own wife or my own daughters to adopt Miss Gluck's style of dressing her hair or clothing her limbs, but I do know that I should be proud of them if they could paint as well as Miss Gluck paints. . .

He went on to say that her 'emulation of masculine virtues' was 'an outward and visible sign of an inward and spiritual grace'.

The critics enjoyed themselves, but were full of praise. 'A less derivative style I have not seen for many a long day' said L.G.S. in the *Art News* (4 April 1926):

It is a curious compound of the masculine and the feminine point of view in art. There is the fine delicacy of the woman artist and the humour and clear-cut vision of the man . . .

and *Drawing and Design* ran a four-page feature which spoke of her vivacity of spirit, rhythm of composition, subtlety of design and of the breadth and detachment of her mind.

The forty-four pictures in the exhibition reflected her life: her self-portrait in beret, tie and braces, with a cigarette hanging from her lips; Lamorna at dawn; Ella Naper at Dozmare Pool; the base of a waterfall on the Moors where rivulets of water bubble into a deep pool; the races at St Buryan. And contrapuntal to the light of the Cornish skies, she painted the spotlit world of the theatre. Ernest Thesiger facing his audience, the contrast of 'On and Off' stage in a scene from a play at the Duke of York theatre, Grock, the clown about to do a backward

Scenes from 'On with the Dance' at the London Pavilion: *Ernest Thesiger*, 1925
Massine Waiting for his Cue, 1925/6

somersault. The show confirmed her reputation as a painter of her time. No word was breathed of her Gluckstein connections.

Her father cannot have liked opening his copies of *The Tatler* and *The Sketch* in April 1926 and seeing large photographs of his daughter in trousers and a tie. Perhaps he was relieved she had abandoned his name. But at least the world declared her work good. He was suffering with heart trouble from which he died four years later. He had had the consolation of his son's return home from the war in 1918. Louis lived at home until his marriage in 1926 when he moved to a house nearby. Ever the dutiful son, he did all he could to please his parents. He even made trips with them to Vichy in their quest for health, as he told Gluck (10 August 1924):

We discuss in the most intimate manner the biliary ducts and general intestinal functions. . . . We are mere units in the liver-cum-kidney brigade which gathers in this small, unpleasantly bourgeois little town. . . . I dislike Vichy. I'm not ill. I don't want to be made ill and I decline to pretend to be ill. . . . I shall remain some two weeks to calm the parental mind at whatever cost to my feelings and shall return to England towards the end of the month . . .

Your devoted and somewhat strung up brother,

Luigi

Louis stayed devoted to his sister for some years after his marriage. He bought her pictures for his home and was proud of her success. Conflict happened after their father's death when he became Gluck's main trustee. It galled her to have her younger brother supervising her finances. His wife, Doreen, a conventional, well-organized woman found both her sister-in-law and mother-in-law impossible. The coolness between her and Gluck grew no warmer as the years passed and Gluck became combative, though surface formalities were always preserved, reciprocal visits made and no birthday or anniversary went unacknowledged.

In 1926 Gluck was flying high. After her exhibition she went on holiday to France where at dawn she painted the sardine boats at St Jean de Luz. The severance her parents wished for occurred between her and Craig, though they remained lifelong friends. Craig was left in the shade by Gluck's success. And at the time of Louis' marriage, Gluck's capital was increased by her father to £20,000 and he bought her the home of her choice: Bolton House in Hampstead. It cost £4000. Gluck moved in with a housekeeper, a maid and a cook. She had her own car to drive to Lamorna when city life became too fast. The Fine Art Society wanted to stage her next exhibition as soon as she could produce enough pictures. She was thirty.

Sir James Crichton-Browne, c. 1930

FOUR

BOLTON HOUSE

Bolton House, Windmill Hill, a tall, red-brick Georgian building on three floors, with a wide drive through wrought-iron gates, was – and is – in the heart of Hampstead village. Gluck favoured houses and communities that offered a pledge to the creative life. By the late twenties she owned Laura Knight's studio in Lamorna, Whistler had formerly worked in her Chelsea studio in Tite Street and Wordsworth, Byron and Sarah Siddons had all stayed at Bolton:

When I dine with my friend Miss Gluck, at Bolton House, Hampstead where she resides, besides those in the flesh seated at the table, there are present the phantom memories of distinguished people who gathered there in the fifty years during which, as the plaque on the front of the house announces "Joanna Baillie, Poet and Dramatist lived here 1801–1851". In the dining room – parlour she would have called it – a quaint little room eighteen feet by thirteen, panelled from floor to ceiling . . . have assembled many a time and oft a goodly company – Sir Walter Scott and his daughter Ann, Lockhart and his wife, John Kemble, Letitia Landor, Mrs Siddons . . . and indeed all the leading men and

'It does not flatter . . .'. Self-portrait with Cigarette, 1925

women of letters of the time, for Joanna Baillie, besides being a poet and dramatist of great note in her day, had a genius for friendship and captivated all who became acquainted with her. She wrote 'Plays on the Passions', but there never was an authoress of sweeter disposition or better balanced mind.[1]

The man in the flesh conjuring the phantoms was Sir James Crichton-Browne. His granddaughter Sybil Cookson, a journalist and writer of romantic novels, moved with her two young daughters into Bolton House with Gluck in 1928. Sir James had been the 'Lord Chancellor's Visitor in Lunacy', for which he was knighted by Queen Victoria. He was a Fellow of the Royal Society, Chairman of the National Health Society, a staunch Scot, editor of *Brain* and author of such works as *Dreamy Mental States* (1898), *The Nemesis of Freud* (1903) and *Prevention of Senility* (1905). He set up the Crichton Institute in Dumfries, a 'lunatic asylum' as such establishments were then called. His family was entitled to a room there in perpetuity.

He visited his granddaughter often at Bolton, admired Gluck's paintings and commissioned his own portrait. Though his wife thought Gluck's picture made him look stern, he was delighted: 'I am stern,' he said. He confided to Gluck that he felt like the creature of a remote past, but that 'friendly messages, like those she sent him, helped to keep him alive'.[2] In 1930 she sent out as a Christmas card her self-portrait in braces and tie. 'I am glad to possess it,' he wrote, 'on account both of its personal interest and of its artistic merit. It does not flatter, but it is very expressive and I shall introduce it to good company in my study here.'

He was assiduous in sending Gluck all the details he could unearth about Joanna Baillie's years at Bolton House – how her uncle, Dr William Hunter 'the first great English teacher of Anatomy', left her the legacy that enabled her and her sister to live there, how her brother Dr Matthew Baillie was a leading physician of his day and how Sir Walter Scott, who admired her plays, always stayed at Bolton when in London. Sir James suggested that Gluck give a 'unique literary entertainment' called 'An evening with Joanna Baillie', with actors reading scenes from her plays and someone singing her songs, such as 'Wooed and married and a'', and 'The Chough and Crow', but Gluck's soirées were not of that ilk and the evening never transpired.

As for his granddaughter, Sybil Cookson, she was about five foot six with green eyes, chestnut hair and thirty-two inch hips. She wore the clothes of a willowy model of the time called 'Gloria'. She had separated in a good-natured way from her husband Roger Cookson, a racing driver with the Bentley team – who drove cars which by 1930 could go at 130 miles an hour. In later years she lived with him again. She was a socialite, a product of the twenties and had a lot of light-hearted love affairs. She published three romantic novels under the name of Sydney Tremaine: *Eve, The Auction Mart* and *The Broken Signpost* and she edited and wrote for a chic weekly magazine called *Eve: The Lady's Pictorial*.[3] She ran a spread of Gluck's pictures in this after her 'Stage and Country' exhibition of 1926. She thought Gluck a genius, wanted to foster her talent and liked being seen with her at parties and shows for they made a theatrical, showpiece couple.

For the magazine, she wrote a column on wedding engagements, show dogs and beauty problems, a satirical weekly page called 'Nights Out' about a wilful society girl called Philippa, and pieces with titles like 'Eve and Her Car' and 'Eve's Golf Bag'. Articles for women advocating self-sufficiency were popular in the 1920s. Universal franchise had been achieved and the 1914–18 war killed off so many young men that one woman in three had, by *force majeure*, to manage alone. In her weekly review of current films she found 'no cohesion and little coherence' in *Grand Hotel*, thought Lionel Barrymore 'deplorably ill-cast' and drily remarked that 'Buster Keaton will amuse his own particular public'.

She had passes to all the opening nights and invitations to the parties. She was far more sophisticated than Craig who had not, until she met Gluck, so much as drunk champagne. She took over the running of Bolton House. When her two daughters came home for the school holidays there were simultaneous parties for the children on the ground floor and for the grown-ups on the first. In summer the four of them went down to Lamorna, to the 'Letter Studio' and the girls stayed in a caravan in the garden. In Lamorna in 1931, Gluck did a portrait of Sybil's daughter, Georgina. It was intended as a surprise for Sybil, but she did not like it and it was sold at Gluck's 1932 exhibition. A Brigadier

'Nothing more delightfully ludicrous has ever been put on canvas.' *Gamine*, c. 1932,
Sybil Cookson's daughter

General Critchley bought it to hang in his breakfast room, remarking that it was such a funny face it would put him in a good mood for the day.

Nothing more delightfully ludicrous has ever been put on canvas than 'Gamine',
the great granddaughter of Sir James Crichton-Browne, who looks out at you
with a pert saucy smile from under a perky felt cap

wrote the syndicated provincial papers. Gluck had painted an earlier picture of

'Georgie' aged about ten in beret and fur coat.

The Tatler of October 1932 commented on Sydney Tremaine's, alias Sybil Cookson's, 'polished journalistic pen and contribution to criminological literature'. The law, along with the theatre and the peace of the natural world, were recurring themes in Gluck's work. In the forties and fifties she did a number of portraits of eminent judges: Sir Wilfrid Greene, Sir Cyril Salmon, Sir Raymond Evershed. In the late twenties she painted two legal controversies of the time, covered by Sybil in a 'famous trial' series for one of the weekly journals. One was the Arthur Rouse trial, also called the 'Blazing Car' trial, a dramatic crime of the day. Rouse had a wife and various girlfriends and got himself into a muddle with them all, so decided to fake suicide. He gave a lift to a vagrant then set fire to the car and jumped free. A Colonel Buckle saw him, and Rouse was tried, convicted and hanged for murder. As the sentence was passed he turned to the public and ran his hand across his throat. Gluck spent days in the courtroom with Sybil following the trial. She did two studies of it:

The Unofficial Jury at the trial of Arthur Rouse

'The Expert Witness' with Colonel Buckle in the box and 'The Unofficial Jury', a caricature of the crowds that hang around the courts, waiting to glimpse the accused.

Sybil also wrote about boxing, which influenced Gluck to paint a number of boxing scenes. 'The Foul' shows the spotlit ring at the Albert Hall on the night of 22 June 1930. The British bantamweight champion, Teddy Baldock, fighting the French champion Emile Pladner, went down in the sixth round from a blow the referee said was below the belt. Protest against the referee's decision, largely from fans who felt robbed by the shortness of the contest, resulted in Pladner, not Baldock, being selected to fight Al Brown for the world title in Paris.

Joseph Gluckstein, Gluck's father, died in November 1930. He preserved to the end an unrealistic hope that his daughter would straighten out and restrained any impulse to punish her financially for the wrong he felt she had done to him, The Family and the name of Gluckstein. He made no special mention of her in his Will, which made her bitter. Knowing he was dying, he put his affairs into order and wrote devoted farewell letters to his wife and his son. To Francesca he wrote:

I hope that our dear Hannah may so develop as to be like her dear mother, which to my mind embraces the wish that she will be a model woman, and as to our dear Louis, I pray he will do well in his profession not only financially but that he will continue to be, as he now is, an upright honourable man and a credit to the name of Gluckstein, which name I feel absolutely sure he will hand down to his children as unsullied as he received it.

I have not made any special bequest for Hannah . . . what has already been provided for her will maintain her handsomely . . . if other and less favourable conditions should arise I know that proper provision will be made for her from the family funds, to the same extent as for the children of my Partners and if this is done you should not provide more for her from my Estate as there is a moral understanding that after your death the balance of my Estate shall revert to the family funds, so that the children of all the partners shall be financially equal.

As regards the financial position of our dear Louis, I am happy in the knowledge that he is amply provided for, but I would like him to remember that money has its duties as well as its pleasures and I have not the least doubt that he will do what is right.[4]

Baldock versus Bell, the Albert Hall, 1927

To his son he detailed the financial obligations he wished to see honoured and said:

... And now my dear boy adieu. I am most grateful for all the happiness you have given to me from the day of your birth. You have been a truly model son and I can say that no son has ever given to his parents more happiness than you have to yours.

I pray you may be recompensed by having a very happy life with your sweet Doreen and that your dear children will give you as much happiness.

Your very loving father

J. Gluckstein[5]

He did not write to Gluck.

After his death, Gluck's brother and mother became her principal trustees. Louis was, by 1931, a barrister, Conservative MP for Nottingham East, on the Board of numerous committees and the father of two children with a third shortly to be born. The youthful intimacy between him and Gluck had gone. He wanted her however to paint his portrait. He went to Bolton House for a couple of sittings, but somehow the picture never got finished.

Gluck did though, in 1930, paint a portrait of her mother in widow's black with tense hands and eyes she described as 'bleached from weeping'. She called it 'The Artist's Mother'. It shows the Meteor with overwide eyes and gaunt face and seems to presage the madness that was to blight the last decade of her life. The family disliked it for its gloominess and did not want it on their walls. After her father's death Gluck phoned or wrote to her mother virtually every day, letters that showed affection, possessiveness, dependency and irritation. They were close but uncomfortable with each other.

... despite our closeness so often making friction nevertheless it is closeness and I love you.... Bless you darling and thank you.... I am in a great rush to dress and go out – thank God fortified by the clothes you made possible for me ...

They were infinitely solicitous about each other's health and welfare. The Meteor strove to give her rebellious daughter everything she could. Gluck was forever telling the Meteor where to get her teeth fixed, or what concoction to take to ward off colds, or advising her on her diet, or telling her not to work too hard, or more loftily, to spurn material considerations and

... concentrate on the fulfilment of the spiritual possessions of which you have such a tremendous store. Bless you –

... I want to tell you not to pay the Normand Garage for the work they did on my exhaust. ... The damned thing broke and trailed in the road before I got to the Hanbury's and I had to have it temporarily fixed with wire to get there ...

... The flowers made all the difference to the dining room and the whole place was very cosy and pleasant to come back to. Thank you ...

... I should think darling even a break of a weekend at the sea might do you good ... the sea is a necessity once a year. Blows all the cobwebs away ...

You know I think you eat too many eggs ... often I have been astonished at the number of eggs you eat. I couldn't do it without feeling like hell. They are very liverish. ... It is more than sweet of you to have the outside of the house and studio painted. ... It means as you say that I can get straight to work when I get back. ... You are very good to me about all these things ...[6]

The Meteor was inordinately ambitious for both her children, generous, certain of their abilities and proud of their achievements. She made no further reference to 'the kink in the brain' but put Gluck's unconventional behaviour down to artistic licence. The tactics of stonewalling used for Craig were not extended to Gluck's subsequent grander lady friends such as Constance Spry and Nesta Obermer, both of whom she liked and respected and with whom she happily took lunch and tea. The Meteor believed, or said she believed, that her daughter had a God-given gift and was something of a genius. She also thought her incapable of managing her own affairs. She acted on the slightest hint that Bolton House might need repainting or the car might need new tyres, or that Gluck might want clothes, or special canvases, or errands run or pieces of furniture acquired. After the death of her husband, she let it be known to the other trustees that she favoured generous treatment for her daughter. What Gluck wanted, after her father's death and before the outbreak of war, in any material sense, she received.

But despite the closeness and regard between them there was at heart a mistrust. Gluck spoke of her mother as being unstable at centre. Though she showed her all her paintings and introduced her to her lovers and friends, she tried unsuccessfully to ward off her continual interventions, which took away Gluck's sense of being in control of her own life. As the years passed Gluck became over-assertive about the most trivial things, as if the drawing of a wine cork or the last word of an argument put at stake her credibility and authority.

She made her mother privy to all that went on in her life and then appealed to her not to interfere. Not to try to promote her pictures, or intercede with The

The Old Stable. Gluck's first Bolton House studio

Fine Art Society, or organize her domestic affairs without being asked. Time after time these appeals were disregarded, for neither of them knew what boundaries to set or observe. Gluck was caught in a familial dependency with which she never really came to terms – by the circumstances of the Trust, by her mother's attitude and no doubt to a large extent by her own feelings.

When she first moved to Bolton House Gluck worked in a small outhouse, formerly a stable for a pony, at the bottom of the garden. She did a picture of it in the winter of 1930, the path from her house cleared of snow, and called it 'The Old Studio'. It hung on her dining-room wall. In 1931, on the site of this stable, her friend the architect Edward Maufe, whom she was to paint in 1945, built her a studio which featured in the design journals as a model of its kind. Maufe had that year won an open competition for the design of Guildford Cathedral. Out of 183 designs, his was chosen. Among his many commissions were Morley College London and, after the war, The Runnymede Memorial to airmen who had died, The Playhouse, Oxford, the reconstruction of the Middle Temple and Gray's Inn, the Presbyterian Church of St Columba's, Pont Street. Gluck paid for the studio out of her own money at a cost of £1500. She walked to it from the house over a stone-paved garden, also designed by Maufe, flanked by flowerbeds and with a central lily pond fed by a concrete fountain.

The design of the studio was economical and elegant. A crescent-shaped entrance with stone columns and double-glass doors opened on to a small lobby with a bathroom on one side and kitchen on the other. Solid folding doors then led to the studio itself, fifteen feet high, warmed by the most modern of slow combustion stoves with a curb of stainless steel and with the whole of the north wall taken up with large metal windows. The walls were insulated and painted in broken white. There were built-in picture racks and bookshelves. The floor was laid in narrow oak boards and the room had exceptional acoustics. Gluck had a

'Miss Gluck is the happy
possessor of an unspoiled
Georgian house and a
completely modern and
efficient studio.' The studio,
seen from Bolton House, 1936

Edward Maufe's plan for
Gluck's new studio

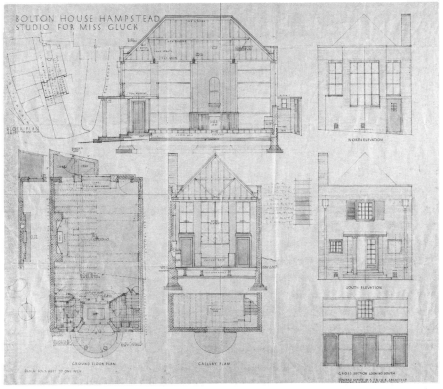

small grand piano in there, and her singing elicited compliments from Crichton-Browne, Maufe and the housekeeper, Mabel. At the south end a secret sleeping gallery was reached by stairs behind concealed doors. Artificial lights were all in recessed niches. The studio boasted every convenience and was much photographed and written about.

It did, however, annoy the neighbours. Mr Brousson from Fenton House, over the wall at the end of Gluck's garden, said it overlooked his garages. His house was grand and old and he disliked the 'modernism' of Gluck's new workplace. He maintained that because the new studio was so different from the old pony stable Gluck had forfeited her right to 'Ancient Lights'. He had, he said, no wish to be unneighbourly; but he threatened to put up a new building or hoarding, just for the sake of it, in front of her studio windows. Maufe challenged him to do his worst, which in the event he did not.

And Gluck in turn panicked when, in 1932 Geoffrey Toye, director of the Royal Opera House, and his American wife, moved into Volta House, adjacent to Bolton, and proposed annexing a music room to her studio. Gluck appealed to Maufe for additional insulation, which he thought unnecessary and he in the mildest of ways dissuaded the Toyes from their enterprise.

The elegance of Bolton House and its studio were a far cry from a simple cottage with the 'Auntie' in the garden. *Homes and Gardens* ran a three-page article in July 1935 on

Miss Gluck, the well-known painter, [who] *is the happy possessor of an unspoiled Georgian house and a completely modern and efficient studio, separated from it only by a paved courtyard, with flower beds reflected in a shallow lily pool.*

It gave numerous details: the upholstery in tea rose and apricot silks, the pigeons in ivory porcelain, the Broadwood piano in Spanish mahogany and ormolu, Gluck's collection of glass walking sticks, the vase filled with arums on a gilt console.

Hampstead in the early thirties offered extreme comfort, a rural landscape, the peacefulness of a village, the liveliness of a special club – and all a cab drive away from the West End. From the windows of Bolton, Gluck looked out over Admiral's Walk where John Galsworthy lived until his death in 1933. A year or so before he died she painted her view of his house, nestling among mature trees, with one of her typical romanticized wide skyscapes, looking like a country manor house with acres beyond.

Among Gluck's Hampstead friends who lived close by were the composer

Arthur Bliss, Eleanor Farjeon whose musical comedies *The Two Bouquets* and *The Laughing Elephant* were on in town, the actor Stephen Haggard, praised for his performances of Raskolnikoff in *Crime and Punishment* and Constantin Treplef in *The Seagull*, and whose portrait Gluck painted, and the artist Arthur Watts. The rich and creative lived in the big houses and the tradespeople in the small terraces. It was unremarkable for there to be a Society painter, a woman of independent means, who looked like Ivor Novello and appeared at soirées in a dinner jacket and black tie. In wider society, lesbianism was neither condemned nor condoned. Victorian legislators, when devising punitive sentences for homosexual men, made no reference to homosexual women. The story goes that Queen Victoria did not believe that women behaved in such a way, so there was little point in outlawing what did not occur. Nor was the donning of men's clothes seen as an act of defiance or subversion. The sexes were polarized in appearance so the assumption was that lesbians who wore men's clothes were simply women who aspired to be men. Many a well-to-do family had one, living somewhere in the country with a 'wife' in skirts, reading the financial pages of *The Times*, drinking brandy after dinner and seeming to appropriate the supposedly male domains of intelligence and activity.

There was none of the intrigued portrayal of an alliance between sexual subversion and power as existed in, say, Berlin at the same period. Analysis was not encouraged, nor the facts of sexual desire mentioned. *The Well of Loneliness* caused a stir in 1928, but was swiftly banned. 'I would rather give a healthy boy or girl a phial of prussic acid than this book' wrote the leader writer in the *Daily Express*. (Gluck had read it by 1940.) The book's author, Radclyffe Hall, a respected member of the PEN Club, dressed in men's clothes and lived with Lady Una Troubridge, the former wife of an Admiral, but such eccentricities were tolerated provided they did not appear to be connected with sex. Men in skirts (other than on the stage, where all folly was contained) would have been whisked quickly away. For her part Gluck provoked an interesting variety of social responses. She got on extremely well with men of the establishment like Sir James Crichton-Browne, or Edward Maufe, or Sir Wilfrid Greene. They commissioned her to do their portraits and shared with her their conversation, brandy and good cigars. To her family she was the difficult daughter, gifted, but as dependent and unreliable as an adolescent child. To her lovers she was the doomed romantic who merged into their worlds. To art reviewers her talent was frequently commended for its 'masculine' strength. As for sexual pleasure of an unorthodox sort, it was thought to be all right for Chelsea and Hampstead.

'. . . an uncommonly clever study of the tyranny of up-to-date fashion.'
Portrait of Miss Margaret Watts, c. 1930

The Artist's Mother, in widow's weeds. 1930

Arthur Watts lived a few doors away from Gluck at Holly Place. His daughter by his second marriage, Marjorie-Ann, had a clear childhood recollection of Gluck walking the streets of Hampstead in the thirties, with cloak, bow-tie and cane, looking like a small, well-dressed, dandyish Italianate man. Through Arthur Watts Gluck first met Sybil Cookson – he had a long affair with her in the early twenties. His satirical paintings appeared regularly in *Punch* and he did illustrations for E. M. Delafield's *Diaries of a Provincial Lady*. He gave Gluck a cartoon of his which she kept throughout her life. Captioned 'The Artist who Loves His Work' it shows a painter in a studio crammed with paintings, producing more and parting with none. Gluck went to great pains to buy back her own paintings after they had been sold. She sold them because that gave her professional credibility, but thought money a poor exchange for her creations. She wanted them near and felt bereaved when parted from them. On occasion she referred to them as her children.

Both Arthur Watts and his eldest daughter Margaret, who became a costume designer, admired Gluck's work. 'Note how modernity is presented frankly, but free from malice, in the sophisticated figure of "Miss Margaret Watts"' wrote the *Morning Star*, 3 November 1932, of Gluck's portrait of her as a student at the Central School of Art. The reviewer described the painting as 'an uncommonly clever study of the tyranny of up-to-date fashion'.

Margaret Watts had a difficult childhood. Her father went to fight in the First World War soon after she was born. When she was ten her mother died and she was looked after in a haphazard way by a variety of 'aunts' – including Sybil Cookson. When she was fourteen her father remarried. She found no place for herself within this new family and it rankled with her to see the furniture and things her mother had chosen melt into their identity. It provoked her father when she came back from Art School dressed in snappy clothes, wearing a lot of make-up and smoking cigarettes. There was tension and at eighteen she left to make her own way – at the time Gluck painted her picture. Gluck understood her need for self-assertion and sympathized with her. They spent a long time discussing the pose of Margaret's tapering fingers. She went on to become a fashion designer, first working for Motley,[7] the stage designers in St Martin's Lane, then setting up on her own and designing costumes for films. *Lion in Winter* and *Anne of a Hundred Days* were among her big commissions. She lived in some style in Kensington, divorced her husband Roger Furse, the theatre designer, had no children and kept an air of reserve and impenetrability.

By 1932 Gluck seemed to have the best of all worlds. She had the perfect studio and was working toward an autumn exhibition at The Fine Art Society.

Her talent was respected and appreciated. She could enjoy the fruits of The Family's efforts without having to conform to The Family's demands and expectations. She had a place in smart society which made few moral judgements and was sexually tolerant. She had the acceptance and company of distinguished men of the Establishment. She could escape, whenever she wanted, to the simplicity of the countryside, the open fields and the clear sky. And yet at heart she seems to have been insecure, as if she had no point of balance, no safe hold on what was hers, no way of reconciling the contradictions in her life. She wanted to be independent, yet was tied to her family for her material needs. She extolled the virtues of the simple life, yet lived rather grandly. She thrived on excitement yet longed for peace. The smallest of everyday transactions raised questions of integrity, yet she showed no moral qualms about infidelity or affairs with other men's wives. The strain told and she was to lose, at different points in her life, her lovers, her sense of home, her relationship to her work.

Gluck painted the people who were close to her, the view from the window, the landscapes that moved her, the flowers from her garden, the news that intrigued her. She chronicled her life in paint. The products of her time with Sybil Cookson were to line the walls of the Fine Art Society in 1932: 'Sir James Crichton-Browne', 'Gamine', 'The Rouse Trial', 'Miss Margaret Watts'. Sybil moved out of Bolton House in a flurry shortly before the exhibition. She found Gluck 'in the wood-shavings' of the unfinished studio with Annette Mills, the designer of children's shows, and later known nationally as the creator of 'Muffin the Mule'.[8] Sybil left Bolton with her daughters then and there and took a house in Cheval Place, Knightsbridge. The children, used to moving, were unperturbed.

FIVE

WHITE FLOWERS

Gluck never went for long without a woman in her life and when the new one arrived she moved quickly into her orbit. Her close relationships influenced her painting far more than theories of art. While she was with Sybil Cookson, she painted Sybil's grandfather, daughter, former lover's daughter and the courtroom dramas about which Sybil wrote. During the years with Constance Spry, from 1932–6, she painted arrangements of cut flowers.

The trade name Constance Spry epitomized refinement and respectability. Monied upper-class ladies turned to her for flower decorations for weddings, churches and coming-out dances. But though her name went with the skills of housecrafts and the polish of finishing schools her own life had not been easy. She endured an unprivileged and not particularly happy childhood, left her first husband who was moody and depressive, had no marked enthusiasm for motherhood and in about 1919, in her thirties, took up with a married man, Shav Spry, whom she married after both he and she had obtained their respective divorces. She met Gluck in 1932 when this marriage too had run into problems. It was Prudence Maufe who effected the introduction:

Lilies, commissioned by Bob Lebus, a friend of Constance Spry

4 January 1932

Dear Gluck

Three things.

1.   The camellias are marvellous.
2.   I am sending you herewith a feather of white velour, which I think is lovely.
3.   Edward and I are giving ourselves the pleasure of sending you up a 'Mixed Bunch' of white flowers for your Studio. I have commissioned my friend Mrs Spry to do it and to ring you up when certain flowers which I have asked for are procurable. She will probably lend you a white marble vase to put them in – she often brings her own when she does not know people's own vases. I think she has a genius for flowers and you have a genius for paint, so that ought to make for happiness. Anyhow, we send them to you with our love and very deep appreciation of your sympathy in work.

Bless you

Prudence Maufe

Constance Spry had not met Gluck when the phone call came through from Prudence Maufe to her shop, 'Flower Decorations Ltd' in South Audley Street. Like her husband Edward, Prudence had trained as an architect. She specialized in interior design and at the time ran a show flat in the Mansard Gallery of Ambrose Heal's furniture shop in the Tottenham Court Road. She exhibited Gluck's pictures in the flat and described the flower arrangements supplied for it by Constance as 'a weekly masterpiece . . . a genius every Monday . . .'.[1]

The 'Mixed Bunch' was intended as a fitting present for Gluck's elegant new studio. Constance was a contributor to the prevailing fashion for white interiors – white walls, upholstery, ornaments and flowers. 1932 was the year when the white craze reached its height, a craze epitomized in the look of the film star Jean Harlow, 'who appeared to have been constructed of equal parts of snow, marble and marshmallow'.[2] Constance wrote of white flowers:

It is in the interplay of light and shade, colour and shape in a thousand variations, that the delight of white flowers lies. It is subtle and distinct, cool yet brilliant and is a matter for endless experiment and pleasure.[3]

Her assistant, later co-director, Val Pirie did the arrangement for Gluck. She drove to Bolton House at the appointed time with a Warwick vase and a box of white flowers; anthurium, amaryllis, arums, tulips. The maid showed her in. It was all very grand and she waited until Gluck came through from the studio in smock and trousers 'looking extremely handsome and cross at being disturbed from painting'.[4] Val Pirie asked for a pedestal and water, then got on with the job. It presented no problems to her for it was a familiar way of using flowers. Suddenly she was aware that Gluck had stopped painting and was scrutinizing the arrangement. This kind of composition was new to her, she was extremely impressed by it and wanted to paint it right away.

It was to be the most painstaking of all her pictures so far. Months followed of replacing each bloom as it faded. The finished picture 'Chromatic' was the most spectacular of all her flower paintings. It was about five foot square and formed the centrepiece of her 1932 show. It was bought by a Mrs Ella Reeves who lived in The Mansion, Leatherhead. After her death it was sold to a dealer. Gluck tried to persuade him to sell it back to her, but he would not part with it. Constance was hugely impressed by 'Chromatic' and wrote of it in her book *Flower Decoration*:

Gluck's painting of this group exemplifies the delicacy and the strength, the subtleties and the grandeur of white flowers. It has another point of interest to those who admire the paintings of the old Flemish masters, since here we have a modern artist painting flowers in a spacious and decorative manner, but with the same delicate precision and feeling that characterized the work of these men.[5]

'Chromatic' was only the first of a series of paintings which reflected Constance's 'genius for flowers'. In all manner of ways the relationship that developed between them influenced Gluck's work and furthered her career. Before they met, she painted cyclamen growing in a pot, camellias or tulips in a glass, poppies in a painted vase. 'Chromatic' and many of her subsequent flower paintings were of arrangements in the Constance Spry manner. Gluck's knowledge of flowers and their characteristics also increased. If they were grand she painted them in marble vases or alabaster urns. Her subsequent notes on flower painting reflected the extent to which she was influenced by Constance's ideas.

Always give your flowers a setting in keeping with their essential characteristics, just as you would a portrait. If you had a queen to paint you would see that her surroundings were as regal as they could be. Flowers have these degrees of flamboyancy and simplicity and to be arbitrary about your setting is to be as stupid and unreceptive as to set a . . . coal heaver in a sitting room. . . . Be very quick at first essentials of character. As much character in a flower however tiny as in a portrait. Same principle as in everything else, but always be on the extra qui vive for the special delicacy of flowers. Impermanency. Feel the direction of growth . . .[6]

Constance's arrangements were light years away from carnations and roses in glass vases. Other florists were tradespeople who delivered sprays, wreaths and bouquets as ordered. She treated flower-arranging as an art and went in through the front door. Many of her clients became personal friends. Each scheme was unique, assembled where it was to be displayed, not below stairs, and often in an ornamental vase or cup from her own collection. She arranged nasturtiums or Roman hyacinths in pearly cockle shells, heaped papier mâché dishes with grapes and gardenias and filled china cabbages with green tulips and orchids.

Her arrangements for the windows of Atkinsons, a perfumery in Bond Street, were a weekly showpiece. The shop was designed by Norman Wilkinson. It was a glittering interior with engraved glass columns, mirrors, and a fountain of tubular glass. Constance filled huge vases with ever-changing displays of lichened branches, wild arum lilies, or moss studded with primroses. The window, spotlit at night, was a conspicuous display, on show to the world of wealth, luxury and fashion.

Le Vert et Noir, a display in the Constance Spry manner

Constance took Gluck into that world. She recognised her talent and how well her paintings would fit into fashionable interiors. She introduced her to her friend and client, the interior designer Syrie Maugham, who was Mrs Somerset Maugham, though not for very long. Syrie Maugham was famous for her all-white drawing room which was featured in the fashion magazines and copied for a

'Gluck's painting exemplifies the delicacy and the strength, the subtleties and grandeur of white flowers', *Chromatic*, 1932

decade. 'Ever since Mrs Somerset Maugham made her white room in Chelsea, one has felt that parties require to be bathed in light,' *Vogue* wrote in 1932. 'White satin drapes, mirrors in white rococo plaster frames, dining chairs in gold and white, white ceramic cockerels, white electric candles, white birds on rings in the windows, silver and white ceramic ashtrays.'

'Our grandmothers' wrote *Homes and Gardens* in August 1933,

in the fashion of their day sat in dark rooms with draped mantelpieces. Our own most up-to-date interiors have been described as rooms in which a white piano would be inconspicuous. Floors, furniture, fabrics, china, have been bleached to complete candour, or, at least, to the ghosts of their former selves. Like the countryside after a hard frost, our interiors shimmer with plate glass and chromium steel against pickled or limed panelling, with fabrics in the natural shantung shades of silks and unbleached linen and cotton.

The article ran a picture of a showroom, at the Dorland Hall exhibition of British Industrial Art, designed by Oliver Hill in off-white shades, with a quilted bedspread of oyster coloured dull silk, a large white rug and Gluck's 'Chromatic' the sole picture on the walls.

Constance worked for Royalty, the aristocracy and the merely rich. It was a time of surface formality when daughters 'came out' into society with lavish dances and parties, weddings were for the most part once-in-a-lifetime affairs and plenty of women spent five or ten pounds a week on flowers for the house. Sir Francis and Lady Oppenheimer were friends and clients. They bought Gluck's pictures and their daughter Betsan was sufficiently impressed by Gluck's white sailcloth trousers to get a pair for herself.

Molly Mount Temple was the grandest and most outrageous of Gluck's new connections. She was stepmother to Edwina, Countess of Burma, and she lived in Broadlands, the Mountbatten home in Romsey in Hampshire. She would phone Constance's shop in the morning and order flowers for the dinner table to harmonize with what she intended to wear that night. She was said to be the first woman in London to paint her nails red. Her husband, Wilfrid Ashley, was the first baron, Chairman of the Anti-Socialist League, and Under-Secretary of State for War in 1923. Molly Mount Temple's town house, Gayfere House in Westminster, designed by Oliver Hill, was an extravagant example of high thirties style. In the bathroom, grey mirror-glass walls reflected a collection of blue opaline glass and vases of white madonna lilies. The floor was black marble, the bath and wash-basin gold, the taps Lalique motor car mascots. The entrance hall to the house had a circular staircase of alternate black and white

Broadlands, 1932. The Mountbatten family home in Romsey, Hampshire

marble steps. Porcelain cats guarded the door and T'ang figures of demons sat on the radiator cases. The onyx dining table was lit from beneath and drapes of rubberized white material festooned the dining-room walls to deaden noise. Molly Mount Temple had a gavel to bang on the table when her guests got too noisy. Soon Gluck was at the dinner parties too and accepting commissions to paint Broadlands and a portrait of Molly. The Meteor lent her daughter her Rolls Royce and chauffeur so that on her first visit to Broadlands, in October 1932, Gluck arrived in style.

Broadlands, the Palladian mansion which had once housed Palmerston, now boasted a polo practice-ground, a golf-course, three tennis courts, eight hundred acres of shooting and room for twenty guests or so. Gluck chose to paint the portico and the sweep of a lawn. She gives a sense of a great deal of private land beyond. Constance described visiting Broadlands in 1932 with Gluck. When asked by Molly Mount Temple to do the flowers for the dinner table, she was uncertain how to match the splendour of the house:

Fortunately [Gluck] . . . *brought to the matter a technically unbiased mind, her eye was arrested only by what she regarded as intrinsically beautiful . . . I got a lesson not only in flower decoration but in the emphatic necessity of keeping a mind clear of prejudice or fixed ideas.*

Red cabbage leaves were the first contribution, followed by curly kale leaves, but only those which had turned slightly towards a yellowy green. These were arranged in two frills round a large shallow copper pan. Then came velvety begonia leaves, again arranged formally and a ring of white scabious. After that a mound of every lovely colour: verbenas, Phlox decussata, *salvia, Bougainvillaea, zinnias, pale flame geraniums, gloxinias, purple carnations and dahlias, mauve, yellow and peach coloured. In the centre were yellow and orange African marigolds, and arranged at intervals the head of the amethyst thistle. . . . It was really exciting, a thrill of colour, satisfying and lovely to a degree. It took a long time, because it involved lengthy and pleasant discussion about the shape and colour of every flower, but it was a great lesson.*[7]

At the dinner party Gluck first met Nesta Obermer, a society woman of charm and style and the second wife of an elderly, wealthy American, Seymour Obermer, whose play *Pigeon Post* had thrilled Gluck when she saw it with her parents in 1918.

The clients for whom Constance arranged flowers began to commission flower pictures from Gluck. Lord Vernon, who lived in Sudbury Hall, Derby and according to *Who's Who* owned about 3500 acres of the surrounding land, commissioned a painting of lilies as an intrinsic part of the design of his new London home, Vernon House in Carlyle Square. 'This house in Chelsea, designed by Mr Oliver Hill for Lord Vernon, is a perfect example of the small luxury house that is so much liked to-day,' wrote *The Lady*, 2 June 1938. Gluck's flower piece, in a frame designed and patented by her, was the sole picture in the drawing room. The walls and the picture frame were in weathered sycamore, the floor in walnut, the upholstery in ivory satin and carefully chosen pieces of Blanc de chine porcelain adorned the wall niches. The green of the lily leaves in Gluck's painting was exactly repeated in the green marble inlay round the fireplace. Lord Vernon paid sixty guineas for the picture and described it as 'the making of the room'.[8]

A similar painting of arum lilies followed for Bob Lebus, whose family fortune came from Ercol furniture. He used to go on holiday with Constance and Gluck to Tunisia. Though Gluck felt herself to be in some fundamental way aloof from society, these pictures, for the expensive walls of expensive people, are among her best. Some of their effect (as with Georgia O'Keefe's paintings of flowers) is sexual. Gluck painted the orifices and protuberances of orchids and lilies and while painting described herself as being like a bee – 'penetrating

Vernon House, Carlyle Square, designed by Oliver Hill, Gluck's *Lilies* the only painting
in the drawing room

them for their sweetness'.[9] She did a painting, now in the Art Gallery, Brighton, of one of Constance's favourite plants, the *Datura* – blooms of unlikely and sinister delicacy on gnarled, twigged stems. The arrangements Gluck painted appeared in Constance's books and articles on flower decoration. Their influence was mutual.

From 1932 until 1936, the two women spent a great deal of time together. Craig and Sybil Cookson still stayed at Bolton House from time to time and in Paris there was the Austrian painter, Mariette Lydis, the Comtesse de Govonne, whom Gluck painted and met frequently, if fleetingly, in a Paris hotel. Mariette Lydis had travelled in Europe and the States then settled in Paris in 1927. She painted portraits of women (her 'Woman in White' was bought by the Museum of Luxembourg), illustrated Colette's 'Claudine' books and Baudelaire's *Fleurs du Mal* and published a collection of etchings on women criminals and lesbians. Gluck noted that an exhibition of hers was held in New York in 1936 with a feature about it in *Harper's Bazaar*. (At some point Gluck destroyed her own painting of Mariette Lydis.)

But most weekends Gluck went to Constance's Kent home, Park Gate in Chelsfield near Orpington, a red-brick Georgian fruit farm with oast houses and acres of garden. Gluck's paintings hung on the walls: her picture of a girl as the essence of Spring, 'Primavera', nicknamed Interflora by the staff from the shop, over the drawing-room fireplace next to 'Spiritual', a study of a negro head. At a party, when talking about painting and light, a friend had remarked to Gluck how impossible it would be to paint a black face against a black background. Gluck advertised in the paper for a black person to model and her picture of him proved this was not true. The title reflected his inner world, the use of light in the painting and the quality of American negro music.

Constance went with Gluck to Lamorna and they visited country gardens and took notes and cuttings. She defended Gluck's taste for 'outré clobber':

Spiritual

motoring down to the Letter Studio, they stopped in a tea room and a vicar made disparaging remarks about Gluck and her clothes. Constance followed him into the road to reprimand him for his prejudice. 'And you a man of the cloth', she said.[10] The two women holidayed together in North Africa and France. Unlike Craig, Constance got on well with the Meteor: 'I hear that Constance had tea with you and she enjoys seeing you always,' Gluck wrote to her mother.

Mid-week Constance usually stayed a couple of nights at Bolton House. Gluck recorded their times together as 'very peaceful and sweet'. Shav Spry had less pacific recollections. Writing in January 1934 to Val Pirie, whom he was to marry after Constance's death in 1960, he described Gluck as fussy and irritating:

The Devil's Altar. Datura, a favourite flower of Constance Spry

She can't settle down to any sort of normal and peaceful life and I doubt if she ever will . . . I gather that she is litigating about her piano. Everything with her is a complication and very restless. I am quite fond of Gluck but I do not like being with her for too long. There is something about the atmosphere of Bolton House that is disturbing to me – as she herself disturbs me. There are always problems and mysteries and tribulations and nothing seems to run smoothly for more than a short time. She is abnormal herself – a queer mixture of childishness and astuteness. The truth is I think she has no real inner peace – nothing to hold onto.

What she had to hold on to was her painting. That was where order lay. In the year she met Constance, 1932, she was preparing for another exhibition at The

Comtesse Govonne, Mariette Lydis, artist and illustrator.
Gluck 'personally destroyed the picture'

Fine Art Society, in November. In this, and in her subsequent exhibition, five years later, she showed an array of new flower paintings – orchids with grotesque heads, heavy branches of white lilac, a huge skeletal display of dead flowers: old man's beard, willow herb, poppy heads, lotus seeds, wild oats and love-lies-bleeding – most of them gathered by Molly Mount Temple from the gardens of Broadlands.

Constance also influenced the way Gluck dressed. Unbothered with her own appearance (she looked rather dumpy and ordinary), she took Gluck in hand and true as ever to the thing itself, turned androgyny into high fashion. The South African couturier Victor Stiebel was a friend – he became a director of her company. He made Gluck an austere long black velvet dress with a white tie, Elsa Schiaparelli designed her a deeply-pleated culotte in black chiffon and in Paris Madame Karinska made her a black crêpe evening dress appliquéd in gold.

Constance also introduced Gluck to the delights of North Africa. Her friends the Hensons owned the Villa Hammamet in Tunisia. Jean Henson, a wealthy

American had, with his wife Violet, created what Gluck described as a garden like 'Eden, with cats, dogs, birds and fishes all living together free and with no danger to one another'.[11] Each morning Gluck was woken at 5.30 by the peacocks. There was a marble courtyard with a fountain playing, a lotus pool, a dovecote, macaws, parrots, Siamese cats.

In later years she talked of the 'languor and hysteria' of Tunisia in the thirties: the stream of visitors who congregated on the terraces, drank iced tea and played halma; the starlit evenings; the sirocco that blew all day and the picnics in the hills.

It is savage, lovely, bare country. Lunch – cold chicken, eggs, white wine, figs and grapes and coffee in the shade of a caroubia tree spreading, with silver-grey low-growing branches and a grey-green leaf.... Flocks of black goats and marvellous looking shepherds passing every now and then, the shepherds shy and accepting with pleasure and eagerness empty Vittel bottles as if they were some rare gift. I rode back – and so home and an immediate plunge into a delicious sea to wash off the dust and sweat. My God I felt good after it. Then iced tea and then people to dinner...[12]

She described wandering round the souk dressed as an Arab. Schiaparelli stayed and got inspiration from the Bedouin robes in the souks of Nabul, and at the time of the abdication there were rumours that the King and Mrs Simpson were to rent a nearby villa. In July 1936, a month after she began the relationship with Nesta Obermer that was to consume her life and divide her from her former friends, including Constance, Gluck went alone and for the last time to the Villa Hammamet on a prearranged trip. She wrote to Nesta:

Today we have a full time. Bathe this morning, then lunch, then siesta ... then three of the most marvellous looking Arab women, the daughters of a minister are coming to tea.... They have an incredible maquillage *and go unveiled to come here.... They wear the most beautiful modern clothes and all have extraordinary histories, so it will be an exotic afternoon. Not erotic pour moi because that kind of thing is not my cup of tea at all and I only admire it aesthetically ... Barbara is after 'the secrets of the Harem' as she writes beauty articles ...*

As soon as they had left I went all Arab myself, put on my snow-white 'excrementals' as Jean calls them (my Arab trousers) – they are white and very baggy – a scarlet Neapolitan sash, yellow shirt and green jacket, geranium behind the ear and Hammamet cap. Jean said I looked the most vicious Arab he had ever seen.[13]

'The flowers are a bright orange-pink-red-indescribably colour . . .'
Pomegranates, painted in Hammamet, 1936

Gluck worked in the afternoons. She wrote of being 'madly excited by the beauty and subtlety' of the skin of an Arab boy whose head she painted. 'He really is delicious – A tiny delicate little head with a sad, far away look in his eyes. . . . God knows whether I shall get any of it. He can't speak French and is very tiny and moves a great deal.' Violet Henson remarked that she would 'make a fortune if any old queers saw it'.[14] Jean Henson helped her arrange in a large shell a group of pomegranates with the flowers still attached:

It is so rare that Jean says people will even question its truth . . . they are the last blooms so the usual rush is on. . . . I shall have to finish it in England because the light is so disturbing here and also I am painting in the general living room with a continual va et vient. The flowers are a bright orange-pink-red-indescribably colour and pomegranates as you know are an exquisite shape and colour.[15]

She began, but did not finish, the head of a Bedouin woman, and a 'conversation piece' of a party on the terrace at night. When it was time to go home, always with stopovers in Paris, she travelled with opium pills for seasickness, rolls of canvas, half-finished pictures, pails in which were turtles for the tanks in Bolton House and 'a particularly fierce kind of fish which breeds babies and not eggs', most of which died and began to smell before she reached Marseilles:

Our departure from Hammamet was marvellous – rows of weeping servants – cats, dogs, and friends and a car packed to the brim with luggage. . . . My cabin is on the deck . . . have just had thé complet. Such noise of sea and people screeching and children tearing about that I have had to put those wax things in my ears to get some sort of quiet . . . the boats have no keels and sail at an angle of 45° . . . I discovered just as I was going to bed last night that all but 5 of my fish had died and it took me $\frac{3}{4}$ hr to take out the stinking corpses and rescue the survivors. The heat and numbers did them in. It was very sad, but there it is and they breed like hell and I think there is one female left. . . . I shall arrive at Dover like a Christmas tree and looking as if I had been fishing for sticklebacks.[16]

Though Gluck's relationship with Constance ended in 1936, her friendship with the Hensons continued until the outbreak of the Second World War. Her exhibitions of 1932 and 1937 record the languor of North Africa, weekends at Broadlands and the cool brilliance of white flowers. The rich and fashionable bought these images for their walls.

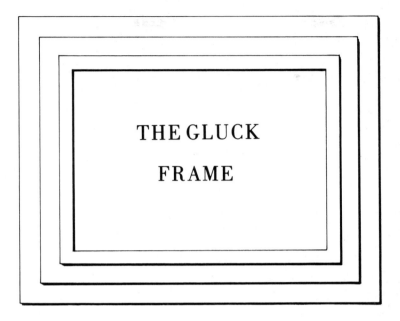

SIX

THE GLUCK

FRAME

In her exhibitions in the twenties, Gluck simply hung her paintings on the gallery walls. In 1932 she designed the Gluck Frame, of which she was extremely proud. With its use she transformed the main gallery of The Fine Art Society into 'The Gluck Room'. She achieved an integrated effect of pictures and setting, so the whole interior became hers. She found heavy gold frames out of place in modern rooms and modern designs unsatisfactory.

One day, feeling quite despairing, I took a lump of plasticine and started trying to make something very simple which, if possible, could be part of any wall on which it might be placed, and in doing this I suddenly realised that what has now become the Gluck frame was the only solution.

This consisted of steps, imitating the costly panelled effect for setting pictures in a wall, but steps of such a character that the usual essence of all frames was reversed and instead of the outer edge dominating, it was made to die away into the wall and cease to be a separate feature . . .[1]

She became suspicious that frames of similar design were plagiarisms of hers,

The Gluck Frame, designed to become a part of any wall on which it might be placed

The Gluck Room at The Fine Art Society, 1932

had the design registered and patented, was assiduous in watching for infringements and employed an antique furniture dealer and restorer, Louis Koch of Cleveland Street as the sole maker.

It was a serious attempt to incorporate paintings into the overall design of an interior. It worked well with decorative pictures like Gluck's in fashionable rooms which aspired to the kind of unity she liked. After her 1932 show it was used in the two major British Art in Industry exhibitions of the thirties: that of British Industrial Art at Dorland Hall in 1933 and by all the shops at the British Art in Industry Exhibition at Burlington House in 1935. This was organized by the Royal Academy and the Royal Society of Arts. It showed 'articles which combine artistic form with utility and sound workmanship'. Gluck had only given permission to Jacksons of Piccadilly to use her frame, but the exhibition organizer, Mr John de la Valette, thinking it 'the best frame he had ever seen', used it extensively – without first asking her. Gluck whisked down to Burlington House but was flattered enough to let matters stand 'only stipulating that the frames should be acknowledged'.

For The Gluck Room at The Fine Art Society she designed an interior of panelled bays and pilasters which echoed the steps of the frames. All were painted white with three undercoats and one finishing coat. An unfortunate Mr Lawrence of The Display Centre Regent Street got the contract to construct the panelling. He had built window displays and exhibition stands for Constance Spry and it was on her recommendation that Gluck used him. She kept an inventory of his firm's misdemeanours. They were supposed to arrive on the afternoon of Saturday 29 October to set up the room, but the lorry driver went to a football match so did not turn up until 8.15 in the evening. He had no screws, no dust sheets, the pilasters were still being made, the carpenter was not there and as the lorry was open it had rained all over the panels which had to have an extra coat of paint.

Mr Lawrence had given Gluck a verbal estimate of £100 for the job. As all work for her infinitely exceeded any estimate, he finally sent in a bill for £165 saying in a restrained if disgruntled way that the sum represented no profit for him, that she had shown no appreciation of his efforts and had taken all the credit. She stalled about paying him anything. Edward Maufe and Constance Spry interceded and she got the service, gratis, of a surveyor who inspected the

Molly Mount Temple and Gluck at the 1932 exhibition, in front of *Broadlands*

work and Lawrence's accounts. The surveyor negotiated a compromise whereby Gluck paid £125 and let Lawrence salvage the wood used in the structure after the show was over. Lawrence wrote Gluck a conciliatory letter (19 January 1933) regretting

that there should have been any cause for misunderstanding or friction. We make bold to say that we shall hope to again have the opportunity of working for you, provided of course that we should have a definite and firm contract for anything which is to be undertaken.

She did not reply.

The room was much admired. Syrie Maugham wrote (5 November 1932) 'Just a line to tell you how much I loved your show. . . . The pictures were lovely in themselves and superbly shown. I have never seen an exhibition so beautifully arranged.' *The Times* thought it offered a solution to the common difficulty of 'how to hang pictures in the typically "modern" interior, with its severe lines and plane surfaces.' The *Sunday Times* said that the exhibition 'reveals an architect as well as a painter' and believed that the paintings were actually let into the panelling.

The guests at her private view were grander and richer than in the twenties. The Mount Temples were there, Syrie Maugham, Cecil Beaton, Lord Portland, Lord Vernon, Oliver Hill, Norman Wilkinson, Ernest Thesiger, Arthur Watts, the Oppenheimers and Nesta Obermer. Queen Mary called in for half an hour on 9 November. Hers was not an entirely impromptu visit. The Meteor, known to the Queen for her considerable funding of charitable works and staunch admiration of all things Royal, had forged the way: 'Knowing how fond her Majesty is of flower paintings,' she wrote to Sir Harry Verney, The Queen's Private Secretary two months before the show,

I wonder if the Queen, in her busy life, could possibly find the time to visit an exhibition being held by my daughter at the Fine Art Society, New Bond Street, from November 1st until the 19th. Perhaps you know my daughter paints under the name of 'Gluck'. Should her Majesty honour me by visiting the Exhibition, I am sure my deep gratitude and sincere happiness will be beyond expression . . .

Sir Harry replied that November was a very busy month for The Queen, but that Her Majesty was delighted to make a note of the dates of Mrs Gluckstein's daughter's exhibition and if she had a spare half-hour,

I know it will give her great pleasure to see some of your daughter's beautiful

work. You must not, however, count on this because, as you will readily understand, it is not easy for The Queen to fit in her innumerable engagements in the short time at her disposal.

Dear Sir Harry

... Will you please thank her Majesty for her gracious consideration in making a note of the dates of my daughter's Exhibition and also convey to her my most grateful thanks for her kindness towards me, always in my work, and this time in what is a really personal matter. I do appreciate that her Majesty's many duties will make a visit very difficult, but I feel highly honoured that she is considering the possibility. I shall hope that fortune may smile on us by giving that extra half hour to her Majesty that she may spend even a few moments at the Exhibition ...[2]

'I would give a lot to know', mused the London Letter of the *Portsmouth Evening News* on 10 November 1932,

whether Queen Mary addressed her as 'Miss Gluck' or 'Gluck'. For Gluck is an artist of the Bohemian kind, wears an Eton crop, affects a masculine type of dress and tells you she dislikes the prefix 'Miss' and prefers plain 'Gluck'. Queen Mary was accompanied by Lady Joan Verney and Sir Harry Verney, and spent a good deal of time inspecting the whimsical pictures on the wall. They are astonishingly clever and not a bit conventional.

Queen Mary apparently gave scrupulous attention to all but one of Gluck's pictures. She surveyed them through her *lorgnette*. When she came to 25, 'The Seventh Veil', her *lorgnette* swooped in an arc of dismissal as she went on to number 26, the portrait of Margaret Watts. 'The Seventh Veil' was of a bosom, no visible head nor arms, with the corner of the last veil turned up, as if about to be tweaked away. Of the fate of this painting there is no record.

On the day of the Royal visit the Meteor delivered by hand to Buckingham Palace letters of fulsome thanks and pleasure to The Queen and the offer of any of her daughter's pictures that Her Majesty might deign to accept. Sir Harry replied

Buckingham Palace
10th November 1932
Dear Mrs Gluckstein
... it is indeed nice to know that you were pleased with The Queen's visit to the

Fine Art Gallery yesterday.

I now write to tell you that I have had the honour of speaking to The Queen about your loyal and kind wish to offer Her Majesty one of your daughter's pictures. The Queen wishes me to say that she is much touched by your proposal, and if you think the picture will not be too much missed from the collection, Her Majesty will be delighted to have the small picture of the tulips.

I feel sure I need not ask you not to mention this matter outside, because The Queen is inundated with such requests from people with whom she is barely acquainted . . .

Yours very sincerely

Harry Verney

But 'Tulips' was already sold, and Gluck became exasperated with her mother's machinations to reacquire it in order to get Royal notice and win Royal favour either for her daughter or herself:

Bolton House
Hampstead
NW3
November 14th 1932

Mother darling

You have been an angel and I shall always remember your faith and generosity, but my part of the 'show' was played when I had painted the pictures, designed the frame and arranged the presentation.

I cannot and will not have anything to do with the 'sales' which is the department of my agents The Fine Art Society and I cannot without killing myself, my brain and my soul enter into the bartering for 'money' or 'honour' of my work.

I am only writing this because I feel that you, who understand so much, do not understand my feelings in this respect. If you once realised what I feel I know you would not 'put me through the hoop'.

The pictures are on public exhibition. As far as the Fine Art Society are concerned the 'Tulips' is sold to Sir Edward Stern – any transaction which takes place in regard to the picture is entirely outside my control and the transaction must be done through Mr Dawbarn – I am not and will not be involved in any way.

I am not giving my pictures away to anyone and will not do so, and when it comes to accounts with the Fine Arts I shall expect two thirds of the price of every picture sold. This is not a question of finance, but of principle and pride.

I could not say all this to you for fear of hurting you, but when you think it over I know that you will think that I am right.

My pictures will find their proper place in due course – there is no need to 'force the pace'.

Mother darling, you have understood so much and shown your faith – understand now – it means a lot to me –

With all my love

Your Hig

'Tulips' was acquired from Sir Edward Stern and given to Queen Mary by negotiations of which there is no record.

The critics received Gluck's exhibition with the usual paeans of praise and the usual comments on her appearance, which inspired a spoof from Constance Spry:

Excerpt from the Feathered World *society news, November 5th 1932*

I have just returned from a delightful little chat with the petite and amusing Miss Gluck. I asked her why she had abandoned her patronymic for the delightful pseudonym to which she replied with a charming moue 'because I prefer it to cluck or duck'. So you see she is a wit! Miss Gluck was dressed in navy blue and wore shoes and stockings; she had had her hair cut at Truefitt's, she told me with a gay smile. I asked her to have a cigarette and she said 'I don't mind if I do'! She is evidently no tyro in the matter of interviews for I asked her to tell me the name of her dentifrice, having observed her beautiful teeth and she archly handed me a sample tube saying 'won't you give this a trial?' We had a frank, not to say abandoned chat about the weather and I then asked her what was her favourite holiday resort, she dismissed my question with a gay little laugh and a sidelong glance which spoke volumes. I said that my paper would be interested in any personal remarks she might like to make – about herself of course – and as this limitation seemed to deter her I helped her by asking if her sister liked cheese. She answered, whimsically, that she had no sister, so I said 'if you had a sister do you think she would like cheese?'. To which she archly replied 'I don't know.'

Of course you will have guessed that Miss Gluck is an artist. She has painted ever such a lot of pictures big and little and they're in ever such nice frames all in white. 'White for purity, you know' said Miss Gluck with a deep note of reverence in her voice, so I asked her if she was a church woman and whether she sang in the choir. She replied in the fine old biblical fashion by asking another question: 'Have you come to see the pictures?' – so quaint of her I thought. And that reminds me, there is one picture which everyone is rushing to see, it is called 'Hors de Combat' because she painted it lying down. Of course I was immediately interested in the artistic aspect of Miss Gluck and asked her to tell me more about her pictures. With an odd little gesture she referred me to her Mother saying, 'My Mother knows more about my pictures than I do, indeed if she were not so busy with her social work she would paint them for me to save my time.'

I then had a confidential talk with her Mother about religion and America.

Just as I was leaving the gallery I caught sight of a picture of Dahlias which reminded me that it was Guy Fawkes day, no less. So I just called over to Miss Gluck to know if she liked Catherine wheels but I don't think she quite heard me for she said something about feeling like that herself.

As I left the gallery the reporter from the Quiver *was asking her if she would be photographed in Yogi costume for publication in next Sunday's issue.*

There was a noise in the gallery and I did not catch her reply.

The show could not have had better reviews or received more attention than it did: 'Gluck is a remarkable genius', wrote *The Star Man's Diary* on Thursday 3 November, 'and her pictures and their setting are arresting in the extreme.' The reviewer talked of her exquisite flower pictures, her breadth of subject matter, her lifelike portraits which seemed about to step out of their frames and thought 'The Expert Witness' 'in Burlington House would easily be the Academy picture of the year'. (In fact Gluck despised the Royal Academy annual exhibition.)

The reviewer for *The Lady* wrote of her 'sensitive brush' and delicate sense of tone, colour and composition: 'no one who loves painting should miss this exhibition. It is perhaps not irrelevant that it occurs at the tercentenary of Vermeer ...' The *Sunday Times* talked of her clarity of definition, clean light colour, feeling for 'stately design' and 'Florentine dignity of composition', *The Times* of her 'suavity of workmanship'. The *Morning Post, Sphere, Tatler, Studio* – all ran pictures of her work and gave enthusiastic reviews.

Twenty nine of her pictures were on show, eleven of them of flowers. The white group, 'Chromatic' was the central piece, many of the others were pre-Constance. There were 'Tulips' for the Queen, 'Dahlias' in a silver cup, orchids she called 'Fleurs du Mal' and 'Chinoiserie', a branch of catkins, seed pods and fruits. Besides the bosom that offended Queen Mary there was a more oblique sexy picture of a swollen lily concealed among fleshy veined leaves. Gluck called it 'Undine' (in mythology a female water spirit who, by marrying a mortal and bearing a child, receives a soul). There were the portraits of Gluck's mother, James Crichton-Browne, Margaret Watts and Georgina Cookson, luminous landscapes from Cornwall and calm landscapes of the Loire valley painted on summer holidays, pictures of boxing in the Albert Hall, of the Rouse Trial and of Gluck's old studio at Bolton House, the pony stable covered in snow. Molly Mount Temple bought 'Oscar', a fat, glistening, china bull.

The show was popular enough for The Fine Art Society to extend its run for a month. All the pictures were bought and The Gluck Room used for the next exhibition – of Dürer and Rembrandt engravings. Gluck designed a narrower and lighter version of her frame for this and had the gallery walls and frames painted a light grey. She bought a Dürer engraving herself and would point it out as proof of the timelessness of her frame.

Mr Dawbarn, director of the Gallery, wrote to her of 'the splendid impression created by the room', how 'worthwhile and satisfying' it had all been and how much he looked forward to her next exhibition. Commissions for portraits and flower paintings accrued and orders came for her special frame. Apart from her mother's appeal for Royal patronage, it had all been on her terms. Her London reputation was secure and Macy's of New York wanted to take the whole exhibition – walls, pictures, frames and all – and reconstruct it in their store. But day by day as the Depression deepened, the market for art and luxury dwindled. The Gluck Room was dismantled in Bond Street and went back to the timberyard.

The life of Gluck's London in the thirties went on relatively undisturbed by the turbulence of international money markets, unemployment at home and German rearmament. She continued to produce ever more polished paintings and her 1937 exhibition was as successful as that of 1932. Two years later war swept away the world of high style she inhabited. She lost her home, her social circle, her sense of direction. She faded from the public eye and was never to regain her early fame. But more violent than war was the onslaught of love. It hit her in 1936 and gave her great pleasure and then great pain. She never really recovered from it.

Paintings from Gluck's 1932 exhibition at The Fine Art Society: *Oscar*, a faience bull,
bought by Molly Mount Temple

Tulips, presented to Queen Mary in 1932 by Gluck's mother

Two views of the Loire valley, painted on holiday with Constance Spry in 1932.
La Loire (above), *Triste Chatelaine* (facing page)

Undine. A water lily

Fleurs du Mal

Hampstead, Admiral's Walk, John Galsworthy's home, as seen
from the windows of Bolton House

PART TWO

LOVE

1936–1944

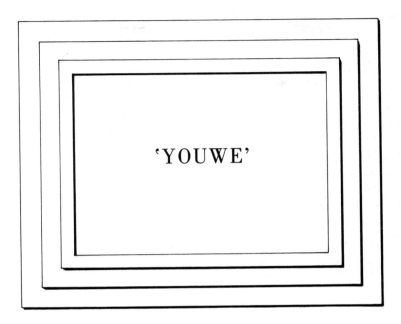

SEVEN

'YOUWE'

My own darling wife. I have just driven back in a sudden almost tropical downpour in keeping with my feelings at leaving you – my divine sweetheart, my love, my life. I felt so much I could hardly be said to feel at all – almost numb and yet every nerve ready to jump into sudden life. I made straight for the studio and tried to be busy and have more or less succeeded, except that everything seems so utterly unimportant that isn't us or connected with us.

I am interested now only in you and my work, a vast interest really and it doesn't leave time or energy for anything else.

Dearest and Best – this brings you my love – my hopes that you have a good journey and every thought and wish for your happiness and health. Take care of your darling self for your own Boy-ee's sake – if not for your own. I love you with all my being now and for ever. Good morning dear heart and goodbye.[1]

'Medallion' is a portrait of Gluck in love with Nesta Obermer. She went with Nesta to Fritz Busch's production of Mozart's 'Don Giovanni' at Glyndebourne on 23 June 1936. They sat in the third row and she felt the intensity of the music fused them into one person and matched their love. She called 'Medallion' the

The 'YouWe' picture. Detail from *Medallion*, 1937

Gluck in her Bolton House studio, January 1937

'YouWe' picture and it stood in her studio in Bolton House while she worked on other paintings for her 1937 exhibition. The gaze of aspiration and direction and the determined jaws have something of the feel of socialist revolutionary art. Nesta's fair hair forms a halo around Gluck's dark head. There is no 'setting'. To describe it Gluck took a quote from Coleridge's *Kubla Khan*:

And all who heard should see them there,
And all should cry, Beware! Beware!
His flashing eyes, his floating hair!
Weave a circle round him thrice,
And close your eyes with holy dread,
For he on honey-dew hath fed,
And drunk the milk of Paradise.

The painting consoled Gluck during frequent weeks of separation while Nesta travelled the world with her American husband, Seymour. Married in 1925 when Nesta was thirty-one, he a widower some thirty years older, the Obermers led a glittering international social life with friends plucked from *Debretts* and *Who's Who*. They wintered in Switzerland for the sports and summered in Venice.

Beautiful, stylish, glamorous, life-enhancing, magnetic, charismatic, silver, are the adjectives used of Nesta by those who knew her. She added style to her elderly husband's life but spoke of the marriage as not meaning much to her. In her youth she had been in love with a Duke to whom marriage was not a possibility. As a child she contracted peritonital tuberculosis which left her unable to have children and dukes want heirs. She was confined to bed for a year:

Brighton on a balcony for a year wasn't at all bad – quite fun looking back. Fun waking at night with snow on my bed, feeling warm. Listening to Chopin's Ballades being played by a pianist very loudly in the drawing room for me to hear – and reading, reading. Also I learned very young to love being alone.

That was good.[2]

Her maiden name was Ella Ernestine Sawyer. She was an only child and her father, a Diplomat, advised her to marry when she did. Unmarried daughters of thirty were a problem to their fathers in the 1920s. Of her mother, the daughter of a judge, she wrote aged seventy-six to Gluck (undated, 1969): 'I can't remember one thing she gave me either in words or example and I know she never really liked me.'

Her early ambitions were literary and in 1921 she published a slim volume called *The Reason of the Beginning and Other Imaginings* – airy pieces about eternity. In her literary pursuits she called herself Nesta Sawyer. Her poems, some of which she set to music, were published and broadcast and she had what she called a 'bedroom' programme, reading poetry late at night on the wireless. Between the wars two of her plays were staged by her lifelong friend the actor-manager Leon M. Lion, *So Good! So Kind!* at the Playhouse and *Black Magic* at

the Royalty. The action of *Black Magic* took place in the 'Morning Room of Chalfont Manor' and starred Franklin Dyall and Athene Seyler. Rowntrees, struck by the title, took it for their boxes of plain chocolates.[3]

'Medallion' celebrated Gluck's 'marriage' to Nesta on 25 May 1936. In subsequent diaries Gluck marked this date as her YouWe anniversary. At some point they exchanged rings. Visitors to the studio understood the implication of the picture and felt its sexual edge. They thought it more Wagner than Mozart and likened the heroic heads to Siegfried, to Valkyrie. 'Vous aimez cette femme,' said the Berlin psychoanalyst Dr Charlotte Wolff, author of *Love Between Women*, when dining with Gluck while Nesta was in St Moritz.

Nesta in St Moritz, January 1937

She knew Gluck and the Obermers and had 'read' all their characters through their handwriting and palms:

My instantaneous reaction was to puke violently. Vomit! *It was quicker than light what I said. I deliberately seized on the word 'aimez' and using it by intonation and inflection and timing in its most hearty British way, said 'Mais oui, certainment. Je l'aime beaucoup. Elle est si gentille et si bonne.' My face, which is a complete mask in one way to her, the way I want it to be to everybody, conveyed only the most ingenuous and naive agreement and interest in what she had said. I twisted completely away from* her *meaning. She was thrown back on her haunches. I almost heard the fall and she just gave it up.*[4]

Leon M. Lion wanted a snapshot of it even unfinished. 'I want permanently to memorise an unforgettable impression!!!!' he wrote to Gluck (15 December 1936). Lady Mary Villiers, who was married to a Rear Admiral and lived in Hatfield Grange, wrote to Nesta (8 January 1937) that she thought it remarkable of her, Nesta, but that Gluck missed herself. 'She has so much beauty in her face she probably doesn't know it.' Though Gluck's narcissism in the picture is disturbing, it gives a better likeness of Nesta. Strength and fearlessness were Nesta's attributes. It was she who lived life to the full, charmed people with her glamour, generosity and understanding, had a go at everything – painting, writing, singing, drove fast cars, got her pilot's licence, did yoga, got gold medals for skating and skiing, and travelled the world. In the picture Gluck has absorbed into Nesta's identity.

Gluck could play at being less than 'ingenuous and naive' when she chose. In January 1937 'YouWe' stood beside a picture she was working on, of tinsel, iced cake and baubles, celebrating the first Christmas she had spent with Nesta and Seymour at their country house in Plumpton, Sussex. Molly Mount Temple ('Emptée, as Gluck and Nesta called her for the way she pronounced her initials) came to dinner with Gluck while Nesta was away. She arrived at Bolton House with a flurry of instructions about the provision of food for her chauffeur and, after drinks in the studio,

became almost hysterical for her with excitement over the 'Noel' picture. Went on and on saying all the right things ...

I realised after the first few minutes that she was deliberately ignoring the 'YouWe' picture which was cheek by jowl with 'Noel'. So I wouldn't let her get away with it and after I had allowed part of the thrill of 'Noel' to pass off, I said 'and what do you think of that one?' She turned to look at it and there was

Noel, 1937, celebrating Gluck's first Christmas with Nesta

a long pregnant silence. Then she said, 'Who is the other?' No answer from me because I thought it too silly to answer. Forced to speak she said . . . 'Oh Nesta'! . . . More long pause then turning decisively away 'No, I don't like it. You have made her too male and you too feminine'! Later she said about it that it was 'Sinister'!! Isn't it comic? I knew it would be a shock and that originally she would be very jealous and I am certain that is the base of her reaction. It's really as a picture entirely her cup of tea, being definite and designed and clean cut. She said what she hoped would destroy it for me.[5]

Gluck enjoyed both the provocative content of the picture and tantalizing people with the relationship it implied. Openness and yet secrecy, bravado, but reticence too. In later years few people knew that the blonde head was Nesta's. They thought, correctly in a sense, that it was an idealized version of Gluck. The image made explicit a crucial psychological problem – her uncertainty as to where the boundaries between herself and others lay. Despite the defiant gaze she melts into another woman. In love she melted willingly if dangerously. In other contexts she battled for self-assertion, as if she was afraid of losing her will.

She thought her love for Nesta strong enough to overcome all opposition, surmount all problems and last for ever. She saw it as a homecoming, an answer to all problems, an end to loneliness and the realization of a romantic ideal. Years later, in her seventies, she confided that Nesta had been the only woman she had ever really loved.[6] And in her old age Nesta was to say that only once had she been in love.[7] Perhaps this love was with Gluck. Theirs was to be an absolute marriage outside of society's terms:

'Oh God, Oh God – There never has been such a thing as Us. We're quite perfect I think don't you? . . .'

'Darling Heart, we are not an "affair" are we – We are husband and wife.'

I have never said or written 'Eternity' before . . . I have never as I have said to you over and over again – felt it before. . . . I was always looking for you, always hoping against hope for you – but never in my innermost heart did I think I had found you until I really did so . . . until you I count my life a dream and do not feel I even became conscious or began to live until I met you and claimed you. And any ditherings I have shown since that moment were only what you call 'top nerves'. Never from that moment did I really deep inside think I could not find my only rest and peace in you. I knew about you and me, all I was not sure about was what life had in store and now I share wholeheartedly your vision and courage about that. Clear? As mud you will say and ask me all over again some time just to have the fun of hearing it all over again – and though it tears me a little because it brings back my mistakes, I will have such pleasure in repeating it all ad infinitum – that to all Eternity again . . .

Good night my most precious. I must just add two lines I discovered in an old notebook. Don't know who wrote them or whence they came . . .

'They have most power to hurt us whom we love
We lay our sleeping lives within their arms'

I love you – I long for you – I want you and I need you. All of you for all of me.[8]

It was on 23 May 1936 that a chauffeur arrived at Bolton House to drive Gluck down to Nesta's home, The Mill House, Plumpton, for the weekend. Gluck and Nesta lazed in the garden, had breakfast in bed, read poetry at night and on the evidence of Gluck's letters, fell in love. From that date on 'N's phone calls, letters, visits to the Hampstead studio, dinner dates and meetings, became the focus of Gluck's diary entries. Most weekends were spent at Plumpton and there were few further visits to Constance's house, Park Gate. When Gluck left, at the beginning of July 1936, for a pre-arranged painting holiday at the Hensons' villa in Hammamet, Nesta saw her off from Dover, fed letters to her and was at the quayside when she returned two months later. They stayed for two nights at the Majestic Hotel, Folkestone, spent a week at the Mill House, then returned together to Bolton House.

Such of Gluck's love letters to Nesta as have survived were all written in 1936 and early 1937. They were among her papers when she died, neatly folded in a red Charles Jourdan shoebox. Handwritten in ink on airmail paper, unsigned – mostly undated except for notes like 'Wednesday morning in bed, 7.15 am' or 'Later the same day' – Nesta, who did not live in the past or hoard possessions, letters or photographs, must have returned them to Gluck after their time together ended. Nesta threw most letters away, but if they were special returned them to their sender. For Gluck they were the 'YouWe' letters, a declaration of romantic love that bridged the gap of continual separation. 'If I was able to write the most divine poetry to you it would still fall short of what I feel.' There is no record of Nesta's letters to her.

The Obermers moved around a good deal. They had the house in Sussex and another in Kensington at 41 Egerton Square. They wintered on the ski slopes, made frequent trips to the United States and travelled the world. In the early years of their relationship, when parted, the two women wrote to each other two or three times a day, sent telegrams and telephoned and longed for separation to end.

Friday night

It's a cruel thing to say but it makes me feel less lopsided to know you are suffering equally, because I thought it would not be so bad for you with so many 'goings on' going on and with me enforcedly alone all days – though I know it would not make any difference to me how much I was surrounded and now I see you are the same.

Alone a lot in her studio, Gluck created the fantasy, common to lovers but insubstantial as a bubble, of divine synchrony:

I have no doubts now that I receive by that curious bond between us waves from you, sad or happy and I like to feel this. Do you remember us leaning against that field fence at Plumpton and looking at the stars and how bright Orion was and how you said you like him so much? Well these last nights every time I came out of the Studio the first thing I saw in the sky was Orion blazing away – the stars have been very bright and he is in the Southern sky at the moment and from there and my bedroom the most prominent. And I see again your darling face quite clear and beautiful in the moonlight. One day I am going to do a picture of that star because it was so lovely. It was so calm and big and we were so close – and poor old Rex [one of Nesta's dogs], *and you being so heartbreaking about him and me having got cross. Aren't I awful! Ha! Goodnight my angel. I adore you – and kiss your hands, your face and your loved body all over – and thus you sniggle up and go to sleep. That's me to you tonight. You will probably read this on a bright sunny morning and that's what time and space can do to thought. Let's forget it.*

This Love was Truth in a universal sense. It was elemental, it merged with the stars in the southern sky, it was beyond harm or accurate expression, it was, like her painting, a God-given gift and it was, with her painting, her world. There were no boundaries, no borders. 'It is because we fused and in every way, that it is suffering as well.' The past was over and the present and future could not divide them. It would escape 'The Rubbish Heap of Time', the world's constraints. It was the original thing.

I think we are like a perfect apple cut in half – the most lovely and significant of fruits and I am sure for that reason chosen as of the Tree of Knowledge.

Gluck, of course, was Adam, and suffering, during a three-week separation, from the hole in his rib cage:

It's shocking how he misses his rib when Eve is not by his side, his heart nearly pops out through the gap that's been left. Today it's a fortnight – *they do say it's the first twenty years that are the worst!*

Nor was it a love that had a moral reference in society's terms, the Truth being beyond morality – 'the greatest bond of all – the most precious and the most difficult in the world of human relationships and I think you will agree our proudest possession'. The Truth, as Gluck felt it, was that Nesta was her inspiration and her wife: 'Love, you are such an inspiration to me, and that you should be my darling wife too is all any man can expect out of life, don't you agree?'[9] The fact that Nesta already had a husband in the ordinary sense of the word and that the world did not define Gluck as a man, were not truths with the same weight as truths of the heart. And if the heart was anarchic, dangerous or destructive, so be it. Writing of Byron and his relationship with his half-sister, Augusta, both women remained unshocked:

Re Incest. No I can't be shocked at it either. What a pity we can't add all this to 'YouWe'. Perhaps we do. It seems to me sometimes as if we have every relationship rolled into one – Just a teeny weeny bit of a shadow of a shadow of incest too, don't you think? Ha! As for you 'bestraddling', glorious word, all worlds, you do, we do. Again a bond. I don't so much as you because my life has been less varied, but mentally near enough to share the detachment and twinkle. Adorable you. How I love you. . . . Oh my darling Love, my Heart, there never has been anything in the world before so lovely and warm and complete as Us.[10]

This was no callow, passing crush. Neither of the women was young. Gluck was forty one, Nesta forty three. Both had packed in a fair amount of living. But for Gluck at least the past was over now. Nesta alone understood her, knew her thoughts and feelings and who she really was. 'We feel and think together whatever the distance – only I wish it wasn't being proved so often because of being parted so much.' At times the sense of fusion and of presence in absence had a hallucinatory quality and life became a waking dream:

At 5.30 a.m. I woke up and you were asleep, your head on the pillow next to mine and I looked at you with my eyes open and I was awake and it was so intense that I got a pain across my forehead – and of course it could not last more than a minute like that. But it comforted me. You were so very much there. . . . I know you had come to me and I know you could only do that in great intensity of feeling and leaving your body.

Separation, even for a week or fortnight, was endurable only through fantasy and fantasy had its edge of pain:

I feel like a balloon this morning so close to you in my spirit, though God knows I daren't let myself think for one minute of such materialization as you suddenly coming into the room, or the feeling of you in my arms, or your naked body lifting against mine in the firelight, because then I ache suddenly with such force I don't know what to do. Just now I am hugging your lovely spirit close to me and feeling you so terribly strongly I wonder if at this moment, which is 9 a.m. you are thinking very hard of me.[11]

Visitors to Gluck's studios in Hampstead and Lamorna commented on how well she looked and how happy she seemed. A neighbour from her Chelsea days,

Evelyn Haworth, who sixteen years previously had lived in the studio above hers in Tite Street, said how young and 'spiritual' she now seemed compared to her time with Craig. Gluck scrutinized her reflection in the glass and concluded that this was because of 'lovely letters and telegrams and feeling surrounded by your love'. Nancy Greene and her husband Wilfrid, Lord Greene, Master of the Rolls, who were devoted friends of Gluck's and great admirers of her work (Gluck was to paint his portrait in 1949) commented so often on her appearance that

I would have become embarrassed if I had not been lapping it up with a grin from ear to ear for 'YouWe'. I have never cared a damn before whether I was good looking or not . . . but now I want to be for you – because it is an outward sign of us, and so as I say I glowed in this acknowledgement to the power of our combined magic.

Molly Mount Temple commented on how much better she liked Gluck's hair, now cut with a hint of curls, and found her appearance a positive distraction:

At one period I was holding forth and she suddenly said, 'Why are you such a good shape, I can't take my eyes off you it's most distracting and I haven't heard a word you said . . .'

It was the 'YouWe' magic. 'Now it is out,' Gluck wrote of their reciprocal love. 'And to the rest of the Universe I call "Beware – Beware!" *We* are not to be trifled with.' And a week or so later, when she was again being flattered on her changed looks, 'I know that our love has given me what everybody cannot help seeing like a lighthouse – because it is a warning too – Beware, Beware!

The 'rest of the Universe' was to steer clear of this dangerous force. Gluck's world was hers alone. She had a perfect studio, admiring friends, was working well for her fourth solo exhibition and was in love – to all Eternity:

Oh darling – I do love you so deeply, so violently and yet so tenderly, it almost suffocates me at times . . . I think we are really very lucky – to have this tremendous mutual love, one of the rarest and most precious things in the world – perfectly balanced in our essential difference and likenesses. . . . What a tangle, what jungles we have had in our lives, and now, anyway to me, it all seems crystal clear and unmistakeable and real, without question, merely with a few roots to stumble over, a few brambles to cut away before reaching freedom and light.

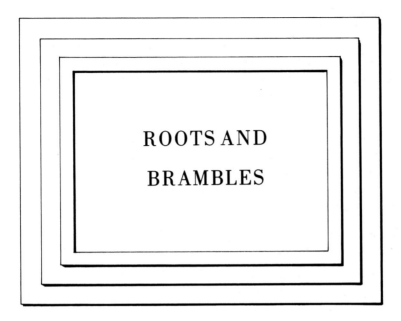

EIGHT

ROOTS AND

BRAMBLES

There were quite a few roots to stumble over and brambles to cut away. Operatic love has obstacles and this love had its share. At the beginning of 1937, while Gluck wrote her bulletins of passion and painted in her studio with the 'YouWe' picture propped always before her like a kind of altarpiece, Nesta was in St Moritz with Seymour. He was in his seventies and enduring bouts of illness. He was a retired playwright, had a considerable private fortune and gave generously to charities. To Gluck he was the Big Bad Wolf, her rival and opponent. She had seen his spy thriller *Pigeon Post* at the Garrick Theatre in 1918. In St Moritz the Obermers were staying at the Waldhaus. Gluck's letters were delivered each day to the Carlton and Nesta collected them on her way to the skating rink.

In Plumpton, Nesta's father was mortally ill and her mother voicing criticisms of what she sensed of the relationship between the two women – who feigned casual contact with each other of the sort that befits good friends separated by frequent travel. While Nesta was away, because of her father's illness, Gluck phoned Mrs Sawyer regularly. On a typical day, when the post had yielded three letters and one card 'my only post and what a feast! ... I thought to find only one and then the whole pile was you – I nearly passed out with suppressed emotion and rushed to the studio and buried myself...', Gluck mentioned, when asked, that she had received only a 'quite ordinary cheerful card (God help me). So now you know. You haven't corresponded except as I have just said. ... In that statement your Mother seemed to find relief and all was well. ... Goodnight again my darling love. I hold you to me.'

And a week later:

Your Mother asked if I had heard from you and I said in a casual way 'O yes, I had a letter yesterday.' 'Is Seymour any better,' asked she. 'I believe so,' answered I. 'I think he took a sleeping draught and felt better for a good night.' Why does everyone rub King Mark under my nose?

Gluck's mother too, though fulsome in her praise of Nesta – 'I am as deeply and fully aware of her charm and sincerity as you are. She is outstanding and I know her real worth' – and guarded at opposing anything that might add to her daughter's happiness, was putting out warning references to society's terms: '... That bloody insistence on S. and you as the "Ideal Couple". ... It bores me,' Gluck wrote.[1]

In January 1937 Mr Sawyer's pulse rate was down to fifty and his appetite gone, he was dozing most of the time and 'sinking slowly'. Nesta wondered whether to cut short her winter holiday in order to be with him. Her mother, troubled by a bad leg, sent depressed bulletins to St Moritz, hoping that her daughter would come home. Gluck tried to interpret the facts:

My heart I want to say something about your Father. ... I have a feeling of responsibility about negating the gloom of your mother's letters. I do think it true that he is getting steadily weaker, that he does not eat enough and is dozing most of the time. But with your stay daily getting your strength up it seems unnecessary to curtail it when this state of affairs ... may continue for a month or more. ... If my impressions are correct I think if you come back when you thought of doing so it will be all right.

Gluck, who revered the concept of truth, colluded in keeping the affair secret in order to avoid pain and scandal. But her sexual orientation was no secret and she could not always hide her feelings. Her jealousy of Seymour, her hatred of being marginalized by his socially legitimate claim to Nesta, and her fear that Nesta was not matching her own passion, spilled out. Bothered by the vagaries of the post, afraid that her three letters a day to the Carlton were not getting through quickly enough, she suggested an alternative strategy, to speed communication. Nesta replied: 'It doesn't matter, as I pass the Carlton daily to go to the skating rink there won't be any delay in my getting your letters, so either way all is well.'

For Gluck, alone with the 'Demon' as she called it, of her artistic ambition, living her life through Nesta and scarcely allowing letters to get through the box before opening them, Nesta's restraint in waiting until morning for a letter that arrived the previous evening, was tantamount to indifference:

In bed, Thursday morning, 7 January (1937)

My one instinct was to fly backwards into nothingness – no contacts, no heart, no feelings. I was furious *with myself having bothered to find out what posts would reach you most quickly. What did it matter – if you didn't get them at night next morning would do.*

Your mother was right, I ask too much – and yet I do not ask what I am not prepared to do and give myself. . . . You will never know the turmoil, the rage, quite cold blooded that seized me – just the same rage that I got at Plumpton when Seymour kept us both hanging about and I did not know when you were coming in to see me.

Don't make any mistake – I know you love me, I know how you love me and I know that nothing like this can prevent me loving you, but my ears went back and I felt that armour close with a snap again round my heart which had become, I suddenly realised dangerously *softened . . .*

I went to bed. There was nothing else to do – I was sick with myself for minding at all. I had so nearly reduced feeling to insensitiveness and now I had let it get all vulnerable again. I determined not to think about it and when in bed took Dial [a barbiturate available only on prescription or the Black Market] *and a purge and hoped by this morning I would find it was all exaggeration and a result of being overtired. At 3 am I woke up with the headache worse than ever and took two aspirin and slept till nine. I felt better and calmer but it would not be possible just the same not to write all this to you. . . . You see darling, when you are near or with me, it's like a warmth that keeps me from analysing and retrospecting and gradually I melt and feel human and creative and happy and all the suspicions bred by my life so far just seem impersonal and of no account and are lulled and I am tamed and safe and happy in it. Then when something like this happens I can feel my ears go back, I can feel my jaw set, I can feel that overwhelming urge to fly – to the desert I know so well it would be, but it seems safe somehow. . . .*

I don't think with all this outpouring of words I have made it clear what I minded. I manage, and you manage, to keep some semblance of our true relationship going, but when you are the chattel, as far as your goings and comings are concerned, of someone else, then I become it too and that, at sudden moments like last night, becomes intolerable. I feel as if I was being hamlugged about, and not to know where you are, so even if I wanted to telephone or telegraph I would be uncertain, or have to duplicate the contact, because of someone who has first claim on you being uncertain and erratic and you having to follow suit fills me with a crazy fury.

Do try to understand. I have understood all your very strong feelings about the clutching things in my life. I suppose it's just the old Adam pouring upward to my brain but you are the only human being I have ever trusted and therefore loved. I do love you and I know what your love is for me and it is true that you sustain my spirits *but I am human after all and if what I have written is small and seems a fuss about nothing, don't forget that it is the tiny things that count and that try as one may to keep the big view they can buzz like gnats and be very disturbing.*

How I wish to God I could say all this with you in my arms and your head snuggled on my shoulder. Having got it out I feel better and closer to you even though it's on paper and Heaven alone knows how and with what a mood you will read it. The sun is pouring into my room on to our bed. Mabel [Gluck's housekeeper] *has just been in to see if I'm alright. I assured her I was grand and just getting up which I am.*

One disadvantage of my job is that it shuts me up in one room and there is nothing to stop a bee buzzing, and to you, constantly on the move and with additional fresh contacts all this eremite drooling will seem exaggerated.

. . . All my love to you as ever – and for ever

That was only pale because I blotted it at once. Not because I feel reticent about it. All my love now and forever.

'What's this dull town to me,' wrote Nesta of St Moritz. But winter sporting is different from working alone in a studio all day. Gluck's news was only of love and work and she feared that the latter at least might bore:

Is all this studio chat too remote and musty for the gay, glittering atmosphere of St Moritz and caravanserai hotels and haute monde? How well I know it all! Perhaps it is a little depressing for you to get all this kind of thing?

Certainly Mrs Obermer cannot have been entirely carefree on the ski slopes –

her father failing (he was to die in April 1937), her mother writing depressed letters, her lover jealous and impassioned and her husband urging her to prolong her stay. He sent Gluck a postcard and the claim he was making threw her into a turmoil and pained her to read:

The hoar frost on the trees and bushes would fascinate you. What pictures you could conjure up here. Another year you too must come. I hope you are satisfied with your work. Nesta looks another person and I too am feeling fine. Nesta's mother writes lugubrious letters about her father and so N. has decided to leave here in a week. I am doing my best to prevent it, as it is doing her so much good and she simply loves the skating. I don't believe it is necessary for N. to return and I have written her mother begging her to send a reassuring letter so N. can remain a few weeks longer. Love Seymour.

Gluck could make no overt claims to the time or attentions of the woman whom she loved and regarded as her wife. She was dependent on endless letters and secret nights. She could scarcely have travelled to St Moritz, explained that Nesta and she were really married, then gone home with her together and for ever. Nothing in law either condoned or condemned her feelings. They were simply beyond the pale. To her, integrity of feeling must have its concomitant in integrity of expression. That was her creative ideal. To go against love so deep was self-betrayal, the ultimate crime. But however confident she felt about love for all Eternity, the pain of additional weeks of separation was more than she could bear.

Years later, when Gluck was in a safe but unromantic relationship, Nesta wrote from Honolulu, where she had moved with her husband, about the difference in their depth of feeling. She believed there was an invisible line which separated the truly talented, like Gluck, from more ordinary mortals such as herself.

Royal Hawaiian
On the Beach at Waikiki
Honolulu, Hawaii, USA
9 March 1952

Beloved Tim

This ain't a fairwell letter coz there ain't no fare-lells, but just to tell you what your friend Charlot said yesterday. They dined with us. I was telling him my theory about the invisible line and that you understood at once, and said you thought the reason I was below it was because I didn't love enough. He thought

Royal Hawaiian Hotel. On the Beach at Waikiki, 1952, Nesta, second left, sits between
her husband Seymour and Charlot (to her right)

*a moment and nodded and then said: 'Also, to be a creative artist, you must be
very good.' 'Good?' I said, surprised. 'But haven't there been many bad men who
were fine creative artists?' He shook his head. 'Not in the final sense.' I thought
of Yeats' line 'And I saw the blessedest soul alive, and he waved a drunken
head, – But he went on: 'Do you know what Matisse said to Braque? He said,
"When you start a picture you must recapture the atmosphere of your first
communion."'*

I nearly bust myself wanting my Tim. It was terrific, wasn't it?

*I enclose – no I don't – I tell you the amended itinerary. Imperial Hotel,
Tokyo. Then Bangkok, Hotel Oriental from April 26th to Tuesday May 4th.
Singapore (Hotel Raffles) only from 4th to 6th and Bali from 6th to 23rd.
Don't attempt any communication to Bali or Bangkok – only Japan, Manilla,
Singapore, Sydney and Auckland. Fiji, Samoa are also hopeless, because even
aeroplanes only come every ten days.*

*So you see Tim was touching the nail on the 'ead when 'ee said I didn't love
enough, and it's only thanks to your thought that I got the added nuggets.*

In their early days together such philosophical conundrums about Love do not seem to have preoccupied them. But there were always the obstructive roots and brambles. Gluck, while living only for the next meeting, was optimistic that a path would be cleared – in much the same way as she set her sights on Eternity while working specifically for her 1937 show. And promises were airily and vaguely made. In 1936 when Gluck was in her studio in Cornwall Nesta wrote: 'It'll be the last time you'll be there without me, d'you realise that.' 'Sweetheart do you *mean* this,' Gluck replied, 'or did you just write it in a sudden spasm? Anyway I love you for it and feel somehow it is true'. Somehow, she felt sure, Nesta would sort it out:

I trust you absolutely to handle your own personal situation with regard to us, *without question. . . . I was greatly relieved to feel you were going to do something to prevent things drifting. It will be much less wearing in the long run. But how or what you do to achieve this I would not presume to advise. I am completely happy and serene about it all. My instinct is to let you be and give you your head – because I can trust your heart. So my Italian Duchess – go to it!*[2]

So Gluck wrote while staying for a weekend with Wilfrid and Nancy Greene at 'Joldwyns', their Cornish home. The Greenes had had years of harmonious married life. It was this ideal of domestic accord that Gluck wanted unrealistically to achieve . . .

they made me ache. I didn't envy them, only felt it a privilege to know them and know my fortune was and might be theirs. Theirs is the real thing, and how rare and precious. And with all my heart I believe it is our possession too, now and evermore.

Questions of context and commitment matter more as love proceeds. Three months later, during the St Moritz separation, when things were quite evidently still drifting, Gluck was alluding to

a plan of campaign, too full of matter for discussion and adjustment for me to write, but the only solution for everybody's peace of mind and future well being. I feel you will approve and agree. It's terribly simple like all good plans – and honest so it can't be defeated (honest up to a point).

There cannot have been that many solutions on offer. They could choose between an affair, with all the excitement and problems of secrecy, separation and feigned casualness. Or they could end their relationship. Or Nesta could leave her husband and live openly with Gluck. It seems as if Gluck thought that this was what would be:

Friday, Thank God, morning, October 23rd

*You say I can never know how much you love me. All I do know is that I could
say the same to you, and I do not believe you will ever know how you fill and
smooth out all the gaps and tears in my heart – making it whole and happy as I
had always longed it should be. . . . I love you with my life. I can't bear to leave
you even like this, or to shut you up in the envelope but I must. You will be with
me truly now and forever, so why should I mind.*

Such absolute feelings, so close to jealousy, possession and pain, bring trouble
in their wake. For more mundane reasons openness was not easy. Gluck lived in
her beautiful Georgian house, had the studio designed by Maufe, the 'Letter
Studio' in Cornwall and two or three full-time staff, but this was all courtesy of
the Family Fund. She had a personal allowance to meet her needs, but no
capital. Her own earnings did not go far. It is unlikely that her trustees would
have revised her income to accommodate, in their view, even more remarkable
transgressions of lifestyle. Her brother, Louis, one of the trustees, was at the
time Conservative MP for Nottingham, absorbed in the problems of cutting
public expenditure and urging the nation to rearm.

Both women moved in social circles where money was the key to the good
life. Nesta, along with her works for charity and patronage of the arts, was
enmeshed in an extrovert whirl of travel, parties, high fashion, servants, and all
the expense of a stylish international social life, financed by her elderly
husband. She had no wish to lacerate his feelings. Divorce was none too easy to
obtain in the 1930s. Separation would have reduced her income and exposed
her to scandal. She kept her marital status perhaps as much for her own sake as
for Seymour's. It was one thing to have an intense and secret love affair while
seeming to conform to society's rules, another, more unpredictable and
isolating, openly to flout those rules and pioneer a different way. Perhaps
separation was never mooted, but words like 'forever', 'Eternity', and 'only you',
do suggest an exclusivity that it requires some strategy to achieve.

NINE

BLAZE WITH A

FIRE

Gluck was so sure of her future that for a week she burned her past. A visitor to her studio at Bolton House in October 1936 remarked that it was like Golders Green crematorium and Gluck thought the simile apt as she fed the fire with diaries, letters, photographs, and reminders of her life. 'My choicest moment today was burning several canvases.'[1] She burned, for example, most of the picture done in the 1920s in Lamorna of Ella Naper raking a bonfire while Gluck watched. But she kept the fragment of herself. And she burned her 'first serious paintbox':

Poor old thing. An honourable and fiery grave. I had had it over twenty years and it was pensioned off about four years ago and now it's gone because that half is gone and nothing is accompanying me now that does not serve.[2]

She was clearing out what she called the 'clinging unrealities' of her life. 'Mabel and Gwen' (her servants)

have been imitating a Greek frieze all day carrying away great stacks of stuff in procession. It is getting dark now and I have not stopped since this morning. . . .

It is the purest heaven to feel so completely above all this possession and outside it all – and to know how bright the future is going to be.[3]

Caution prevailed when it came to burning too many of her canvases:

You see dear Love just now I want to start such a new life that anything even vaguely smelling of the past stinks in my nostrils, but then it might not do so so much in other people's, so I must I suppose be a bit careful. . . . What would it matter if I destroyed everything. There is more, as I said crazily before, to come and we hope better.[4]

She felt a sense of freedom in the unencumbered rooms with all the problems of the past reduced to ashes and in possession of Love that 'makes me blaze with a fire that I do not believe even Death will be able to quench'.[5]

The relationship with Constance ended at this time. Hitherto, Gluck had spent her weekends at Constance's home, Park Gate, now it was Nesta's home at Plumpton. After the fateful May 1936, Gluck made only a couple more visits to Park Gate. On one of them Constance said she was 'bored about everything to do with flower pictures', and Gluck walked in the park alone. On the other, after Gluck returned from summer with the Hensons in Hammamet, she went down to Kent for lunch and tea. 'C. very stuffy to begin with and not much better after. Relief get home. Bed. Telephone N. 10.30. N. telephones me 11.20. Dial.'

And for Constance the regular midweek dinners and nights at Bolton House ended. She stayed once in June, a month after Gluck's 'marriage night' with Nesta: 'C. dinner and night B.H. Talk and say no more *', was Gluck's blunt diary entry for 24 June 1936, and once in November: 'Awful evening Thursday', was how that was recorded. A week later there followed a cryptic, confused exchange, the evidence of which Gluck saved from the flames and filed away. Mabel wrote Gluck a phone message 'Flower Decorations rang up. Mrs Spry would like to spend Thursday and Friday evening with you.' Gluck phoned the shop to say no (she was spending both evenings with Nesta). Constance's private secretary, a Miss Lake, rang to say 'No one rang from Flower Decorations last night. A mistake has been made.' And both she and Constance sent letters.

'Darling Gluck,' read Constance's (24 November 1936),

I've just had such an extraordinary message – 'Miss Gluck sorry she can't put you up on Thursday and Friday.' It's Greek to me! I haven't dreamed of such a thing. It must be someone else. You must have thought me a perfect damned nuisance. We've tried to get you on the telephone to explain – or Miss Lake has –

with no success and I've got to go off without having it explained to you. Love Constance.

And from Miss Lake on the same day:

I assure you that no message was sent to you on Mrs Spry's behalf last evening. The shop was closed at 7 o'clock and Mrs Spry herself left here at least an hour earlier. Any message being sent from Mrs Spry or for her would definitely go through me and no other person here would have any knowledge of this.

On the same day Gluck sent back Constance's nightdress with a letter. The following Monday Nesta called to see Constance and whatever the purpose of the visit it prompted a grateful reply:

My dear Nesta
I really cannot tell you how I value what you did yesterday. It was a very generous, a very wise and a kind thing to have done. More of your spirit would help everyone.
I look forward to seeing you again, and I'd like you to feel very sure of me – of my friendship, of my wish to be of use and of help if ever that were needed.
I love courage and clear cut action – and anyone who has the first and behaves the last fills me with affection and respect. Excuse the grammar, the paper and the dirt!
My affectionate thanks
Constance

On the evening of Nesta's visit to Constance, Nesta and Gluck went to a concert at Wigmore Hall. The following evening it was Covent Garden, the night after, the première of *Ladies in Love* followed by a cabaret. They dined mid-week at Bolton House and on 5 December – Constance's birthday (now scratched out of Gluck's diary) a Rolls Royce arrived at the studio to take Gluck to Plumpton for the weekend.

Whatever the circumstances (and Val Spry's understanding was that Gluck had become so demanding of Constance and difficult, that Shav Spry forced an end to the relationship, for fear that Constance's career would be hindered), a fatal rift happened at this time. They simply did not meet any more. It was the end of a friendship that had encouraged Gluck's talent, furthered her career and taken her into the heart of thirties smart society. The relationship was reduced to ashes along with all the other burning.

One of Nesta's first presents to Gluck was a gramophone and the songs of the day struck a special chord. 'These Foolish Things' was a favourite:

By the way I have ordered a new record – Cole Porter, very sentimental but clever, he's the man who wrote 'Miss Otis'. It's sung by Virginia Bruce and is called 'You've got under my skin'. [sic] I think you'll like it. It's not a dance record so it will do for us when we sit it out.[6]

Gluck went, while Nesta was away, to a season of surrealist films at The Everyman, Hampstead, and to an exhibition of eighteenth-century wallpapers at Sandersons which she found 'beautiful and somehow consoling'. She saw Mae West in *I'm no Angel*. 'Gawd! I was fascinated but never want to see her again' and the Dionne Quins in *The Country Doctor* which she found marvellous, amusing and fascinating.

She tried to cut down on smoking, forty a day of Players Medium Cut ('It's the Tobacco that Counts'), and tried to cut down on Dial, but very often it was her only way of getting a good night's sleep. She endured frequent visits to the dentist, a Mr Simpson, who told her he had never met anyone with such sensitive teeth. She bought new turtles for the fish tank, which she cleaned out regularly, but with equal regularity the turtles died. To salve the pangs of separation Nesta sent photographs of herself which Gluck scrutinized under a magnifying glass: 'the little haze of mist round your mouth which is your beloved breath on the cold air – I nearly died of that in the side view one'.

Nesta bought an eiderdown for the studio bed which was a great success. Mabel thought it 'looked so light as if it would fly up any moment'. It was not quite big enough so Gluck wanted to pay for an extra one. 'Then it is really and truly household, isn't it?' The idea of shared domesticity was important to her, as visible proof of their relationship, though it would be hard to imagine two women less interested in domestic chores.

Gluck bought an anchor for the punt in which they spent their romantic afternoons on the lake at the Mill House 'specially made and a chain to match ... I think it ought to make quite a difference to our pleasure and comfort.' She painted them lazing in it, she leaning against Nesta, the end of the punt stretching out across the water like a bright path that leads nowhere. (The director of The Fine Art Society thought the picture suggestive and would not have it in Gluck's 1937 exhibition.) They went with Leon M. Lion and Lord and Lady Hollenden to H. G. Wells's seventieth birthday party at the Savoy in October 1936. It was given by the PEN club and there were 500 guests. (No doubt Edith Heald, a founder member of the club, with whom Gluck was to live

The Punt. Nesta and Gluck lazing on the lake at the Mill House, Plumpton, c. 1937

for thirty-five years, was there.) They went to the first night of *Boris Godunoff* at Covent Garden, to *Cosi fan Tutte* at Glyndebourne, to supper at the Savoy, to the Café Royal. Molly Mount Temple came to dinner, as did Ernest Thesiger, Osbert Lancaster, the Maufes, the Villiers, the Toyes, the Greenes. And above everything, in the whirl of it all, Gluck worked. The eighteen-month build up to her fourth exhibition, in November 1937, was an extremely productive time. She tackled a whole range of new work and completed canvases already begun.

'Just this Beloved, nothing but happy pictures since Youwe', she wrote to Nesta. In 'Noel' she wanted to reflect her new sense of freedom. It was unlike anything she had worked on before. She did not draw first, but painted directly, delighting in conveying the textures of the things she was painting, feeling very 'robustious' as she put it and cracking crackers to get in the revelling mood. She got the streamers and blue frilled paper from Woolworth and the sinister mask is one she had torn as she put it on Nesta's head the previous Christmas. She

Miss Susan Ertz, popular novelist of the thirties and friend of Gluck and Nesta

The Lady Mount Temple, c. 1936, dressed by Schiaparelli, an M for Molly and Mount
Temple engraved on the buckle of her belt

worked at the picture for three or four months in 1937, one day painting a pale pink cracker, the next a little silver ball and, for days on end, the striped damask tablecloth. She strove to make the whole thing look as if it had been dashed off in a moment. She wanted the cake to look wobbly and unprofessionally made. There are little silver edible decorations, piped icing and a precarious robin. At times she thought it the limit of banality, but in the end she declared herself pleased, gave it 'satisfied and slightly bloated looks' between sips of tea and writing to Nesta, and wanted it to hang beside 'YouWe' in her 1937 show.

Two of her best portraits of women were to appear in this. There was 'The Lady Mount Temple', dressed by Schiaparelli in the absolutes of black and white, her hat perched on her head at an angle of conquest, her jewellery worn like military decoration, the veins in her hands revealing her age, her head cocked to one side as she looks down on her viewer with the arrogance and authority of her class. Equally telling psychologically, and technically better, was the portrait of the best-selling novelist, Susan Ertz, a friend of both Gluck and Nesta. Her serenity and elegance are emphasized by the muted browns of her clothes and the pale green silk of the upholstery. Her husband, Ronald McCrindle, commissioned the painting in 1936, but thought it made his wife look ten years too old. Gluck waited ten years and then offered it again through a letter from Nesta. Susan Ertz hung it over the drawing-room fireplace of her Kensington house and insisted on giving Gluck the original commissioning fee of £50.

The flower groups in the 1937 exhibition all showed Constance's influence – the considered displays and careful choice of vases. The large-scale 'Nature Morte', or 'Dead Group' as Gluck called it, the skeletons of flowers and grasses in an alabaster vase, all delicately painted in pale silvers, greens and browns, reflected Constance's view that anything from the hedgerow could provide material for an arrangement.

Gluck was aware of a sexual element in many of her flower paintings. Of 'Lords and Ladies' a picture of wild arum lilies, she wrote to Nesta, 'How can these flowers be female? Anything more male than this prominent feature I cannot imagine.' As she painted the flowers she wrote of 'loving them and stroking them with my most chosen brushes'. Of the blousy display, 'Lilac and Guelder Rose', Lord Villiers remarked, 'It's gorgeous. I feel I could bury my face in it.' Gluck called a painting of flowering chestnut 'Adolescence' and, with her typically unusual application of sexual stereotype, described the two blooms as a boy of eighteen and a girl of sixteen. The 'girl', she wrote, was wistful, slimmer and higher up in the picture so that the 'boy' has to reach up to get her.

Nature Morte, dried flowers from the gardens of Broadlands,
the centrepiece of Gluck's 1937 exhibition

She cut the two branches for the picture from the chestnut tree in the garden of her neighbours, the Toyes, while they were away. 'The bits I cut were taken from where it didn't make any difference to its divine shape – and Oh how lovely they are!'[7]

While working on this picture she wrote to her mother (13 December 1936), urging her to recapture her adolescent self 'the real you . . . was what you were before you married. . . . One's adolescent ideal is the core of one's spirit and what else matters when we come to realise the values in life.' Not the sort of letter that mothers in their sixties find terribly helpful, but an insight into Gluck, who stayed close to adolescent rawness of feeling and resisted maturity with its suggestion of compromise.

She ran into trouble with the quality of this canvas, a presage of the battle she was to wage for decades with the manufacturers of artists' materials. It was grainy and full of knots, the paint sank in and became dead, and subtle differences of colour and texture got blurred.

She finished the cornucopia of pomegranates begun in Hammamet and the head of the Arab boy. Mabel said he looked better without a cap, so bareheaded he remained. She finished the charcoal drawing 'In Aid Of . . .', lampooning a society gathering for whom a charity occasion is just another cocktail party. She showed it only to Molly Mount Temple and Nesta and swore them to secrecy because many of the people in it – the women who look like hens and the bored men – were apparently recognizable.

She did a quirky picture of a lovelorn rhinoceros, which she titled 'Frustration'. He, like Oscar the faience bull exhibited in her 1932 exhibition, was bought by Molly and hung along with Gluck's portrait of her at Broadlands. After Molly died the pictures were disposed of by the Mountbatten family, with whom she had not been popular.[8] The portrait turned up in 1973 in the cellar of Molly's sister's house. A friend wanted to buy it from her, but she gave it to him, remarking that she already had one portrait of Molly and one was enough.[9]

On a Monday in February 1937 Gluck and Nesta drove to Southease, a village in East Sussex in the valley of the river Ouse. They had a picnic in the car and Gluck began a landscape of the river at a point where it changes course, as she felt she was herself changing course, and flows to the open sea. She called it 'Sulky Spring, Southease'.

In June they went to Poole in Dorset, to an island they called 'their Shangri La', and Gluck painted one of her best seascapes, 'The Sands Run Out, Poole Harbour', looking inland from the sea with the sun breaking through the rain. Nesta had various broadcasting commitments in London, talks and poetry

In Aid Of...

readings with the BBC, so she travelled back and forth on the train. 'Marvellous and happy day, work at big picture.' 'Lovely day, bad weather. Cannot work.' were typical of Gluck's diary entries at this time.

In August, while staying down in Plumpton, she spent two weeks in the open air painting Falmer Church and graveyard: the church, its reflection in the water and the wall and towpath form the shape of a cross. Nesta spent several days with her and wrote a twenty-page sketch called *A Painter's Day* about interruptions from trippers of a different social class:

MAN: I s'y! Look at that now. 'e's pynting the church.
SECOND MAN: So 'e is now. *And* the water.
MAN: Wouldn't I blinkin' well like to be a painter instead of drivin' this blinkin' bus.
SECOND MAN: S'pose 'e'll get pots of money for that.
MAN: That's right. Pots. Some people's got all the luck.

Sulky Spring, Southease, 1937. The valley of the river Ouse, East Sussex,
a picnic spot for Gluck and Nesta

The Sands Run Out, 1937. Poole Harbour, Dorset, the setting for
'happy days . . . some of the happiest'.

Work and fun merged. There were games of badminton, teatimes spent lazing in the punt on the lake, enough days and nights together to keep dissatisfaction at bay and too much to do to be jealous for long. Everything was geared towards making a success of her show.

As in her 1932 exhibition she again created The Gluck Room at The Fine Art Society and as in 1932 this led to a great deal of fuss. Ernest Dawbarn, the director, kept out of the way and simply established the dates available for installation and when she must have the place cleared. A Mr Westbrook of the Camden Joinery Mill, Camden Town, got the job of constructing the room. He was experienced at building exhibition stands and displays, and confident of his work. He had no appetite for lengthy correspondence.

Gluck perfected the design used in 1932. The room, measuring approximately thirty by fourteen feet, and the frames, were this time to be in grey alder wood. Seven foot high pilasters, stepped vertically in the same way as her frames, divided it into bays and a boxed skirting, one foot six inches high and ten inches wide, ran round the circumference. A four foot six inch wide door separated The Gluck Room from the rest of the gallery.

Her relationship with her framemaker, John Footman, at the antique furniture dealers and restorers, Louis Koch in Cleveland Street, was good. If people got on amicably with Gluck over her business affairs, they were open with her, realized she was needy, did their best and were blessed with exceptional patience. As Mrs Guy, who did housework for Gluck and Edith Heald in later years when they lived in Steyning, Sussex, put it 'You could lead her, but you couldn't drive her. She had to think it was her idea.'

Mr Westbrook was a busy carpenter. The contract for The Gluck Room, though interesting and worth some £150, presented no particular problems. Gluck did. The colour of the alder was, she said, wrong, some of the fittings were an eighth of an inch out, there was confusion about the price of additional items and labour and the meaning of remarks that were or were not made. By the end of it all he lost his temper:

November 30th 1937

Dear Miss Gluck

Many thanks for your unlimited correspondence. I have wasted enough time and money on your job so far. I think it time I called a halt. Definitely your invoice stands as I have forwarded viz: a total of £148/15/6d. This sum you either pay or tell me you will not.

When you care to explain to me why you broke your part of the contract by refusing to have my name inserted in your catalogue as you definitely promised, I may feel inclined to answer further questions. Meantime I shall be very pleased to hear what you intend doing as regards to payments? I would refer you to your own letters of October 2nd, last paragraph, November 1st, second paragraph, November 3rd, first paragraph. An early acknowledgement of this letter and its contents will oblige.

Yours faithfully

A.J.Westbrook

She was getting as good as she gave – a formula which got her nowhere, time after time.

Accompanied by Nesta and the actress Leonora Corbett, who was starring in *To Have and to Hold* at the Q theatre, Richmond, Gluck made several visits to the tailor for her exhibition menswear. She arranged the lettering for the flag to be hung outside the gallery in Bond Street proclaiming her show, sorted out titles of pictures for the catalogue and supervised the printing and distribution of 2500 invitation cards. And a month before the show opened, she attempted to resolve a less practical problem – Mother. She wrote the Meteor a cautionary letter:

October 6 1936

Mother darling

I do hope you will read this letter very carefully as I am going to do my utmost not to write anything that could be misunderstood by you or that could possibly hurt you.

For at least a year, as you well know because I have often burst out about it to you, I have tried to show you how vital it seemed to me to avoid, especially in my Exhibition, any connection whatever with the family name. It is twenty years now since I have called myself Gluck and made it what it is, an independent and not entirely unknown name.

As you well know, there will be innumerable press people about, and that's the difficulty. You have been very sweet in wanting to help me as much as you can, but I have had repeatedly to refuse because no one can help me except in very small and personal ways, but now darling, I'm going to tell you frankly the ways you can help me. They are terribly important to me, though they may not seem so to you.

First of all, do remember to call me Hig instead of Hannah. It really worries me to think that at the Show, or any time we are with people, out will come the hated name. Do please make a tremendous effort for my sake.

Then I know you genuinely think it will help me to have some of the Royal Family at the show. For a very long time now, I have tried to tell you it is a matter of indifference to me about whether they come or not. Though you do not seem to realise it by your many remarks, my paintings have nothing to do with royal patronage, but a good deal to do with Time! And Time is a dignified affair and does not truckle to temporary things. If you had been a personal friend of the Queen it would be different. Even Queen Mary is different because you have had some sort of connection with her, but for the others you would have to write explanatory letters and immediately the comment 'why Gluck and Gluckstein' would come up at once.

The Brookses I should like to meet, because they are nice people and are sweet to you. For no other reason at all. As they are not taking the Royalty matter out of your hands and you would have to do it all yourself, I really do not want you to. If you do, I don't wish to hear another word about it, for to me it seems undignified, and we cannot run around explaining why I took the name of Gluck – and there it is!

I am putting all I have into this exhibition, every ounce of myself, and I do want to feel that you are in complete agreement with me, and not hindering me simply because I had not made everything clear to you. What I feel is that the people who come through knowing you with your name of Gluckstein can only be a source of danger and distress to me. Please try and see this, and when you send out the cards, do not put your name on as well as mine.

I am more than happy that you as my mother will be able to be at my show. You'll look a knock out and I shall be very proud of you. But it must be as my mother and not as Mrs Gluckstein. D'you see?

Anyway, if you truly love me you will do this to help me and give in to my wishes, even though they may disappoint you, so please darling let me recapitulate them once more.

1. Unless the Brookses can hand my cards to the Queen or any members of the Royal Family in the ordinary way of friendship or acquaintance, do nothing about it.

2. When you come to the show, tell no one you are Mrs Gluckstein. Just tell them you are my mother. You will help the sale of my pictures more than you know, because then I shall not be labelled 'rich amateur' and your personality will not be swamped by the name either.

3. And... 'HIG' darling. 'HIG' for ever more!!!

Bless you. Don't be disappointed, but now that you realise how much this *means to me, tell me that you understand and will do all I ask for my sake.*

Your very loving Hig

It was the letter of a child anxious that her mother might prove an embarrassment on prize day. Like a child, Gluck felt that the power her mother had over her would extend to others too. It was not the letter of a forty-two-year-old woman, of considerable professional standing, brazen enough to wear men's suits. Behind the wolf's clothing there lurked a sheep or even lamb, the victim, not the aggressor. Gluck was afraid, as ever, of losing her will, of 'being swamped', by the mere mention of her family name.

On Saturday 13 November she got her hair cut in the morning then met Mr Westbrook and his men at the FAS for the erecting of the alder wood room. They worked all day Sunday too, until he and his foreman left in annoyance, leaving Gluck to supervise the work alone. On the Monday she arrived at the Gallery at 7.30 in the morning for the hanging of her pictures the day before the show opened. 'Terrible day', she recorded in her diary, an observation with which those who knew her pre-performance nerves and perfectionist standards, would not have demurred.

The Gluck Room at The Fine Art Society, 1937, the walls and frames in pale grey alder wood

TEN

THE QUEEN WORE

PEACOCK BLUE

Gluck's 1937 exhibition ran from 16 November to 13 December. When it came to the staging of it, the Meteor did not stay as reticent as Gluck had hoped. The whole event had a distinct sense of an action replay. Mrs Gluckstein was more concerned in 'truckling with temporary things', like again getting Royal notice for her daughter's work, than in waiting for the uncertain 'dignity of Time'. She expended a great deal of energy in prompting the Queens Elizabeth and Mary to put in an appearance at The Fine Art Society. She exhorted Lady Clare Brooke, her friend at the Palace, to help. Lady Clare took the opportunity to elicit a 'small donation' for 'a jumble sale for one of the Queen's charities', sold Mrs Gluckstein tickets for a children's party: 'Do take your grandchildren. . . . The Duchess of Kent will be there and perhaps you could persuade her to come to your daughter's show' and, as two good turns deserve one other,

asked the Admiral about your small problem and he says you should approach Queen Mary through Lord Claud Hamilton and the Princess Royal through her Lady-in-Waiting. He is afraid the Queen may not have time to come to your

daughter's show as she has every moment of her time planned out, but do send
him the card with dates etc and if it can be arranged you know he will do his
best.[1]

That was before Gluck's plea for dignity and severance from the Gluckstein name. But, unable to resist doing what she felt to be best, two weeks after receiving Gluck's letter, the Meteor wrote again to Sir Harry Verney (20 October 1937) telling him of the exhibition and urging him to prompt Queen Mary

to honour my daughter once again with her presence. Her Majesty was so
gracious in coming to see Miss Gluck's previous exhibition and I felt most
happy, thrilled and excited at Her Majesty's kindly expressions of approval of
her work. The Press Day is November 16th and the Private View the following
day. If I might suggest it, I think the Press Day would be the best to get a review
of her work.

Sir Harry made known the invitation to Sir Gerald Chichester, Queen Mary's Private Secretary, who wrote direct to Mrs Gluckstein. His reply was terse: '... in view of the many engagements she has already entered into for November, it will not be possible for Her Majesty to have the pleasure of inspecting Miss Gluck's pictures.'

The Meteor in her work for charity was renowned for her persistence. 'Not possible' was an unacceptable answer:

October 23rd 1937

My Dear Sir Harry

Many thanks for your sending on so quickly to Queen Mary's Private Secretary
my letter. Alas! I am sad at the reply received, a copy of which I herewith
enclose. Perhaps I am to blame as I did not mention the exhibition was open for
a month until December 12 or 13th.

I am writing to the Hon. Gerald Chichester, acknowledging his kind and very
charming letter and rectifying my mistake by sending a card, like the one
enclosed to you and Lady Joan and it will show that the 13th is the last day.
The situation is indeed a rather delicate one. But I should indeed be sad, if by
my own error, my daughter should be deprived of the great Honour of a visit by
Queen Mary – who is so deeply interested in Art and has such a wonderful
understanding of the technical side as well. I hope it is not too late to correct my
error and that her Majesty Queen Mary may still find time to honour the

exhibition with Her Presence at her own time and convenience.

With my deep appreciation of your kind and ever ready help at all times and with best wishes and all kind thoughts in which my daughter unites to you and Lady Joan.

Sir Harry's recommendation was that she should not approach Sir Gerald again. 'If I had a chance I would say a word. But no one knows better than I do how terribly full up these next few months are.[2] In the event it was Nesta, a personal friend of Helen Graham, a Lady-in-Waiting to the Queen, who effortlessly scored the *coup de théâtre*. A word and all was arranged. Lady Graham called at The Fine Art Society, lunched with Gluck and Nesta at Bolton House and two days later wrote:

23 November 1937

Dear Miss Gluck

I told the Queen about your pictures yesterday and Her Majesty has said that she would like to look in quite privately and informally at the Gallery at 148 New Bond Street tomorrow (Wednesday) about 12.30.

Her Majesty does not wish any preparations made, or any visitors disturbed who may be going round, but I thought I would just let you know privately that the Queen was coming as I know she would like to go round with you.

Afterwards of course it will be quite in order for you to say that her Majesty has seen your Exhibition if you wish to.

Yours sincerely

Helen Graham

'The Queen', announced the 'Court and Society' column of the *Daily Mail*, 25 November 1937,

accompanied by Lady Helen Graham, paid an informal visit to the Fine Art Gallery to see the exhibition of painting by Gluck yesterday morning. Her Majesty, who was wearing a swagger suit of peacock blue velvet with a hat of the same colour, spent a considerable time in the Gallery, discussing the pictures with the artist.

Apparently Her Majesty found the pictures 'decorative', was 'much amused' by 'Noel' and 'greatly interested' in 'They Also Serve . . .', painted on George VI's Coronation Day, 12 May 1937, by Gluck from a fifth-floor window of the Cumberland, and showing crowds of people and lines of soldiers at Marble

Falmer Church, 1937

Lords and Ladies, c. 1936. 'I feel like a bee . . . penetrating them for their sweetness'
Gluck wrote, when painting these wild arum lilies

Arch, waiting for the procession to pass. After the Royal visit, Gluck went on to lunch with Nesta and Molly Mount Temple at Gayfere House. Godfrey Winn was there, noting for his 'London Letter' in *Everywoman* the Court gossip and the size of Lady Mount Temple's aquamarines. On the following day Queen Mary, accompanied by the Dowager Countess of Airlie, visited the exhibition, as she had in 1932, and stayed for about three-quarters of an hour. There were no contentious paintings of bosoms this time to make her *lorgnette* slip. Comment on the Royal visits was made by all the daily papers, and each Queen had a page to Herself in Gluck's Visitors' Book.

Gluck's friends rallied to make the occasion all it might be. Wilfrid Greene wrote the Preface to her catalogue, praising her freshness of thought, remarkable versatility, vigorous imagination, inherent simplicity and classical quality unspoilt by any trace of imitation. Nesta worked her social magic and encouraged the interest of critics and buyers: 'Mr and Mrs Seymour Obermer', announced *The Times*, 17 November 1937,

are giving a luncheon party at Claridge's today in honour of Gluck. . . . The guests will include: Viscountess Davidson and Viscount Davidson, MP, Sir Philip and Lady Gibbs, Major-General Sir John Hanbury-Williams (author of The Emperor Nicholas II as I Knew Him*), Lady Rumbold, Mr and Mrs Charles Morgan, Lady Mount Temple and Sir William Reid Dick (a trustee of the Tate Gallery). Afterwards a visit will be made to the private view of the exhibition.*

And the Meteor was chastised by her daughter for getting in the way when the furniture arrived in the Gallery on the Press Day.

The alder room and the exhibition's design received wide praise. 'The result is tranquil and attractive', said *The Sketch*. The large 'Nature Morte' of seeding plants was the focal picture in the show. 'Youwe' was shown alongside 'Noel', as Gluck had wished and Molly Mount Temple's portrait hung by the entrance above the carved table, where 700 or so visitors signed their names with a quilled pen in Gluck's red leather visitors' book. The furniture, all from Louis Koch's, was for sale, but nobody bought it.

The people in Gluck's portraits were themselves in the news. Susan Ertz had brought out her latest novel, *No Heart to Break*, Joan Swinstead was being warmly reviewed for her performance of Lysistrata at the Gate Theatre and Stephen Haggard acclaimed as Marchbanks in Shaw's *Candida*. (He was to die, aged thirty-one, in the impending war. Gluck's portrait of him was also destroyed.)

Thirty-three pictures were shown on the limited wall space with more in

They Also Serve... 1937. George VI's coronation, painted from a fifth-floor
window of the Cumberland Hotel

reserve. There were Gluck's usual themes: the stage, society people, flower
pieces, idealized landscapes, and her lovers – this time Nesta, and the painter
Mariette Lydis. Selling was brisk. Prices ranged from £20 to £300. Reviews
spanned the art, society and gossip columns. 'A brilliant exhibition of painting',
Bystander called it (24 November 1937):

*I do not remember for years seeing such a display of versatility. Gluck's flower
paintings would be her strong point if her landscapes were not so brilliant, and
her landscapes might get the top marks if it were not for her portraits or her still
life.*

Her pictures were reproduced in *The Sphere, The Bystander, The Tatler,
Studio, Apollo, Arts and Crafts, The Artist, Homes and Gardens,* and a splash
of seven of her best portraits in *The Sketch. The Times* (27 November 1937)
commended her for the 'clearness of her sense of form, her subtle use of colour
and curiously reserved emotional content.' T. W. Earp in the *Daily Telegraph*
called her crowd scenes 'little gems of humorous perception' and the *Daily
Sketch* in a personal interview described her as having 'the profile of a Greek

god' with eyes that 'shone like black diamonds'.

There was less comment about her name, Eton crop, plus fours and ties than in 1932. She was fêted at cocktail parties and at dinners with prospective clients. She went to tea with Sir William Reid Dick. There was success to celebrate with Nesta. They went to *The Prisoner of Zenda* and *Mourning Becomes Electra* and to parties with friends. And in the wings, but not entirely unobtrusive, the Meteor continued to involve herself in regal machinations to further her daughter's career. Under the guise, totally fictitious, of acting as agent for a rich American benefactor, she bought, for £500, four of her daughter's best pictures: 'They Also Serve . . .'; 'Lilac and Guelder Rose'; 'Falmer Church' and 'Lords and Ladies'. 'I have much pleasure in accepting your offer to purchase the pictures on behalf of a friend, who is to remain anonymous,' Ernest Dawbarn wrote to her. 'I understand that the purchaser would like these paintings to be placed among the Public Galleries and we will do our best to find Galleries who will be glad to accept them.'

The City Art Gallery, Manchester, was pleased to accept 'White Lilac and Guelder Rose' if bemused as to whom they were thanking or displaying. 'My committee', wrote their Curator to Mr Dawbarn,

*were delighted at the gift and regretted that they could not express their thanks
to the donor on account of the desired anonymity. Perhaps you will do so for
them. . . . Does the artist prefer to be known simply as Gluck without any
Christian name? I know that this is how she appears when she holds exhibitions,
but I wondered if, on the tablet affixed to the picture she should be known by her
real name.*[3]

An effusive letter of thanks was forwarded to Mrs Gluckstein from the Gallery Chairman, and the *Manchester Guardian* recorded, on 18 December 1937, the acceptance by the Galleries' Committee of the anonymous painting along with various dolls' clothes, dress accessories, and an eighteenth-century French woven shawl from Miss Whitehead of Bowdon. The Birmingham Art Gallery expressed delight in being given 'Falmer Church', but the Tate Gallery dithered over 'Lords and Ladies' and despite many members of the Committee wanting to acquire it, in the end the Trustees declined.

As for 'They Also Serve . . .', well, The Queen *had* hesitated before it, which must mean its proper place was on a palace wall. To get it there, the Meteor and Nesta were in cahoots, concealment deepened and the truth got further stretched. While the Meteor directed, Nesta pulled the strings. Nesta wrote again to the Queen's Lady-in-Waiting:

A private view. Guests at The Fine Art Society, 1937, in front of
White Lilac and Guelder Rose

14 December 1937

My Dear Lady Helen

An American collector has bought four of Gluck's pictures. One he has presented to the Tate, one to Manchester and another to Birmingham. The fourth one, the Coronation picture 'They Also Serve . . .' he feels strongly should be presented to Her Majesty The Queen if she would be willing to accept it, for it is such a personal picture and would remind Her of a unique moment in Her Life.

In his opinion, Gluck is the one young artist of outstanding genius in this country today (he has never seen her, he only knows her work) and he feels Her Majesty might like to have a specimen of her painting.

He has gone to America today and has left the picture in charge of Gluck's mother, so in the event of Her Majesty being willing to accept it, she would bring the picture whenever you wished.

Isobel came in the last day of the Show and simply loved it! She too feels that the coronation picture should be kept in the family!

Thank you so much for asking me to tea next Monday but alas we shall be in

Plumpton and won't be back until after Xmas.

Yours very sincerely

Nesta Obermer

Darling Meteor

Here's the copy. I sent the letter this morning. Not a word *to Gluck!*

Much love

Nesta

The Palace was not anxious to accept anything from anybody. In her reply to Nesta (21 December 1937), Lady Graham said she needed the name of the American collector before she could 'bring his offer before Her Majesty' . . .

I fully appreciate his thought that the picture would be a very interesting and fitting souvenir for the Queen to have of that unique occasion, but there is always the difficulty of accepting a gift of this nature from an unknown and, in this case – un-named donor. . . . Whatever the outcome may be, I am sure the Queen will be touched at the kind intention which has prompted this offer . . .

Nesta withdrew from the charade and gave the Meteor the letter to deal with as she would. She wrote to Lady Graham (27 December 1937) saying how deeply she regretted it, but she had promised the anonymous donor not to divulge his name:

. . . but as all arrangements are left to me, and so far the picture has not been paid for, I have decided under the circumstances to buy the picture 'They Also Serve . . .' so I can truthfully say it will be Gluck's mother who has the great honour of asking Her Majesty's acceptance of it, and I am sure the un-named donor will not mind.

I had the honour of presenting a work of my daughter to Her Majesty Queen Mary at the last Exhibition and it would give me great pleasure and happiness to offer for Her Majesty Queen Elizabeth's acceptance a remembrance of what must have been a most interesting day in Her Majesty's life.

The Palace, passing no comment on the tortuous convolutions accompanying this act of generosity, graciously deigned to accept the gift:

Her Majesty is waiving Her usual rule in such matters, but the two facts that have weighed with her are: firstly that the Queen warmly appreciates your wish to present her with a specimen of your daughter's work and, secondly, that this particular picture has a close connection with Their Majesties' Coronation.

I am to assure you, therefore, that the picture will be greatly appreciated by the Queen and I am commanded to convey to you Her Majesty's very sincere thanks for your kind thought.[4]

The picture was in the frame Gluck had designed. 'Time marches on', remarked the framemaker, John Footman, at the notion of this frame on a Royal wall. As for the Meteor, her gratitude was beyond words:

... I am unable adequately to express to you what I would desire to convey. How deeply touched and grateful I am at the Queen's gracious acceptance of my dear daughter's painting. Will you please convey to Her Majesty how honoured I feel and how much happiness it has given me. I am sure Gluck's heart will be gladdened at the knowledge of Her Majesty's acceptance and the Queen's appreciation of her work.

... May I wish their Majesties and the members of their family a happy and peaceful New Year and add how truly the King and Queen have reached the hearts of their loyal subjects by human understanding and personal help and sympathy ...[5]

Gluck suffered some kind of depressive reaction after her exhibition, went to bed and would not speak to her mother. She spent Christmas down in Plumpton and then went off with Nesta for a week in Lamorna. When they returned, Nesta wrote to the Meteor:

January
Private and confidential

Dearest Meteor

... She is furious about the Queen getting the picture because she thinks your name has got mixed up with it!! I have looked completely 'Blah' and I pretend to know nothing about it. But I keep telling her that you've done a very fine thing in getting it where it will be appreciated.

Watch your step though, because she is really annoyed at the moment and says she is not going to say one word to you about it, so don't you say anything either! Just let her simmer down! She is very nervy though she makes gallant efforts to master her nerves. ... I do think there is something wrong physically for she looks so white and drawn ...

I was interested to see how much more peaceful she became when she got to

Cornwall. I think it's a gloomy place to stay alone in, and I told her so, but she has such a real, solid affection for that part of the world that I think it would be a great mistake for any suggestion to be made at present to get rid of it. Let her get strong first.

All my love and don't forget this is a very private letter! She is so annoyed at the moment about your name and the Queen that she's not writing to you. But you know well enough it all means nothing and I really do think she is ill and tired into the bargain – though happy!

Much love dearest Meteor

Nesta

Gluck must have wondered quite whose exhibition it had been. The Meteor was unable to leave her alone at centre stage. Out of a desire to promote Gluck's reputation, and perhaps her own, she had made an undignified display. Her actions left Gluck uncertain as to where her own worth lay. The inference of her mother's determined efforts was that artistic worth could be got from Buckingham Palace or the national galleries. Gluck wanted her pictures to speak for themselves. They were all that she had to say. If they were to receive praise she wanted it freely given, not coerced. She had asked her mother unambiguously not to interfere. Her words had gone unheeded. Gluck could defend herself by changing her name and her appearance, but she could not change her mother who caused her to fight with superhuman force for a will she might call her own. She could not achieve her mother's standards of perfection. Nor, for that matter, as the years took their toll, could she either in life or art achieve her own.

ELEVEN

'THE BRIND AND
THE WHEEZE'

After the razzmatazz of the Bond Street show, Gluck's first thoughts were to take time off for a holiday with Nesta: 'The hoar frost on the trees and bushes would fascinate you. What pictures you would conjure up here. Another year you too must come.' So Seymour Obermer had written from St Moritz in January 1937, to Gluck as she pined in her Hampstead studio for his wife. The next January Gluck joined them in the mountains. She conjured up no pictures in Lenzerheide, but was crazy about Nesta's forte, skating:

Grand Hotel Kurhaus, Lenzerheide
February 20th 1938

Mother darling

... skating has taken such a hold of me that I can think of nothing else. ...
Nothing like an absorbing new occupation for putting things in proper
perspective. Yesterday I tried to waltz with Nesta and it didn't go too badly. She
is a crack skater – quite the best here. In fact she has given the professional
teachers many tips. ... It is such a graceful, lovely thing and so rhythmic to go

Waltzing in Lenzerheide, Gluck
and Nesta, 1938

round with the music which consists of a gramophone with loudspeakers and very good records – so you see my horizon though limitless is also bounded and I almost dream skating at the moment – you must forgive the obsession. My ankles, which I always had thought too weak are getting stronger . . .

I have only been on the ice three weeks next Monday. I have a lesson every day professionally, so something ought to 'marche' soon. On Friday we are going to take an expedition to the top of the mountain – Nesta on skis with two other skiers and Seymour and two Englishwomen we met on the rink and I on snow shoes. There is apparently a marvellous view at the top.

Goodbye my dear . . . I have literally no news because my whole existence at the moment is concentrated on skating . . .

Always your very loving Hig

The following year the trio went again to the same place. Seymour evidently accepted Gluck as a holiday companion. The months during which the world rumbled toward war were, for Gluck, happy, hedonistic, low on work and high on fun. In the early thirties she had entered Constance's world of hard work and high style. Now she moved into Nesta's life of outdoor sports, house parties and no work routine at all. She spent more time at The Mill than at Bolton.

Sporting crazes came and went. Horseriding in Plumpton followed skating in Lenzerheide, 'Fourth lesson – learnt about bridles and saddling at stables' was her diary entry for 20 September 1938. A couple of days later she wrote to her mother (23 September 1938): 'Riding goes on apace – Yesterday, my 5th lesson I rode some events with other pupils and came in first twice. I shall hate stopping to come back to London.' And, to complete the country image, she acquired a dog, a Weimaraner:

Mother darling

. . . I have a stupendous piece of news for you! I have a dog!! It is one of the most beautiful creatures you have ever seen. Its father is a champion. . . . It has the sweetest nature and will be a grand guard when I go out sketching. . . . I have always loved dogs as you know, but felt I ought not to have one until life seemed more settled. Now I feel the moment has come.

Now comes the very important part of this letter and please *don't forget about it. Nesta has given him to me – but we have told* Seymour *and* everybody *that you* have *given him to me because it seemed more politic from every point of view – She has been far too generous really and he is a 'show' dog and for that reason she felt she would sooner no one knew she had given him to me. You are the only person to know and you must never divulge the secret. I expect all this will amuse you, but with your experience of people and life you will certainly see eye to eye about it I know.*

The dog, Zar, in his short life became uncertain as to quite where home was. Perhaps Gluck was uncertain too, despite her claims to feeling settled. Those who knew her in her later years say she had little rapport with animals – that she was sharp with dogs and they disliked it.[1] Zar was boarded out for a good deal of the time. And Nesta seemed uncertain as to quite whose job it was to look after Gluck, if looking after was what was needed. An arrangement had been made, to mollify Seymour, whereby Gluck spent alternate weekends away from the Mill House with Nesta's mother, who lived in the nearby village of Uckfield but this became problematic and before long Nesta was writing to the Meteor with another proposal:

'I have a dog'. Gluck and Zar

Dearest Meteor

. . . I've been thinking hard about you and Gluck and the summer. As you know, she has been spending alternate weekends with me and

with my mother. My mother is rather a society fly-about really . . . She is the kind who took up Gluck like so many have done and now Gluck has made herself at home and lays down the law a little (you know!) she does not take into account the workings of genius, but is getting a little restive. Nothing is wrong yet, but I, knowing my mother, can see it coming! I have said nothing to Gluck about it naturally.

Now. She has often bemoaned the fact that your life and her life are so utterly apart . . . and suddenly last night I thought what a marvellous idea it would be if you got a house in the country and let her come down every other weekend to you . . .

. . . If you did this you would have to find the house on your own and when it was all ready say casually, 'I'm trying this for a month come down some weekend!' I know that really she would far rather be with you than anyone. My mother's is only a pied a terre. . . . The country which Gluck says is very paintable is Rye and round that part of Sussex. Or where there are very large fat trees! If you think anything of the idea tell me and I will keep my eyes open . . .[2]

What the Meteor thought of the idea is not on record. But it came to nothing and on the face of it more houses and seeing more of mother, were not what was needed.

However unsettled her sporting life, Gluck was having fun. She spent a good deal of time trundling back and forth between Hampstead and Plumpton in her 1935 Hillman, registration BUL 700, to which she was devoted. It kept going wrong but the Meteor, for the most part, footed the repair bills. The summer of 1938 was spent holidaying, mainly with Nesta, in Dorset, Devon and Cornwall. 'It's rather fun to mess about like this before I start work again in earnest,' Gluck wrote to the Meteor (23 August 1938). She stayed for a week with Nesta's friends the Hollendens at their South Devon home, Matt's Point. (Lord Hollenden had bought Gluck's picture of the chestnut branches, 'Adolescence', at her 1937 exhibition.)

It is one of the most spectacular places I have ever seen. The house is halfway down a cliff. . . . And then there are hundreds of steps and paths down to the sea and swimming pools in the rocks and beaches and caves – the whole headland belongs to them so it's peaceful and untroubled and quite lovely. . . . It's just possible I may do some work here . . .

And a couple of months were spent at the 'Letter Studio' with a host of house guests. Work remained a possibility.

A gruff word from Ernest Dawbarn of The Fine Art Society, in October 1938, went unanswered: 'I hardly feel that what we have left from the exhibition does justice to you, and thought, perhaps, by this time you might have been able to let us have one or two new pictures.' The only picture she recorded working on between the end of her 1937 exhibition and the outbreak of war was a commissioned portrait of Peter Giffard in January 1939. He was seventeen and she did a profile of his knobbly Adam's apple, chin and nose with his hair like a thick thatch.

The Giffards lived in Chillington Hall, Wolverhampton, inherited through the direct male line, for nine centuries, from Walter Giffard. He, so the legend ran, came to England when William the Conqueror invaded – riding alongside him as it was his hereditary right to hold William's stirrup when he mounted or dismounted his horse. His reward for this, and presumably other services of conquest, was Chillington and all its lands. Some years ago Gluck's picture, still at the Hall and in its original stepped frame, was affected by a form of mould which made the hair colour fade.

Gluck took three weeks over the portrait then hastily packed for six weeks in the snows of Lenzerheide with the Obermers. This time she took up skiing as well as skating. She had seven lessons before breaking her thumb, which ended her sortie into winter sports.

After skating, skiing and riding came sailing – for a while. She bought a boat and a 3/6d how-to-do-it book from Lillywhites, put the boat on her car roof and drove it down to the lake at Plumpton:

August 9th, 1939

Mother darling

... The day before yesterday having practised different rope knots and read my book I felt I must go a stage further, so rang up a friend of Nesta's, a retired Colonel cracked about sailing who came across in his old clothes. It was blowing and pouring and we spent a happy messy wet afternoon crouched in the boat on the lake. He was very sweet – a bad limp and a big tummy and was like a boy about it all – from 3.30 to 5 pm he sat crouched and could hardly stand up when he got to land. He taught me a lot and said he wants to take me sailing at Newhaven. Isn't it exciting. He gave me a small examination at teatime and I didn't make any mistakes. I have been dreaming knots and tackle and am truly very thrilled about it. I have always loved water and boats and it's like a very pleasant dream come true.... It's done me no end of good to have something so

bracing to be interested in as I must get fit and less jumpy before I can paint again . . .

As soon as I give this to the postman you can imagine me rushing to the boat – so 'yo ho ho and a bottle of rum', Quite crazy you see, as usual. Goodbye darling. Take care of yourself. Forgive all this nautical news – as Nesta said in a lovely spoonerism the other day "The brind and the wheeze" are calling!!

My best love as ever
Always your loving Hig

Gluck moved as far as she could into Nesta's life. They went to the Plumpton Races at weekends, to the Dog Show at Olympia where Zar was exhibited, to cocktail parties, Glyndebourne, art exhibitions and the first nights of the theatre people whom they knew. At times Gluck noted the precise number of hours and minutes of the week she and Nesta had spent together, with the rueful implication that these might have been more.

For most of 1939 they worked together hectically on a fund-raising project of Nesta's. This was to raise money for the Heritage Craft School, in Chailey, Sussex. The school, dependent on charitable finance, provided education and hospital care for disabled children. Nesta's idea was to organize an exhibition of antiques, loaned by Royals and aristocrats, which the public would pay to see. It was a project after the Meteor's heart. The title, which took up a quarter of the headed paper, read:

EXHIBITION OF ROYAL AND HISTORIC FURNITURE
AT 145 PICCADILLY
Graciously loaned by
THEIR MAJESTIES THE KING AND QUEEN AND QUEEN MARY
THE DUKE OF CONNAUGHT, K.G., PRINCESS LOUISE, DUCHESS OF ARGYLL
PRINCESS ALICE, COUNTESS OF ATHLONE, PRINCESS HELENA VICTORIA
AND OTHER MEMBERS OF THE ROYAL FAMILY AND OTHER OWNERS
IN AID OF THE HERITAGE CRAFT SCHOOLS, CHAILEY, SUSSEX

Princess Alice was President of the exhibition and Lord Hollenden its Chairman. 145 Piccadilly was the London home of George, Duke of York, until he became King in 1937. Nesta whisked Gluck from palaces to stately homes persuading the rich and regal to lend their chattels. But Gluck had no history of interest in collecting money for charitable ventures, that was her mother's domain, nor any true zeal for organizing exhibitions other than her own. 'Life seems to start at 6.30 and go on to midnight these days,' she wrote to her mother in May 1939. 'I am never in after 9 in the morning at Bolton House and don't get back till about 11.30 or 12. What a life! There's one consolation, it can't go on for ever but must stop soon –'

And stop it did. The exhibition opened on 28 June 1939. It ran for two months, raised a substantial amount for the Heritage and earned Gluck more Royal notice – from Princess Alice who wrote commending her on her 'marvellous triumph, ability, untiring energy and self sacrifice for Chailey'. On the 3rd of September Gluck's laconic diary entry was 'War declared. N. at BH.' She spent the next few days returning the Royal furniture, closing the exhibition at 145 Piccadilly, and packing up Bolton House to go down to Sussex. She appeared more concerned at not seeing enough of Nesta, than at the threat of war. 'Saw N only by own efforts for a few minutes after Wednesday.' 'Stay night only by saying too tiring to leave so early for meeting next day' were her disgruntled diary entries. Gluck's preoccupations were with Love and Art and her own feelings. Her battles were within and her war was to come a little later.

Nesta at the opening of the Exhibition of Royal and Historic Furniture, 1939

Within weeks, Bolton House was commandeered by the Auxiliary Fire Service. She handed the whole thing over to her Trustees to sort out, kept the studio as a London *pied-à-terre* and moved in with Nesta's mother, Mrs Sawyer, while searching for a house close to Nesta's to rent. Mrs Gluckstein, mindful of the hints Nesta had dropped of her mother being less than enamoured of Gluck as a house guest, wrote to thank Mrs Sawyer. 'I do not want thanks when it is a pleasure to me to have Gluck,' Mrs Sawyer replied.

The upheaval and uncertainty unsettled Gluck and she felt Nesta was not helping all she might. 'My looks say I am well, my spirit is a mess at the moment and my body and nerves almost at the end of their tether', she wrote to her mother (24 September 1939). But she soon found a house and because of petrol rationing got herself a bicycle, which she quickly learned to ride. Nesta bought a motorbike, which she rode round the lanes at alarming speed.

'Millers Mead', in Plumpton, was about two minutes away from Nesta. It was small, not at all on the scale of Bolton, and a simple outhouse in the garden was to serve as Gluck's studio. She took it 'for the duration' at a rent of £218.8.0d a year and moved in with a married couple, the Fitzgeralds, as her servants. There were numerous letters to mother, appealing for an iron, a bell for summoning the servants, a supply of liquor – six bottles of claret, Chateau Durfort Vivens, 1929, six of hock and a quantity of spirits – cans of salad oil, a bedside table and a lawn mower. She got hens and hives of bees and prepared herself for the privations of wartime.

And she began working again. A commission came from the Bougheys, cousins of the Giffards. They lived in Malling, a big early-eighteenth-century house on the Sussex Downs, near Lewes. Their twenty-year-old son, John, had been called up to fight with the Coldstream Guards and they asked Gluck to do his portrait before he left. Though they lived only eight miles away, because of petrol rationing she moved in with them to do the work, eighteenth-century style. She was nervous about the commission. She did not know them and it was, as she put it, 'my first painting for many moons'.

Her stay was a success. 'I have never met such sweet and kind people as these', she wrote to her mother (14 October 1939). She found it a strain for she was out of practice and anxious to do her best. They turned the fives court 'a vast echoing building' into a studio for her. She stayed for two weeks and Nesta called over a few times to see how she was getting on. It is not technically one of her better portraits, but with its background of oak leaves the Bougheys felt that it caught the boy's patriotic spirit. And it perhaps symbolized the broad-shouldered, innocent-eyed young men who were to fight and, as in John

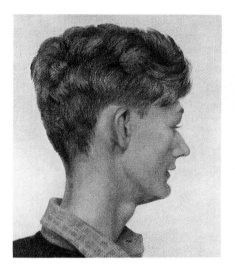 

Portraits commissioned in 1939:
Peter Giffard and *John Boughey* – who was killed in the war

Boughey's case be killed, in the war against Hitler.

Of the visit, John Boughey's sister, Hermia, remembered candlelit dinners, her father opening special bottles of wine, a great deal of laughter and Gluck's lively conversation. And their mother, Lady Boughey, wrote Gluck a long letter of thanks both for the consolation of the portrait and for what she felt to be 'the great and wonderful gain of a friend . . . which is precious and I know enduring.' The family were to remain devoted and lifelong friends of Gluck's.

The next commission came from Nesta. It was a portrait of her mother, Ethel Sawyer, known to friends as Boo. Gluck began it while staying with Boo in October 1939 and finished it when she moved into her new studio at Millers Mead. Boo was elderly and at times illness made her tearful, but in her portrait she puts on a brave face. She looks the epitome of a respectable English gentlewoman: veiled hat, no-nonsense smile, pearls, mayoral collar and bright if rather watery eyes.

Gluck could have picked up any number of portrait commissions. The war sharpened people's awareness of the tenuousness of human life and they wanted consoling images of those whom they loved. The solicitor who drew up the agreement for the renting of Millers Mead was impressed with Mrs Sawyer's portrait and wanted one of his eldest son. The Maufes hoped for three – of Prudence, Edward and their son. Friends of the Bougheys offered her

Portrait of an English Gentlewoman. Nesta's mother Mrs Ernest Sawyer

commissions. Word went round about her work. 'Not that I want all these portraits,' she wrote to the Meteor, 'as you know I find them a terrible strain, but just the same it's marvellous in these difficult days and I am grateful really to help my diminishing income.'

Early in December 1939 she went to Chillington Hall, Wolverhampton, to do a portrait of Diana Giffard, who later married the MP Airey Neave.[3] She travelled by train to Wolverhampton with all her gear and the Giffards met her at the station. 'It looks a bit over life size', Gluck wrote to her mother of the house. She described the Hall as a 'bracing place 500 feet up'. Everything was on the grand scale. Even the private driveway was two miles long which played hell with the petrol ration and presented problems with the post. The place was so vast that footmen bicycled through the hallways from the servants' quarters when the front doorbell rang, in order to arrive before visitors grew too disconsolate. A fire was lit for Gluck each night in her room. She slept well, enjoyed herself, worked hard, and thought the Giffards charming and sweet to her. 'Last night they started to teach me to knit and we became nearly hysterical with laughter in the process. It's rather fun.' It was a pair of mittens on four needles. She did not get far, and Diana Giffard finished them and gave them to her for Christmas.

Gluck worked out something of a formula for her commissioned, flat-fee portraits – a head and shoulders with an uncomplicated background took her two weeks. But now she again ran into problems with the quality of the canvas:

Every day I do a tiring good day's work and the next day it all looks as if water had run through sand. Nothing to show for it. . . . It's one of the things I've got to settle when I get to London. I can't go on like this any longer. This is the third experience and a new guaranteed canvas. . . . It has all taken at least four times as long.

She was back in London in time to do her Christmas shopping at Whiteleys department store and to arrange for the transfer of her piano to Millers Mead. It was a snowy winter, the water pipes at the Mill House froze and the hens declined to lay. Gluck bought a flying suit so that she could work in the icy weather. 'I just pull it on over very few clothes, zip it up and am so warm it's almost too much. It looks very dashing so I feel quite smart at the same time.'

She had collected together what she could of her world and brought it as close to Nesta's as was possible. Close as this was, it was by no means as close as she had dreamed and hoped. But she believed, fatalistically, that things would work out as they must, and she was prepared to wait and see. She spent her fourth consecutive Christmas at Plumpton with Nesta, Seymour, the Villiers and the new addition, Zar. And on New Year's Eve Nesta went over to Millers Mead. The two of them had supper together, danced and saw in the New Year. Nesta who had a bad cold left at 7.45 a.m. on New Year's Day.

Convolvulus, 1940. 'One of my best flower paintings'

TWELVE

THE WAR EFFORT

In March 1940 Gluck became ill. Love, for which she had burned her past and on which she had staked her future, was not working out. 'Dearest Meteor,' Nesta wrote (7 March 1949),

Gluck had a most terrible brainstorm yesterday and tried to jab her wrist with a knife . . . she shouted and raged for an hour, in which time she called me a Liar, Callous, Selfish, had done nothing for her etc. . . . She put on her heavy flying suit when I went to take Zar for a walk and scared everyone by disappearing. I looked everywhere – even rushed the car to the Downs. It was nearly dark when I discovered her walking in the fields. She had been walking for an hour and was absolutely done. I've told the doctor he must be drastic. Of course you must know nothing . . . the more she works herself into these fits, the worse her heart will get.

The year began peacefully enough for Gluck. Her first painting, to 'christen' her new studio, was an idealized drawing of Nesta's head. She called it 'Madonna', or 'Nativity' and it speaks only of repose and love. With Gluck as her tutor, Nesta, too, set up a painting studio down at the Mill House. Grounded by the war, exotic travel and winter sports denied her, she turned for recreation to art. She proved a keen pupil and painting became a lifelong enthusiasm. She made no great claims for what she produced – Gluck in later years referred to her efforts as 'daubings' – but she had panache and was prolific. At some point one of her paintings was bought by the Los Angeles Gallery of Modern Art. Called 'The Clutching Hands of Every Day', it showed 'nothing but hands writhing – holding one back from all things one wants to do!' In a matter of months in 1940 she produced forty-five canvases, which she sold at an exhibition in the Reading Room of the Village Institute in Plumpton to raise money for the Red Cross. They were mainly landscapes and portraits and certainly free-flowing. 'I am very proud of my pupil,' wrote Gluck to the Meteor (18 September 1940), but she showed little interest in the exhibition and only went to it after Nesta criticized her for not doing so.

The winter of 1939–40 was sufficiently cold to allow skating on a friend's pond, a small compensation for being kept from the Alps. A hen laid the first egg – cracked – on 27 January 1940, the second – cracked – on the 29th, the third – cracked – on the 30th and the fourth – whole – on the 31st. Gluck again resolved to give up smoking, this time to pay for Zar's food, a resolve she again did not keep. Requests for commissioned portraits continued to come in. The Maufes kept hoping for theirs, Ida Copeland, former Unionist MP for Stoke-on-Trent, Commissioner for the Girl Guides and wife of the Director of Copeland China Works in Cornwall, asked Gluck to paint both her soldier sons before they were posted overseas. She lived in Truro and Diana Giffard and Christabel Pankhurst were staying with her in March 1940 when she was urging Gluck to 'come without delay'. 'She looks rather like an insignificant little black beetle,' Diana Giffard wrote to Gluck of Christabel (18 March 1940), 'I simply can't imagine her chaining herself to lamp-posts and being sent to prison.'

At Millers Mead Gluck was close to Nesta with enough work in the offing. The Meteor used her powers of persuasion on the Chief Petroleum Officer, Tunbridge Wells, to ensure her daughter's ten-gallons-a-month ration got doubled so that she could motor with all her gear to fulfil her various commissions. But something was wrong with Gluck. She was suffering from what seem to have been anxiety attacks, her heart palpitating, worrying obsessively about practical matters, unable to get down to work.

The catalyst to the outburst described by Nesta came in March 1940 with Gluck's servants, the Fitzgeralds. They lived in and she paid them £120 a year for all general duties. On the morning of the 2nd March, after a fraught weekend of rows with the Meteor over business matters, she told Fitzgerald to clean the windows. He refused, saying the sun was on them. She asked if he was refusing to carry out her order and he replied, yes. She asked him to repeat this in front of Mrs Fitzgerald, which he did, adding a few unrecorded insults. The couple were out of the house by 2.30 p.m. The doctor was summoned. He ordered Gluck to bed, told her to forget about work and gave her Haverol Oil capsules and an injection of 'one of those very good vaccines' – a dubious medicinal concoction of arsenic and iron – 'made by Allen & Hanbury, recommended for cases of this kind by Sir James Purves Stuart, the great nerve Consultant'. On Nesta's recommendation, a resident nurse was brought in. 'When I saw her I gave a gasp of joy', Nesta wrote to the Meteor (9 March 1940). '... I *knew* Gluck would like her. Tall, iron grey hair, grey eyes and a strong quiet face. Took command quietly. Gluck obeyed like a lamb!' The doctor wrote to the Meteor telling her not to visit her daughter who was 'on the verge of a serious breakdown', that her heart was feeble and intermitting and that were it not for the help and support of Mrs Obermer matters would be worse.

The Meteor paid for the nurse – three guineas a week – sent down a revolving garden sun hut, large enough to take a day bed, put £1000 of Defence Bonds into Gluck's account, paid a ten-shilling fine for her, incurred by driving through a red traffic light and wrote her sweet letters telling her to 'forget about the war, the chickens, me and everybody'. Nesta organized replacement staff, looked after Gluck's affairs and sent progress reports to the Meteor. Perhaps Gluck courted such responses to her neediness. But her illness was real enough. The upheaval of war and relinquishing Bolton House had left her insecure, and moving to Millers Mead, just down the road from Nesta emphasized how close to her she was, but showed also that she had scant hope of getting closer.

Gluck stayed in bed for a month and wrote notes collected in a folder called 'Book' about her theories of painting – about being true to vision, receptive to the identity of the subject painted and painstaking in the execution of work. Though repetitive and oratorical – she urges her reader never to work simply for money or in a way that feels compromised or false – the core of her ideas (see pages 42, 54, 89 and 192) is profound and heartfelt.

She cancelled the Copeland portrait, which would have brought her in a hundred guineas, and went instead, after a month of complete rest, to Bournemouth for a week in April 1940 with Nesta and Mrs Sawyer. In her diary she noted seeing a rainbow, reading Blake, restful days and not sleeping well when she and Nesta were given hotel rooms on different floors.

By June she felt strong enough for what was intended to be the first of

Facing: top, *Sir Edward Maufe*, 1940. In the background is his sketch for Guildford
Cathedral. Below, *The Pleiades*, 1940–3. Above, *Violets*, 1940–1

three portraits, husband, wife and son, of the Maufes. 'Three small portraits to go with their family ones – one of the most honouring commissions I have ever received.'[1] She began with Edward. The other two did not get done. Though Maufe had won the competition for Guildford Cathedral in 1931, the foundation stone was not laid until 1936. The war then put a stop to building, and the Cathedral was not consecrated until 1961. Gluck used his winning signed sketch as the background 'brainwave' to her picture and shows him drawing the plan of the cathedral on his worktable. She captured his tall, willowy elegance and episcopal looks. He and Prudence were accomplished dancers and he was said to be charming, exquisitely mannered and shy. The joke ran that he was so shy that on arriving at a party and announcing 'I'm Maufe', his host's reply was 'what already?' After Maufe, Gluck painted a delicate flower piece – white convolvulus in a stemmed glass. It took her five weeks of solid work. The flowers wilted within hours and she scoured the hedgerows for replacements. She painted it in the summer of 1940 at the time of the blitz on Britain, air raids and dog fights in the sky. She regarded it as one of her best flower paintings. It was bought by the owner of Millers Mead, a Colonel Hale, whose son eventually took it with him to Rhodesia.

Though uprooted and unsettled by the war, Gluck was neither deflected from her artistic vision nor made afraid. 'People say to me, "what dreadful times to live in ..." I don't think so. They are inspiring and spiritual times, earthly and material values not meaning a damn thing any more, because they are so insecure.' She saw an enemy plane brought down in flames over the downs, heard the 'goings on' of bombing all around, and went to air-raid practice, a first-aid course, and jam-making mornings at the Village Institute. The hens went broody and supplied her with twenty-seven chicks and the bees seemed regularly to sting her and Nesta, but provided them with honey too. Rabbits were added to the home farm, eggs pickled, vegetables bottled. The next set of servants, the Uptons, left at a moment's notice, but somehow replacements were again soon found. Gluck trained as an emergency ambulance driver and volunteered to house a pilot for forty-eight hours' leave twice a month – no pilots appeared. When in September 1940 she heard of the death of John Boughey she drove straight over to 'Malling' to be with his family. They are thankful they have the portrait,' she wrote to her mother,

but I now feel if only I had the tongue of an angel ... I did my best, and if it wasn't worthy of the full greatness of the boy, at least it got something of his

quality. I cannot bear to think of it and I feel so sad and unhappy for his
wonderful and lovely family.

She tried to work as if nothing was wrong. A war she thought just was being fought, but it was not her war. And behind the self-sufficiency – the hens, the rabbits, the bees – a kind of personal loneliness was compounding. Her relationships with her constantly changing staff seemed to worsen. She watched them like a hawk and criticized their every move. Time after time they left hurriedly after explosive scenes. It was a roll call of disaster. After the Uptons came the Burdens, who left amid scenes with her and the police. Then Mr Williams, Mrs Stevens, Miss Scott, Margaret, and Beatrice who stole some onions and silver and was at once dismissed. Then Mr Holloway who got an ulcer, ended up in Chailey Hospital and was viewed with suspicion by Gluck's Dr Richards. He wrote to her (6 February 1941):

This man's a damn sight too psalmy for my liking . . . for an out of the way place
like Chailey and Plumpton there have been an enormous number of bombs
dropped and I do know the police are on the look-out for suspicious people in that
neighbourhood, although the railway has been suggested as a possible cause.

Then Miss Ward, followed by Mrs Drury, both of whom stuck it for a week. Then Mrs Payne, Mrs Richards who suffered from hysterical symptoms of tightness in the throat, and her son whom Gluck helped with his spelling, Mrs Beard, Mrs Dennett, Mrs Facey, Paula, Mrs Caspell, who was not a good cook and cried all day after Nesta gave her a dressing down, Isobel, Dora, Mrs Reed, Miss Foster – all fled or were fired with indecent speed.

Nor was Gluck managing with Zar. He took to disappearing for hours at a time and would show up three miles away or go down to the Mill House for the night. She punished him by withholding his food or ignoring him, which did not make him a more obedient dog. And worst, and at root, there were cracks in her relationship with Nesta. They were lovers in the afternoons or in hotels. They always saw the old year out together and the New Year in (in 1940 Nesta arrived at Millers Mead on her bicycle at 10.30 on New Year's Eve and at midnight they had oysters and champagne), but she seldom slept at Millers Mead, Gluck now had no excuse for staying at the Mill House and the Love to all Eternity of 1936 seemed far away.

Gluck went on producing good work though she took to spending longer on each picture. The deadline of an exhibition or the pressure of a commissioned portrait made her paint quickly. Left to herself she worked with a sense of timelessness and with exquisite precision. To visitors to her studio, she would show, under a magnifying glass, the silken undersides of petals of flowers painted in six colours with brushes pared to a few hairs. A painting of violets, begun in November 1940, took her about seven months. The villagers of Plumpton came to see it when it was done. The Bougheys commissioned it and paid her a hundred guineas. She described her 'vision' of its shape – a votive offering in a bronze vase, formal in composition, clean and cool in colour, the violets wiry and strong despite their delicacy.

After 'Violets' came a tangle of pink convolvulus and grasses. Called 'Pleiades', it is a small piece, 19×24 cm. She worked out of doors, crouching for hours over the same patch of weeds, until her back ached and her hands, already showing signs of the arthritis that bent her frame in later years, got cramp. It is rich in hidden detail. The grasshopper on a leaf and the drops of dew on a web come as a suprise. The tangle of leaves gives a sense of cover, of life going on in the dark world beneath what is seen. As in 'Noel', she created order, rhythm and harmony out of seeming disorder. She worked again at it in June, July and August 1942 – 'N. comes at 3.15 and leaves at 3.50. Very depressed and find gossamer very difficult to do.' was her diary entry for 26 July 1942. She lamented to her mother:

. . . if I don't get it done before September is over I am dished – and there are two waiting prospective purchasers. Anyway I am not anxious to face it again a third year and the work in it is terrific. I can only do very little every day and it is a great strain on the eyes. It is certainly going to be worth it when finished, but when will it ever be finished!?[2]

She did face it for a third year and finally finished it, or at least let it be, in August 1943.

Early in 1942 she did a commissioned portrait, 'George Hardinge Esq.' He lived nearby at a house called Sheffield Park and liked bridge, billiards, the races and the Church. He was a difficult sitter and she had problems in getting canvas and paints of decent quality. He got very tired, and as one of the sittings was on a Sunday, went off to church for a couple of hours in the middle of it. In his portrait he looks difficult and Old School, his collar starched and white and his moustache and what is left of his hair, neatly groomed. He looks well cared for though, no doubt by Mrs Hardinge, who provided Gluck with supper and champagne and showed her round the garden.

Gluck met him through her association with the Sussex Churches Art

Council. The Bishop of Chichester, President of the Council, officiated at the Thanksgiving Service and lunch, given in Gluck's and Nesta's honour, in the Chapel of the Heritage Craft Schools, Chailey, in gratitude for the money they raised from the Exhibition of Royal Furniture in 1939. Each Christmas the two women went to a service at Chailey Chapel and sat in the front pew with the Schools' founder, Dame Elizabeth Kimmins. In 1942, the Bishop, impressed by Gluck's painting, social connections and ability as a fund-raiser, invited her to become an executive member of the Council committee. Duncan Grant and Edward Maufe were on it. It aimed, grandly, for the fusion of art and the Church which existed in the middle ages.

Gluck had cast off her Jewish background (her brother was President of the Liberal Synagogue in St John's Wood). She believed though that the true artist was a servant of God and she wrote several poems on this theme:

> Let me be pure of heart
> And always ready to receive all beauty.
> As stretches of unbroken sand
> Are patterned by the mighty sea,
> So let my soul be graven by Thy hand,
> And let all beauty print its shapes in me.
> Let my ears ever like the twisty shell
> Be tuned to all sweet harmonies,
> And Lord give me the power to give
> Thy gifts to others, so they too may live.[3]

She accepted the Bishop's invitation with excitement and wrote to him (5 March 1942) of 'the vital need to mankind of the arts and the artist's vision'. 'We are going to prevent the hideous things that have been allowed to ruin so many lovely buildings and going to raise the standard of taste in towns and villages' she told Mrs Bromley-Martin, a wealthy lover of Art and God, urging her to take out a seven-year covenant.[4]

Gluck did advisory work, submitted designs, recommended other artists and exhorted those she knew – such as 'Golly' Yglesias, a Basque painter in Lamorna, and later Edmund Dulac – to contribute designs of tryptiches and madonnas for the love of God and very little money. Through her working association with the Council Chairman, Bertram Nicholls, who lived in Steyning, about ten miles from Plumpton, Gluck first established contact with that town. In 1945 it became her home and remained so until she died.

Gluck would show her paintings when she finished them to the Plumpton villagers. Early in November 1942, forty-nine people came up to Millers Mead

The View from Blackdown, 1942. The highest point in Sussex

George Hardinge Esquire, 1942

to see a small landscape of Blackdown, the highest point in Sussex. Edith and Nora Heald, who lived in the Chantry House, Steyning, journeyed over specially. Nora was editor of *The Lady* and Edith, her younger sister, a well-known journalist. They spent three hours with Gluck and she described it as 'a good quiet time'. This was the beginning of her friendship with Edith, with whom she was soon to live for the rest of her life. Nesta had a bad boil and was in bed all day, so Gluck took the picture down to show her at the Mill House after the sisters left.

Gluck disliked abstraction and 'isms' in art. She showed her work only in solo exhibitions and shunned comparison with other painters. She saw no anomaly in painting convolvulus with the sound of air raids blasting in the distance. She was unafraid of death and unswerving in her painting style. 'If you honestly have the sort of vision that sees blue and pink trees or whatever the diversion might be' she wrote in her 'Book',

then go to it. If you don't it is as if seeing the truth you preferred to tell a lie. . . .
When I look at some of these patchy, painty modern landscapes I get the strong
sensation of the painter having worked as hurriedly as he could to remove any
suspicion that he could be guilty of such a solecism as to see a tree as a tree. The
oak must bend to the blast of his 'ism' or snap. It usually snaps.

So, while Graham Sutherland painted red landscapes and black landscapes, David Bomberg mauve and orange landscapes and underground bomb stores, Henry Moore frail figures sheltering from bombs in underground shelters and Paul Nash bleak, unpeopled, desolate warscapes, Gluck painted the most short-lived of wild flowers, violets and convolvulus, and the people whom she knew. It was her personal world beyond the reach of politics. The war went on outside as Virginia Woolf, living a few miles away at Lewes, noted in her diary: ' "They're at it again" we say as we sit, I doing my work, Leonard making cigarettes. Now and then there's a thud. The windows shake. So we know London is raided again.'[5]

Gluck was no pacifist. She wanted to make a contribution to the 'war effort'. Kenneth Clark, then Director of the National Gallery, thought she might work for the War Artists Committee which, financed by the Ministry of Information, gave commissions to artists for war paintings. 'In her Brueghel manner,' he wrote to Wilfrid Greene (2 May 1942) who was asking about canvases for her, 'there might be many scenes of war-time life that would be valuable to us.' He also wrote directly to her (2 June 1942) suggesting that her crowd scenes would

The Eighth Army Canteen, Plumpton, 1944

In England's Green and Pleasant Land, 1944. The village hall, Plumpton

be appropriate or a scene inside a British restaurant. Gluck wanted such commissions and sent off photographs of her work for the Committee's scrutiny: 'I am interested in rough working types,' she wrote to Clark, 'or as seen in contrast with others of a different class. I do not know what part of the war effort might give this, nor if it would be possible for me to get a permit to see the more dramatic type of war factory or docks, such as have, for instance, very large machinery that dwarf the figures serving there.'

The Committee did not employ her, but sent her a general permit for sketching freely out of doors. She travelled no further for inspiration than the nearby Home Guard canteen. In 'Canteen, Plumpton' soldiers drink tea, play billiards, smoke and lounge around in the cold. For another picture Gluck went to the Women's Institute, Plumpton, and painted the awesome respectability of certain country women in 'In England's Green and Pleasant Land'. The thick-ankled conductor has split her seam trying unsuccessfully to inspire her impassive choir with Blake's *Jerusalem*. In front of them lie cups of tea, the true focus of their vision, and on the walls behind them a map of the war-torn world. Gluck's society portraits and paintings of the Cochran reviews linked her work to the twenties, and her white flowers to the thirties. These Home Guard scenes capture something of the local spirit of villagers during the war years.

The last painting which linked directly with Nesta's life was of her mother, Ethel Sawyer. Gluck's second picture of her showed her as she lay dying in 1943. The next year Gluck and Nesta were to part. The painting was the flip side of the YouWe profile. Resemblance between mother and daughter is strong, but now the eyes are closed, the face tired of life, creased with pain, all vision gone. Somewhere in Gluck's psyche it had registered that Eternity in love is hard to find. 'Nothing but happy pictures since YouWe', she had written to Nesta in 1936. Seven years later she was painting the death of her lover's mother.

Mrs Ernest Sawyer

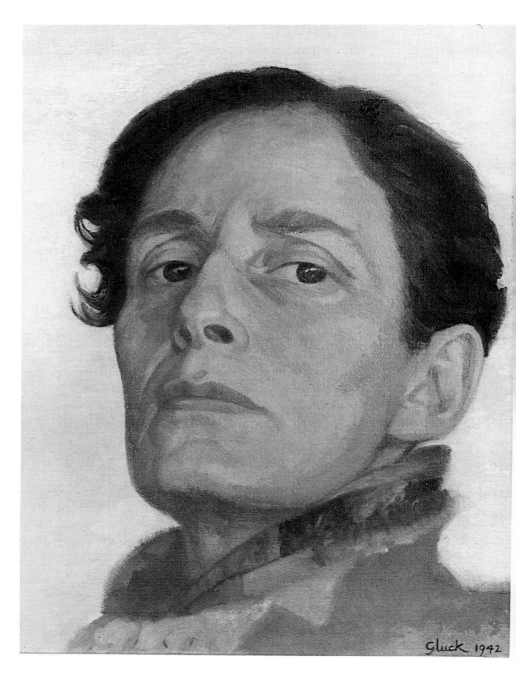

Self-portrait, 1942

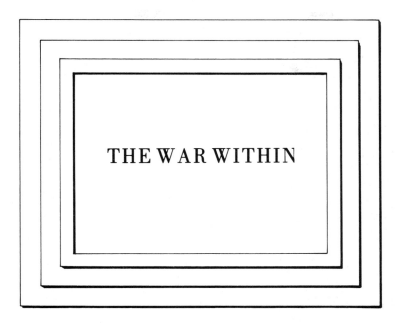

THIRTEEN

THE WAR WITHIN

Gluck's personal battle, during the war years, was with her trustees over the management of her affairs. She wanted autonomy and to handle her own money. There was nothing she hated more than being told what to do and when to do it. She presented herself as a man, a person of power, authority and strength. To The Family this was a masquerade. She was a woman, a girl, and by their social definition dependent and with no authority. From her father's point of view, when he drew up the terms of her inheritance, she was his difficult and rebellious daughter. He wished to ensure that she would always have a roof over her head and adequate funds which she could not squander. Had she been, in the accepted sense of the term, a conforming man, as his eldest child she would have been a member of The Fund and a director of the business. As it was she had to defer to her brother, her cousin Sir Samuel Gluckstein and her mother. It strained her relationship with them all.

The trustees agreed to the rent of Millers Mead when Bolton House was commandeered in September 1939. But the Auxiliary Fire Service moved out in July 1941, stopped paying rent to Gluck and left her again responsible for the rates. Left empty, the house suffered. Rainwater seeped in because the gutters were blocked with leaves. The whole place needed extensive repairs and there was a wrangle between Gluck, her Trustees and the Fire Service, about who should pay.

In the thick of the war, Gluck was responsible for the upkeep of three houses, income tax was ten shillings in the pound and her net monthly income had been substantially cut. Her cousin, Sir Samuel Gluckstein, one of her trustees, urged her to limit her expenditure to the absolute minimum. 'I am not endeavouring to read you a lecture', he wrote (while doing just that), 'but I am endeavouring to help you to avoid getting into financial distress.' (30 July 1941)

Her mother and brother were deeply involved in the war effort. The Meteor, awarded the MBE in the First World War for her work for Belgian refugees, again immersed herself in the fight for right. Frugality came easily to her. She closed up her flat in London, put her belongings in store, and lived in one room in the Cumberland Hotel, snatching meals as and when she could. (She lost two-and-a-half stone in the war years.) During the blitz she slept on a camp bed in the hotel corridor. For economy's sake, she used scrap paper for writing letters. Her chauffeur went to make aeroplane parts, so she garaged her Rolls-Royce, handed in her petrol coupons and travelled by bus. She continued her work as a Justice of the Peace and worked avidly for charity. In London War Weapons Week she personally collected £27,000 in five days. Her son, now a Major after active service in France, worked in the army legal service and continued as an MP. He was intensely patriotic, an uncompromising negotiator and a hard-liner who was on Hitler's death list in the event of German invasion. He advocated 'blunt methods' of reprisal bombing and opposed the notion that some towns and cities should be spared. At home he did a great deal to organize the reconstruction of the lives of refugee children. Neither he nor the Meteor wanted to spend much time corresponding with Gluck about her rent and rates.

The Fund made its discretionary decisions about financial help for the family in an ad hoc, democratic way. In the war years Gluck was overdrawing on her allowance by some £100 a year which invited consternation and reproof from the Trustees – and worried her too. 'My finances are a little on the wrong side,' she wrote to her mother (1 June 1942). She was genuinely unclear quite what her responsibility was over the upkeep of Bolton House. To boost her income, she wanted to put the furniture in store – if the house was empty, she was absolved from paying rates – and let it for the duration of the war. She wanted to keep on the studio in case she got commissions in London. The Trustees, or her brother certainly, doubted that she would use the studio until the war was over, advised her to save money by storing the furniture in the studio gallery and foresaw further problems if the house was let. Gluck wrote endless letters, with carbon copies to all and sundry, in part businesslike, true and accurate over detail, in part reflecting her current emotional hurt and insecurity and in part aggravating old wounds and resentments:

December 13th, 1941

My dear Luigi

You wrote to me in December 1938 as follows:—
'You have been told many times that there is no income apart from the Trust Funds available for the maintenance of Bolton House and your other properties. If the total income is paid to you, you must be responsible for the upkeep.'
    You wrote on December 5th 1941 that:—
'As the Trustees are responsible for the condition of the property, the Schedule of Dilapidations is their concern and I accordingly do not propose "to instruct Trevors to let you see it at once".'
    Though your use of the word responsible appears to be haphazard, and these two statements taken together appear contradictory, there is no doubt from your 1938 letter that I am expected to pay for the upkeep of Bolton House as my responsibility and as accounts I have had to pay prove; but from your letter of 1941 I am to gather that despite having to pay, I am not to be allowed to see that for which I am paying. The Schedule of Dilapidations, having direct connection with the upkeep of Bolton House, is very much my concern as well as that of the Trustees, and there cannot be any valid reason for refusing me sight of it.
    I had to struggle for four years from 1934–1938 before getting a yearly statement of my financial position. My reason for wanting this statement was the same as for my requests now, to enable me to arrange my life with complete knowledge of my affairs. The Statement should have been a matter of routine and ought never to have become, as it did, a matter of lies, intimidation and a cause for grievance on the part of the Trustees against me . . .

The Meteor sent her a great deal of maternal advice, most of which went unheeded. 'I cannot,' she wrote (25 May 1942),

either understand or cope with this continual correspondence with copy letters to Louis and Mr Dyer, but I would like to make this perfectly clear . . . Today everybody's income *has been reduced to exactly half . . . If you were to write a thousand letters you would not alter this, and I do think, in these very strenuous, nerve racking days, the less correspondence you and anyone has the better . . . I am sure if you and Louis met more often there would be greater mutual respect and understanding instead of this continual waste of time and letters. You were always very devoted to each other . . . I do not get younger and these things make me very unhappy.*

Sir Samuel was short-tempered with her, called her Hannah, and treated her like a difficult child. He wrote with a truth untempered by tact to her mother (8 January 1942) 'she must be made to understand that she cannot carry the burden of three establishments plus storage, contrary to the advice of her Trustees, and expect that she is going to be free from anxiety.' Her brother tried to avoid replying directly to her about her affairs, and when forced to do so, was curt and to the point. He warned that 'a final breach between us must follow' unless she changed her tack. 'The word "final" astonishes me,' she replied (20 May 1942), 'as I did not know any breach existed. In any case I cannot see why a breach should occur as a result of letters asking reasonable questions upon Trust matters that affect my income.' All three of her Trustees thought she was being impossible and wasting their time in the middle of a world war. Her mother tried to be placatory, generous and helpful, but irritation kept creeping in. Her brother was totally out of temper with her and her cousin, dismissive. 'I am really very sorry for you and Louis,' he wrote to the Meteor (16 December 1941).

The whole atmosphere became electric with bad feeling. Gluck, while purporting to want only the facts and autonomy over her own affairs, wrote of mishandling of affairs, unfriendly and unconstructive letters and of attitudes that were 'inimical and trampling'. 'If,' she wrote to her brother (13 December 1941),

your interpretation of your functions of a Trustee and as representing the other Trustees, is to continue to obstruct every request I make, to instruct your agents to do likewise and to adopt a carping attitude towards me, such as assuming knowledge of my lack of participation in the war effort when you know nothing about my life, then I can only say that I find living under such conditions intolerable, and will consider myself free to act in the future in accordance with the situation you will have forced on me.

Her mother kept asking her to meet and talk things over amicably rather than to write endless pernickety letters. Gluck had employed a secretary, a Mr Stanley – another expense – to deal with the voluminous correspondence she generated. When Gluck, her mother and her brother did meet to talk about

Bolton House, at the Trocadero on 6 August 1941, they rowed horribly. Referring to the meeting four months later, Gluck wrote to her mother (9 December 1941): 'This talk was of a nature so disgusting and shocking to me that it became clear that I cannot discuss any matters connected with my Trust affairs without a witness and a shorthand writer being present.'

The more she ignored the Trustees' recommendations which were sharp, but not punitive – such as that she should store her furniture in the studio gallery to save paying rates on the house – and went her own way, the more implacable and unsympathetic they became. The more obsessive and demanding her letter writing, the more she was stonewalled. By 1942 communication had reached such an *impasse* that it was difficult to see how any of it could be put right. The sub-text was far too complicated. She could not have said that she wanted to keep Bolton House studio uncluttered because it was her special space, or that love had gone wrong and left her feeling lonely, powerless and dependent, or that it galled her not to be treated like a man, when she was by no means a typical woman, or that she did not know where quite to call her home. She tried to present herself to the Trustees as a force to be reckoned with, high on principle, a hard negotiator, an *homme d'affaires*, the master of her fate and the captain of her soul. The wrangle happened at a time when she was suffering acutely from disappointed love. It soured her feelings about Bolton House and she was never to return there.

I cannot be expected to take an interest in the property when I am refused information with regard to its upkeep and my liabilities in connection with it. . . . were Father alive today, which unfortunately he is not, he would have been the first to welcome my interest in the subject and my desire to get it straight.[1]

Worries about love exacerbated Gluck's combativeness. After five years of so-called marriage, in 1941, she was chronicling in her diaries Nesta's daily news as if it were her own. Nesta's visits to Brighton, sore throats, colds, headaches and lumbago, her badminton games with Seymour, the day she lost her dog Mr Chips in Brighton, lunches with her mother, dinner guests, broadcasts, poetry readings and charity commitments were noted down as if indivisible from Gluck's own activities and concerns. And as time went on she took to recording, with obsessive precision, the hours they did or did not spend together. Nesta was travelling the country talking at Women's Institute and Red Cross meetings on Anglo-American relations. 'Wings for Victory' was one of her talks. She saw less of Gluck whose diary entries became a litany of pain: 'Do not see N. all day.' 'N. comes to see me 4.20 to 5.30.' 'N. dashes in for a second on way to Lewes.' 'No letter from N. Very unhappy about it all.' 'N. comes from 11.30–12.30. Lay in hut and read Chinese poems. Got very upset by them.' 'N only came in for ten minutes. Very short. Was most depressed by her. She went to Boo for day. Came to see me however at 8pm for few minutes. Was very sweet then.' 'N. comes 6.30 but only for $\frac{1}{4}$ hr.'

When, in 1941, Nesta went to Newcastle for ten days and Gluck received only four letters, three phone calls and a telegram, she became extraordinarily miserable and depressed. 'Send telegram. "Plus que moi" etc.', she recorded. And she wrote poetry that reflected her hurt – sonnets in Shakespearean style:

> I heard the sea and the incoming tide,
> I felt your heartbeats throb against my own.
> I thought I held you fast . . . but from my side
> I found that you and all delights had flown.
> Then I remembered how you lay at rest,
> And heard the gulls cry in the tremulous day
> I saw your dear hair tumbled on your breast
> And languorous vigour of your darling clay.
> And how your eyes, as you lay quietly sleeping
> Were shadowed by one graceful arm flung wide,
> The passionate night your gentle form belying. . .
> Oh God must I forever be denied
> Such life with you – Must we forever part
> And I go lonely, with an aching heart.

Nesta's absences highlighted how isolated Gluck was in Plumpton. This was her exclusive relationship. She had staked everything on it and it was not so much going wrong, as not going anywhere. Her life in the thirties in Hampstead had been social and fast. As time went on at Millers Mead she dined more often than not alone. Few people visited her in an everyday way. Seymour, if he came to pick up Nesta, did not come in. Craig stayed with her for a month or so in November 1943, but Gluck was horribly nervy with her and burst out about how hopeless everything seemed. When the Meteor visited for weekends she and Gluck argued constantly about the Trust. On several occasions Gluck wrote to her mother not to discuss business matters when they met; all that, she said, could be dealt with in writing and she wanted to preserve their relationship apart from the Trust. But the subject was too pressing to avoid.

Gluck noted down her profound worries with a cool regard for the truth. This was how it was. She wished for things to be different but did not know what to do. It was not the world war that threatened her. She bought blackout paint for the windows, walked to see bodies brought from a German plane shot down less than a mile away, and did not wake when nearby aerodromes were bombed at night. Her worries were about love, money and where she could call home. She was abstracted and lost things – the cigarette case Nesta gave her, her lighter, her shooting-stick, her fountain pen. Dr Richards warned her to be very careful. And she did a self-portrait of herself looking for all the world like the Duke of Wellington, arrogant, combative to a hostile world, allied to masculinity as a definition of hardness and pride. This was not at all the cheeky chappy of her 1926 self-portrait, and not at all the face of a person who would write again and again in her diary, as she did, 'no telephone calls, no letters, terribly upset about it all'.

Though on a crucial level she was unhappy, life was not all gloom. She had a distractable disposition and quick-changing moods and if fun was on offer, she liked to have it. There were still with Nesta the games of badminton, shared walks on the Downs, times spent reading aloud in the hut: *Paradise Lost* or *Moby Dick*, Yeats, Blake and Plato; or listening to music, or singing duets, or sunbathing in the nude – though the fads of sailing, skating and riding had faded forever. Often enough she would note, disarmingly, 'a lovely day'. Her good friends were there though it is doubtful how much they knew of her problems. When in February 1941 she was both feeling miserable and having problems with staff, which meant that she had to make her own tea and feed the chickens, Noel Boughey phoned her every evening to see how she was getting on. Gluck stayed with Wilfrid and Nancy Greene at their wartime home, 'Wilderness', in Holmbury St Mary, near Dorking, messed about in the garden, listened to Haydn and Beethoven on their gramophone and went with them to tea with Max Beerbohm and his wife and had a happy time.

It was not that Nesta neglected Gluck for long or was ever angry with her in other than a passing way. It was simply that she did not have the disposition for exclusivity. Years later she talked of 'the tyranny of friendship'.[2] She knew that she drew problematic people to her, and then could not be the answer they desired. She was so much the opposite of Gluck, which was perhaps where attraction lay – so unobsessive, easy with people and physically fearless. She believed in Gluck's exceptional talent, gave what she could and wanted her to be happy. Each Christmas she bought her a diary and inscribed it with all hope for the coming days. 'To my Tim' she wrote in Gluck's 1943 diary 'with so many large hopes that the days be filled with large joys (and small too) small as Tiny Tim'. Gluck would always drop work to have time with Nesta. She resented interruptions from others and longed for them from her. As the war went on,

Nesta took on more and more speaking engagements and, as suited her, travelled the country – often on her motorbike. She had been awarded an OBE in the first war for similar charitable works. She resisted telling Gluck her every move and to Gluck such evasions were betrayal and lies. Gluck was again having arsenic and iron injections and taking sleeping pills. But her true drug was her moments with Nesta. Those moments elated her, she deflated when they passed.

By April 1943 Gluck seemed thoroughly depressed and discordant. With ever-changing help in the house and her smallholding now sizeable, she had to do more chores herself. On Good Friday she parted with Zar with whom she clearly was not coping: 'Very upsetting day. Zar's last day. Very unhappy. Did not work. Difficult day.' she recorded. A fortnight later the kennels phoned to say that he was ill and should be destroyed. '*Zar put to sleep*' was her diary entry for 7 June 1943. The settled life he was supposed to symbolize and be part of had never come about.

She completed work, in a sporadic way, on 'Jerusalem', 'Pleiades', two small landscapes and a triptych for the Sussex Council of Churches. In connection with her work for the Council, she made several trips to Steyning to see the Chairman, Bertram Nicholls. On those trips she visited the Heald sisters at the Chantry House. She lunched with them, sometimes stayed overnight and met their friends, the fashion editor, Alison Settle, the writer and editor of the *London Mercury* Rolfe Scott-James and his wife Violet. Nora Heald, then in her early sixties, was editor of *The Lady*. Edith was fifty-eight, ten years older than Gluck, when they met in 1943. A friendship started, shaped by mutual need. Edith had had a close relationship with the poet W. B. Yeats and was desolate when he died in 1939. She and Gluck looked at books, listened to music, visited Chichester Cathedral and then Edith stayed at Millers Mead. They walked in the woods and Gluck missed her when she left. It was respite from her desperation over Nesta. She saw Nesta on Christmas Eve 1943, the atmosphere was sad and she went to the Chantry House for the holiday – the first time in eight years that she had spent Christmas apart from her 'darling wife'.

Gluck held an exhibition of her paintings in Steyning Grammar School in February 1944. Edith helped her set it up, and they had lunch and tea together and looked at books on Rembrandt. Edith was sympathetic to her unhappiness and arranged distractions. They went to Brighton for a week and stayed at the Beauport Park Hotel. Gluck bought a Redouté watercolour of pansies and they had tea in the Pavilion. They visited Winchester and Rye, Hastings and Battle. Nesta phoned Gluck in her hotel room most nights.

The Report Post. Edith as firewarden, Steyning, 1945

On a sunny weekend in May, when Nora was away, Gluck stayed at the
Chantry House alone with Edith. They read in the garden and in the evening
danced. Gluck began a portrait of her, of which there is now no trace. She
struggled with it for weeks, scraping out the face and beginning again and again.
Edith made frequent trips to the Millers Mead studio for sittings and they sat up
late talking and listening to the gramophone. Clifford Musgrave, Director of the
Brighton Art Gallery, was impressed by the picture: 'It is very true and has an
inner life of its own, the sort of phantasmal quality of some Chinese paintings.
What a task it must have been building up the surface!'[3] He asked Gluck to
exhibit her paintings in the Gallery's autumn exhibition.

Gluck took to spending most days and nights at the Chantry House. Edith's
war contribution was to serve as a fire warden in Steyning and Gluck started
another painting of her at work in the makeshift office, dozing over a book at

1.30 a.m. They had quiet, consoling times together. On the last Saturday of
June 1944 both Nora and Edith stayed at Millers Mead and asked Gluck if she
would like to come and live with them and paint in one of the cottages on the
estate. Gluck sat alone from midnight until three in the morning pondering the
invitation and the next day said yes. The following week Edith invited her to go
on holiday to Lyme in Dorset in August with her to meet her friends Edmund
Dulac and Helen Beauclerck. Nesta was jealous and distraught. 'N arrives at
5.10 pm has tea with me. Offers * but I say no.' In tears about it all, Nesta went
alone for a day to Newhaven, to walk by the sea. When Nora and Edith came the
next day to stay at Millers Mead, Nesta rode up on her motorbike after
midnight, put notes under the door for Edith and Gluck, and phoned in the
small hours of the morning.

There were scenes and there were tears. 'I am very nervy and cannot decide
about going to Steyning' Gluck noted in her diary, weeks after having said she
would go. She told Nesta all she felt. Nesta took off her 'wedding' ring, then
later put it on again. On the day before Gluck left for Dorset with Edith, she and
Nesta had a 'pretend' birthday – Gluck would be forty-nine on her holiday.

The problem was of course that she was in love with Nesta and it was an
unshakeable fact. The holiday was not an unqualified success. Edith caught a
cold, Gluck had a fainting turn and headaches and got a boil in her ear. All she
noted of Dulac was when he had a headache and when at dinner he made a
perfectly shaped duck from a pellet of bread. He did, though, draw up Gluck's
horoscope. Like Yeats he was interested in things occult, though his analysis of
her work seems to have more to do with simple opinion than the stars:

... *The Flower pieces are herself at her best – her happiest, most detached mood.*
Neither passion nor protest intervene directly.

The portraits come next. Her sitters have some of the objective values of
flowers for pattern making but the externals of dress, likeness etc, impose
themselves upon subjective direction and control. . . . The landscapes represent
the Romantic escape. The arrangements are 90% subjective . . . Composition
and design are very strongly biased by romantic emotion.

Relief from 'conflict' expressed in terms of more or less obvious caricature she
gets from her 'character scenes'. The less detached her emotions are the less she
allows facts and objects to collaborate.

. . . while she is exceptionally gifted to deal with her emotions there is
somewhere a hiatus . . . independence has led her to a blank wall and she doesn't
know how to get through it . . .

Helen Beauclerck, with whom Dulac lived, pronounced it 'a not very lucky horoscope, but most interesting'.

Gluck was extremely pleased to be met by Nesta at Plumpton station three weeks later. As soon as she got back, and in the middle of all her frayed and confused feelings, Wilfrid Greene gave her a commission which she could not, out of friendship, refuse. He was resigning as Principal of the Working Men's College, after years of service, and had been asked to present a drawing of himself to the College.

I would not want to be drawn by anyone but you . . . and I am writing to know whether (1) you would honour me by accepting the commission and (2) whether you would please us by coming to stay here for a few days and then and there accomplishing it . . .[4]

When she arrived at his house 'The Wilderness' in Dorking, Rayner Goddard, who became Chief Justice two years later, was staying too. She thought him very nice. Both he and Lord Greene were enthusiastic about the drawing she did and they all made large bonfires together in the garden.

Her peace and concentration were broken by a phone call to 'The Wilderness' from Edith, who was in great distress because Nesta had gone to see Nora in London and 'been beastly' about Gluck. Nora had then had a row with Edith – presumably about the impending move. Nesta phoned Gluck too but made no mention of the visit.

On 6 October Gluck moved into the Chantry House. It was understandable but it was to prove most damaging. She went there largely because she did not know where else to go or what to do. Her suffering because of love took away her confidence and happiness. She had declared her love so often, so passionately and wholeheartedly. It was not independence that led her to a blank wall but a broken heart. And her painting suffered. She faded from the public eye and produced very little. Others were to suffer too, including Edith. It is hard to be on the receiving end of a rebound from such love. Unlike Nesta, Gluck could not let go – not of things, not of arguments, nor issues, nor the past. In old age she wrote of her YouWe days in a shaky hand:

> Count not the years
> The laughter or the tears
> What was, still is, and ever shall so be;
> Count only this – my heart belongs to thee.

Sentiments that she stored within her, like letters in a shoebox.

PART THREE
THE FACTS
OF LIFE

1945–1978

Bookplate for the Heald sisters, by Edmund Dulac, showing the Chantry House

Weekend parties with the Heald sisters prior to the Gluck years. Edith is on the right

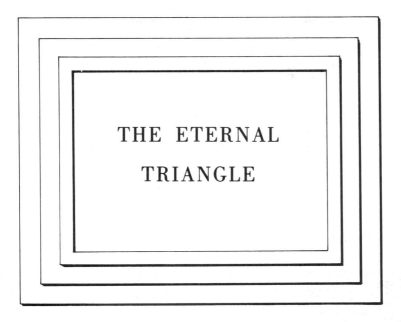

FOURTEEN

THE ETERNAL
TRIANGLE

In Steyning Gluck moved into an established home. The Heald sisters, Nora and Edith Shackleton, bought the Chantry House in February 1934 when Edith was forty-nine and Nora was fifty-one. They intended well-earned, elegant country living for their middle age. The house was empty, near-derelict and covered in ivy with broken windows and leaking roofs and the gardens were overgrown. They rented a place nearby, Smugglers Cottage, and worked at Chantry's complete renovation. The original sixteenth-century building had been the home of priests from the chantry chapel in Steyning Church. It was enlarged in the style of a Georgian country house in the early eighteenth century. Nora and Edith opened it up and made it light and warm. They took out the back staircase, put in new walls, windows and floors, ripped out the old larders, had a new kitchen built, new bathrooms, a new roof. They moved in at the end of May 1934. 'Tidy at last' was the caption in their photograph album for the 'before and after' transformation of the house. They took with them their antique furniture, paintings, glassware, rare carpets, rugs, ceramics, books, and huge collection of gramophone records. By summer Mr Hole, the

'Kokoscha, the little kitten', drawing of Edith Shackleton Heald by Edmund Dulac

gardener, was gathering figs and pears from the pruned fruit trees in the now orderly walled orchard.

Nora spent week nights in London in a flat above *The Lady* offices, Edith worked from home. There were house parties most weekends where the conversation, food and wine were reputed to be good. Edith complained that most of the household decisions were left to her, but there were servants to do the chores and it was to all appearances a harmonious and enjoyable life. They took frequent holidays together, motoring in Europe, chauffeured by their nephew Ivan, staying in inns and sightseeing.

Both sisters were successful and highly respected journalists at a time when it was exceptional for women to have such careers. Edith began, in the early 1900s, as a freelancer with stories in the *Manchester Sunday Chronicle*, where her brother Ivan was assistant editor. She used her mother's name, Shackleton. (The family was distantly related to Ernest Shackleton, the antarctic explorer.) By her early twenties Edith was a special correspondent on Beaverbrook's London *Evening Standard* – she was the first woman to go into the Press gallery at the House of Lords and she covered events in Paris during the First World War, the struggles for Irish independence and the setting up of a republic by the *Sinn Fein* in southern Ireland in 1919. During the 1920s both she and the poet Edward Shanks worked as leader writers on the *Standard*'s 'Londoner's Diary'.

'I sometimes suppress the fact that I write leaders for a daily paper when being condescendingly questioned by the inhabitants of the outer world' she wrote in an essay, 'Women in Fleet Street',[1]

rather than face the disbelief or alarm which follows. Though journalism is one of the professions in which women and men get equal rates of pay for the same work (thanks largely to the National Union of Journalists), and in Fleet Street a woman usually finds friendship and a fair share of the hard work among her men colleagues, news editors still keep up the tradition that anything written by a woman has an especial quality of rareness, as though women observed and recorded as seldom as dogs walk on their hind legs . . .

In the 1920s she wrote opinion pieces in the *Express, Sunday Express* and *Daily Sketch*. Her writing was free-ranging, whimsical, sharp and with a feminist bite. She had been a suffragist, was an advocate of equal pay and a founder member of the PEN club. She wrote about the myths of female passivity and male superiority and extolled the virtues of spinsterhood and late love: 'There are other and better bouquets than those we get at our first dances . . .'[2] She considered the marriage promises 'wild and improbable', and provoked a heated correspondence in the *Sunday Express* (October 1925) by advocating that 'the wisest and most eloquent women should be allowed to occupy the pulpits'. She wrote of the iniquities of violence against women, maternal mortality, snobbish boarding schools and censorship, and warmly about all things Lancastrian and the delights for women of short hair, sensible clothes and driving their own cars. She was romantic about talent and love: '. . . novel writing is like marriage – you should never do it unless you feel that otherwise you will be unable to go on living at all . . .'[3]; and dismissive of domestic calm: 'the secret of a joyful life is to live dangerously,' she wrote, quoting Nietzsche, in the *Sunday Express*, 19 July 1927.

In her whimsical words she tweaked at the Establishment's tail. 'Adam was rather a poor creature' she wrote in the *Evening Standard*, 25 April 1929, in response to an MP who lamented that women's independence made men lose their manners, 'but one likes to believe that his sons have steadily grown out of his sneaky way of trying to put the blame on somebody else . . .' And in a piece ostensibly urging economic independence for partners in marriage she mischievously remarked:

Edith as a young journalist

I believe there is something divine in marriage, but I believe also that there is something divine in many other human relationships. David and Jonathan appeal for no legal assurance that one shall support the other or be responsible for his debts, as long as they both shall live, even though their friendship breaks. Why should Edwin and Angelina?[4]

She was for a time the *Evening Standard*'s drama critic and the only woman member of what was known as the 'Critics Circle'. In September 1931 the paper appointed her as their book critic:

In offering Miss Shackleton the control of this important feature we have been influenced by her reputation as one of the best-known women journalists, by her high standing in the literary world, and by the wide popularity of the many articles she has contributed to this journal in the past.

Three months later, for some unexplained reason, Edith left and went to Greece and the job went to J. B. Priestley.

Nora was both a journalist and editor. She started as a music and drama critic, then became editor of the women's pages of *The Daily Herald*, editor of *The Queen* and from 1930 to 1953 editor of *The Lady*. Edith did a weekly book-review page for *The Lady* and a humorous, informative and extremely popular opinion page 'With Prejudice', under the name of 'Clio'. Nora took into *The Lady*'s stable the fashion writer Alison Settle (who also moved to Steyning in the 1930s and was a close friend of the sisters), Stella Gibbons, the author of *Cold Comfort Farm*, and the writer and book reviewer, Elizabeth Coxhead.

The Heald sisters had lived together harmoniously for most of their lives. Mother, to whom they were devoted, lived with them until her death shortly before the move to Chantry in 1934. She was in later years a dumpy figure rather like Queen Victoria and had a reputation for making the best coffee in London. Before moving to Steyning they owned a fine Regency house at 24 St Petersburg Place, near Hyde Park, with a red Riley in the garage and a flat for the chauffeur at the top of the house. (Edith was an erratic driver, known to go to sleep at the wheel.) They earned their standard of living through ability and hard work. They were not, like Gluck, born into money. Their family, originally from Larne in County Antrim, Ireland, moved to Accrington in Lancashire. '. . . my Lancashire great-grandmother smoked a pipe among her men folk and joined in their discussion on that startling fellow Tyndall and the possible effect of the newly projected Atlantic cable . . .' Edith wrote in the *Sunday Express*, 19 July 1927. Throughout her life she kept up the Irish connection. She had a cottage in Rosapenna, in Donegal, and she and Gluck went on walking holidays there. In later years Gluck painted landscapes on these Irish holidays.

There were two brothers, Harry, who became an engineer, and Ivan who was killed in the 1914–18 war. Each year after he was killed, until the end of her own life some sixty years later, Edith put an *In Memoriam* tribute in *The Times*. He too was a journalist; he wrote humorous, satirical pieces for the *Manchester Guardian*. An anthology of his work, *Ivan Heald: Hero and Humorist*, was published when he died in 1917[5] a collection of lighthearted, youthful pieces on such topics as Americans in London, philately, an Anarchist meeting in Newcastle, or 'How to Buy a Straw Hat'. In the war he was commended for conspicuous bravery and devotion to duty. He sent his mother and sisters reassuring letters from the graveyards of Alexandria and Gallipoli:

When we arrived we found the trenches strewn with dead Turks and bits of dead Turks. It is not really half so ghastly as you would think, or maybe it is that we have lost all of our sense of these things. . . . I think I can stand it all better than anyone here and I am never despondent. I do hope you won't trouble about me whatever happens. . . . I want you to send me some garden seeds like nasturtiums and calceolarias and things so that I can have a wee garden. Also another drawing pad and a modern Greek primer and some Japanese water colours and things. And some whiskers and moustaches for the national theatre that I hope to start here.

Father was never mentioned. Mary, their mother, left him, though she had no money, when the children were in their teens. Rumour had it that he drank and womanized. None of them subsequently saw him and on an occasion when Nora was drawing up a family tree, she left him off it with the remark 'We don't mention him.'[6]

In an article for the *Daily Express*, 10 August 1929, called 'Men Who Interest Me', Edith cited the King, Albert Einstein 'a man who thinks in immensities . . . his mental adventures seem to me more terrifying than journeys to polar silences or solitary Atlantic flights . . .', Edmund Dulac '. . . he could have been just as famous as a musician or a writer or an actor, and can cook a chicken with the same perfection with which he draws an Arabian princess in an enchanted forest', G. B. Shaw and H. G. Wells, whom she described as

attractive . . . but too reasonable to be mysterious and do not excite my curiosity as much as Mr W.B. Yeats, whose grave manners and melodious conversation seem to take one back to a more spacious ancient world, who can be as practical

W. B. Yeats, Edith and Dulac in the
gardens of Chantry House

*as any other Irishman (which is
saying a lot) and yet sees the
fairies and has dealings with
spirits ...*

It seems that Edith was the last of Yeats's lovers. She first met him when, aged twenty-one, she was in Manchester attending a lecture of his. Of their early relationship there is no record, but after Gluck's death in 1978 about sixty letters from Yeats to Edith were sold to the Houghton Library, Harvard. Personal and passionate in tone, they date from 1937 until his death in 1939, keep her informed of all aspects of his work, invite her comments on the progress of his poems and cover such matters as his radio broadcasts with Dulac, the affairs and disputes of the Abbey Theatre, his family, friends and contemporaries. In 1937, when Edith was fifty-three and Yeats seventy-two, he was writing to her (29 May 1937) sentiments that echoed her own views on the 'better bouquets than those we get at our first dances'. He wrote, in words that commend the romantic sensibilities of older people, of how, had Edith been younger, true intimacy between them would have been impossible. He told her he thought the finest bond of all occurs 'when we have outlived our first rough silver' and of how sweet this bond can be to the old and the half old. He spoke of his profound hopes for their friendship and of how peaceful the understanding and sympathy she accorded him made him feel.[7] In a letter to Maud Gonne in June 1938 he described Edith as 'one of the best-paid women journalists in the world. She found she had no leisure so she gave up the most of it.'

He stayed for months at a time in the Chantry House. Edith evidently revered him and provided him with an ideal environment for work. The 'Yeats Room', as it was called, was kept just for his use. He wrote many of his later poems and plays for the Peacock Theatre there and discussed his work with her: 'When we meet at the end of the month I shall have much poetry to read you . . .'[8] When in England he would stay first with the poet Lady Dorothy Wellesley (who, though married to the Duke of Wellington, had a sexual preference for women) at her home Penns in the Rocks in the village of Withyham, about thirty miles from Steyning, and then move on to the Chantry House.

By 5 February 1938 he was writing to Edith that in England she alone mattered to him. They went on holiday to the south of France – to Monte Carlo and to Cap Martin, where they stayed at the Hôtel Idéal Séjour.[9] On these trips Edith looked after him – he was suffering from a heart condition that made his ankles swell – and acted as his chauffeur.

His letters to her became quite impassioned – a mixture of friendship, timidity, romance and longing. They showed a growing dependency on her – her love of his work and understanding of it, the peace and comfort of the Chantry House, the quiet of her personality and her talk.

By 15 March 1938 he was writing of how, after a sleepless night, he wanted her arms to make him sleep. On 25 June he told her that what was left to him in life was hers. On 5 September he wrote of needing her as earth needs Spring and of how, in his fantasy, he began with timidity to hold her. On 12 September he wrote that he longed for her in body and soul, that his feelings for her transcended speech and that he wanted to say to her the kind of foolish things sometimes read out in breach of promise cases.

His wife, George Yeats, was unperturbed by his interest in Edith. 'You won her goodwill,' Yeats wrote to Edith of George and spoke of having her blessing for them to go away together. George Yeats wrote sharp letters to Edith from her home in Rathfarnham in Dublin about ensuring that WB took his medicine:

Do please extract from him his prescription for the digitalis mixture and make him take it twice a day while he is still with you. . . . He needs so much intellectual stimulus that you and others can give, but he unfortunately also needs that heart stimulus. And nobody can feel more passionately than I that he has to return to this desolate place.[10]

Both Edith and George shared a vigil over Yeats's body the night after he died on 28 January 1939 at the Hôtel Idéal Séjour in Menton in the south of France. '. . . I watched over him until 4 a.m.' Edith wrote (26 August 1968). 'His features had become even more noble and beautiful than I had known them. It was a wonderful southern night of stars and I remembered that "the heavens themselves blaze forth the deaths of princes".'[11] To commemorate him Edith put a plaque on the wall of Chantry House: 'William Butler Yeats 1865–1939 wrote many of his later poems in this house'.

Edith was generous, appreciative and nurturing of talent. Her book reviews, too, were receptive, informed and filled with insights. She gave to Gluck the same loyalty and devoted appreciation that she had given to Yeats. She thought her gifted, referred to her genius, and made allowances for her impossible temperament. Gluck noted in her own diary a comment, that perhaps alleviated her guilt over her own difficult behaviour, made by Yeats to Edith: 'We who create have to cultivate our wild beasts; most people have to subdue them.' The theatre critic and diarist James Agate, who knew Edith well, wrote in his *Ego* diary volumes 'Edith is a tower of sympathy to people in trouble and spends her quick and noble mind generously.'[12] The writer, Anne Scott-James, whose parents often used to stay at the Chantry, until Gluck moved in, described Edith as an intellectual and a good conversationalist. People thought her reserved, rather self-effacing, with a droll sense of humour, and given to making pithy asides. She remarked, for example, as a dull, newly-married couple left a tea party at the Chantry, 'How nice that they've married each other, and not one of us.' And James Agate recorded lunching with her and the publisher Alan Dent at the time of Edward VIII's scandal with Mrs Simpson, and Edith commenting: '*Peter Pan* is a charming play for children. It is not a rule of conduct for a great nation.'[13] She had a kittenish, mischievous smile when saying such things, so Edmund Dulac nicknamed her Kokoscha (Russian for little kitten). He did a drawing of her to capture that expression.

Gluck entered the sisters' intellectual, civilized world five years after the death of Yeats. Nora evidently had reservations about the *ménage à trois* from the time when Nesta called in to see her at *The Lady* offices in September 1944. Edith was adamant at wanting Gluck to live with them and thought it would work out. For Gluck, whatever her feelings about Edith, the move seemed to offer solutions to her problems. It took her away from the pain and disappointment of her relationship with Nesta and it resolved her struggles with the Trustees over the upkeep of Bolton House. Bolton was sold, after a few more rows, in 1945 to a Dr Martin Pollock of the Medical Research Council and the money reverted to Gluck's Trust. But she kept on the studio and had a wall built at the end of the paved garden, at a cost of £50, to separate it from the house.

Gluck felt, too, that Chantry would provide an atmosphere conducive to work. Here were professional women who had made their own way, depended on no one else's money and had earned their success. It was away from the West End whirl, the Meteor's pressures, Nesta's dilettantism. Here was solid professionalism where she could, above all things, work.

She moved in on 6 October 1944 still smarting from Nesta's 'beastly about me' visit to Nora the week before. She brought with her, her Broadwood piano and mahogany four-poster bed, seven-foot long, five-foot six wide, with reeded columns. The Yeats' Room was cleared as her study and a cottage in the grounds became her studio. She wrote a letter to Nesta cancelling a proposed visit to the Mill House. Nesta replied and sent a copy of whatever she wrote to Nora, which upset Gluck a great deal. For a few days after moving in, Gluck felt terrible with heart palpitations and what was probably an anxiety attack, but it passed and she declared herself happy.[14]

Friends of the Heald sisters from the outset expressed discomfort at Gluck's arrival. The atmosphere quickly became awkward and their visits tailed off. In 1945 Gluck endured a kind of breakdown, diagnosed as neuritis. She went to a private rest home in Middlesex. Rayner Goddard, who the following year was to become the Lord Chief Justice, had written to her on 24 January asking her to accept a commission from him to paint Wilfrid Greene. He intended presenting the picture to the Inner Temple. 'I of course leave everything to you, but I confess that I should like nothing so much as a replica in oil of the drawing – it was so excellent a likeness and I could see every side of his character in it. At any rate you will give me something as good won't you?' Because of illness Gluck had to postpone the sittings and did not deliver the picture until 1949.

On first arriving at the Chantry, Gluck did little but try to get strong and adapt to her new circumstances and to separation from Nesta. The initial friction and resentment at parting passed, and their deep loyalty resurfaced. Gluck was never far from Nesta's thoughts or affections. With the war over, Nesta and Seymour resumed their travelling life. In New York Nesta visited the actress Leonora Corbett, who had moved there toward the end of the war. 'The first thing I saw when I went into her bedroom was "The Glory of Mud" looking *beautiful*', she wrote to Gluck. This was a seascape, of which there is now no trace, done in Dorset in the 1930s, on an island they called their Shangri La. 'You can imagine how warming it was to see my Tim smiling at me. It recalled happy days on that island. Some of the happiest.'[15] From the 'Boca Raton', between Palm Beach and Miami, she wrote to Gluck (23 December 1945) thanking her for a cutting of a photograph of sheepdogs, shepherding little children. 'And I especially liked to think somehow of my little Black's small fingers (with the little brown mole just below the first finger knuckle) cutting it out, all serious, and folding it up and making a little star with ink to show it wasn't the other side you meant with the American fashions!'

At the Chantry House life soon became problematic. Gluck took to recording Edith's preoccupations as well as her own: the anniversaries of the deaths of Edith's brother Ivan on 4 December and of Yeats on 28 January, Edith's attacks of lumbago, visits to town, to the hairdresser or to friends. Alone together they had peaceful times. As a threesome the atmosphere was impossible. It was evidently intolerable to Nora that Edith and Gluck were having some kind of an affair in what was, after all, her house. The writer Marjorie Watts, widow of Gluck's friend the *Punch* artist Arthur Watts, remembers the expression of disgust and pain on Nora's face as, in the offices of *The Lady*, she voiced her horror that Edith could be behaving this way.[16]

Tension and battle of wills took the place, for Gluck, of depression. Years later she would say that she was the one who ought to have moved out of Chantry, not Nora, but that Edith wanted her to stay. Alison Settle and other friends found Gluck's presence in the house unbearable. Gluck's diary entries tersely chronicled the tension, week in, month out.

Alison to dinner, very rude about lampshade.

Write letter to Alison.

Alison comes round but does not come in. Nora upstairs.

E. goes to talk to Alison, who ran away, about not coming in night before. I tackle her, and E. and I refuse to go Saturday for drinks before lunch. Nora accepts.

E. and I alone. Lovely evening.

Nora returns 5 pm. Very grim.

Nora awful all day. Very rude at tea. Alison rings up and asks Nora to drinks at 6. Does not return til after 8. E. and I have drinks alone.

E. starts shingles on Tuesday. Dr Dingemans comes 11 am and gives Pethadine injection. Makes E. very ill and sick. Nora horrible to me and E. Deluging rain.

Alison calls for first time to see E. Nora behaves like a fiend.

Have scene with Nora about E. and her behaviour to E. then ask Alison to see me in cottage. A. rude and insists on seeing me in road. E. upset and crying.

N. does not come back till 1 am. I tell her what I think of her.[17]

At the time of these scenes, in 1946, Gluck was fifty-one, Edith sixty-one, Nora sixty-three. It was not the settled harmony of middle age. For Nora it was a nightmare. There were tensions and shrieking matches. The situation struck a wedge between the sisters and then Gluck came to Edith's defence against Nora. No doubt Nora felt betrayed by Edith. Gone were the shared holidays, the house parties and ease of life. Nor that year did Gluck earn any money from her painting. Her sole professionally earned income for 1946 was three shillings and ninepence – royalties on the sale of postcards of one of her flower paintings. Edith remarked of the cheque that things were looking up, which made Gluck laugh.

Gluck's only painting in 1946, done in what she called the garden studio, was *England*. It was a romantic expression of the postwar calm she hoped for through her move to Steyning. A background plate shows a tranquil scene of a church and two figures and in the foreground are roses from Edith's walled rose garden. But whereas previously Gluck had painted perfect blooms, these roses are blousy, some of the petals blighted and one broken bloom lies dying away from the group. Maybe it was a reference to those who died in the war, or a valediction to her love for Nesta.

Gluck and Edith went to Lamorna for a month in the summer, made bonfires, cooked lobsters and chicken and took long walks round the coves. Home life had not improved on their return to Chantry. 'Return from Cornwall at 6pm. Nora awful.' was Gluck's laconic diary entry for 5 October 1946. It was a conflict of feeling that could not be resolved. Nora felt unable to invite her friends and work colleagues to the house. She was, after all, editor of *The Lady*, which did not countenance ladies behaving in quite this manner. The feud became territorial. Gluck and Edith went to look at alternative houses and studios but in a half-hearted way. When Gluck put forward a proposal to have a prefabricated hen incubator reconstructed as a studio in the garden, Nora opposed the idea bitterly. She cried and would not give her agreement, but the scheme went ahead, none the less. When Gluck moved some of her things into one of the attic rooms in the Chantry House, unused for six months, and started to use it as a workroom, Nora took the key from the door and sat in the room. No castle would have been large enough to house them together. Letters and insults were exchanged. Nora's friends found the situation shocking and sided with her against Gluck. Though a fatal rift was being driven between the two sisters, it seems that Edith was absolute in wanting Gluck to stay. When, however, Nesta, on a Plumpton stopover, visited Gluck alone in her studio cottage for an afternoon, Edith and Gluck then had a 'dreadful upset' – an intimation of the jealousy that was subsequently to plague their relationship.

Nora took to not going home at all, or going straight to bed after supper and staying there until after lunch, or escaping round to Alison Settle. When Gluck spent Guy Fawkes night, 1946, with Nesta at the Mill House, Nora and Edith, alone together at Chantry, did not speak. The servants quit, unable to stand the atmosphere. Nor did Nesta help. When dining at the Ivy, in London, with Lord Londonderry, a former Leader of the House of Lords, she overheard a conversation critical of Gluck and affairs at Chantry House. She relayed this to Gluck, who sent letters to Alison and Nora. Christmas at the Chantry House that year was on the frosty side.

In such an atmosphere Gluck cemented her relationship with Edith. It had more to do with striking an attitude than real compatibility. Gluck wanted a home and Edith was determined to provide her with one. They had good times – they went to the Theatre Royal at Brighton and saw *Lady Windermere's Fan*, *Murder in the Cathedral* and Valerie Taylor in *Anonymous Lives*. They went to Glyndebourne for Benjamin Britten's new opera *Albert Herring* and to London – occasionally – to visit the art galleries. Gluck kept on with her work for the Sussex Council of Churches and both she and Edith took tea with the Bishop at Chichester Palace. They visited the Bougheys, the Greenes and the Dulacs. Susan Ertz and her husband Ronald McCrindle came to stay and Gluck spent the occasional weekend with Molly Mount Temple. On Gluck's birthday, on 13 August, Edith brought her red roses and nectarines with dew on them on her breakfast tray. 'Darling Grub', she wrote when Gluck went into Hove nursing home in July 1947 for an operation on a tooth abscess '. . . I played our record at the time I thought you were under in case you were disembodied enough to drift this way . . . I will come at 3.30, Love E.'

Gluck was taking a completely different focus on her professional life. She seldom visited the Bolton House studio and made no contact with The Fine Art Society. She was not working toward an exhibition or in any thematic way and had left the buzz and pressure of London life behind. The tensions and dramas of the Chantry House obsessed her now. Nora and Gluck were scarcely speaking and there was deep bitterness between the sisters. 'Nora makes terrible scene with E. before supper. I hear it but stay upstairs. Nora insulting to E. about her job.' 'E. working hard. Nora goes in and makes scene on her at 11.30 when she's working. E. tells her to go away.'

In October 1947 Gluck sold the Letter Studio in Lamorna after some pressure from her trustees about her continuing to hold properties she seldom used. The loss made her extremely miserable. All that she once had was slipping

England. Gluck's only painting in 1946

away. Nesta, free as a bird, sent letters from Italy, Zurich, Lenzerheide, Mexico, New York, until Seymour had a minor stroke in November. Then she came back to Plumpton for a while. It would have confirmed her worst fears had she seen Gluck in this hothouse of emotional discord. Nora accused Gluck of spying and called her and Edith 'disgusting people'. Gluck thought Nora 'treacherous' and 'crazy'. Nora, in her sixties, was scared of losing her home – a home that she had done so much to create, and Gluck, in her fifties, was scared of not finding a home and facing loneliness. And perhaps, more ominously, there were old scores to settle for the pain and loss that triangular relationships had caused her.

There were no oysters, champagne, or dancing on New Year's Eve, 1947. Edith cooked a goose because the kitchen staff were away. Early the next year the division of the linen, furniture, glass, carpets, pictures and records took place. The Trust paid for half of the value of Chantry House on Gluck's behalf and Nora, with that money, moved out to another house in Steyning, at Wyckham Close, on 14 February 1948. She was sixty-five. Though in the years that followed some reparation took place between the sisters, Nora never visited Chantry again.

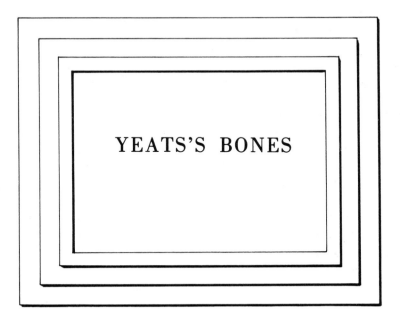

FIFTEEN

YEATS'S BONES

With Nora ousted from Chantry, Gluck had a responsibility to make the *ménage à deux* work. The demands of the house soon dictated the structure of her life. It became in one way the settled home she had always wanted and in another a curtailment to her talent. A housekeeper, Mrs Gurd, joined them in 1949 and stayed with them, like the gardener Mr Lovett, until they died. Robert Lovett, a former postman, first went to the Chantry in the early fifties and did not mind stretching Gluck's canvases and listening to her woes as well as pruning the trees. Whereas to Nesta Gluck had been the 'darling boyee' now she began for all the world to seem like a patriarchal father – the father Edith never mentioned. She was protective of Edith but dominated her totally. It was Gluck who sat at the head of table in a dinner suit, carved the roast, pulled the wine corks, checked the household accounts, hired and fired the kitchen staff and monopolized the conversation at mealtimes. Everything was spotless, ordered, formal but the atmosphere of the house changed.

Burying herself at Steyning did not help Gluck's career. It was a small market town, rather well-furnished with nursing homes. With the sale of Bolton

House her links with London became tenuous. She seldom if ever used her Hampstead studio, and eventually sold that too in 1949. To compensate, in 1953 she bought the 'Dolphin Cottage' in St Buryan, Cornwall. Mr Dawbarn of The Fine Art Society, who so liked her work and encouraged her in the thirties, retired after the war. For the next thirty-five years Gluck had little or no contact with the Gallery and she and her work were all but forgotten by them. And the trend in postwar art was toward abstraction, which she regarded as a passing fad. She believed in the universality of classicism – that it revealed nature and human character 'in all their depth and nakedness, freed from the fashions and hypocrisies of time and place'.[1] She found herself out of kilter with the times.

Commissions for portraits and flower groups still came from those who knew her and a clique of people remained as convinced as ever of her worth, but the sheer *joie de vivre* of the thirties was gone both from her and society's élite. Art was now for public museums rather than for stunningly designed rooms in private houses and 'Prints for Pleasure' of the old masters were available for the average drawing room wall.

Society had drastically changed. Nationally, the postwar years were a time for reconstruction. The polarities of the thirties – joblessness, deprivation and hardship for many; money, daring and style for a few – were dulled. There was a Labour government and a spirit of egalitarianism. Few individuals now commissioned pictures of perfect blooms for their walls or perfect floral displays for their dinner-party tables. Constance Spry kept her shop in South Audley Street, but 'weekly masterpieces' of flower decorations for fantasy interiors like Atkinsons Perfumery were no longer wanted. She diversified into teaching homecrafts – cookery, housekeeping, flower arranging, gardening and needlework. With her husband Shav she bought a rambling Georgian house, Winkfield Place near Ascot, and opened it as a college for girls. She lectured nationwide and wrote books and articles for numerous magazines.

The Villa Hammamet in Tunisia, the setting for hedonistic summers in the thirties, got occupied by the Nazis during the war. Jean Henson was incarcerated in a Silesian prison, starved, and for years eluded the searches of the Red Cross. His wife Violet stayed imprisoned in the Villa, cooped in a couple of rooms. After the war the couple reunited, but the élan and magical years of endless summers, peacocks strutting in the marble courtyards and games of halma on the terraces were gone for ever.

Gluck's brother, Louis, took over as Steward of The Fund in 1940 – the key job in administering the complex structure of trusts and investments, claims and practical problems of the Family dynasty. He lost his seat as Conservative

MP for Nottingham East in the Labour landslide of 1945, but despite his parliamentary disappointments he was to hold a plethora of public offices: President of the Albert Hall, President of the Marylebone Conservative Association, President of the Liberal Jewish Synagogue, Chairman of the GLC. He was knighted in 1953. As the years passed he got more busy, autocratic, uncompromising and impressive. The jokiness shared by him and Gluck when young evaporated and they continued to try to avoid direct negotiations with each other over her financial affairs. There was a bond of kinship, Gluck stayed with him when in London, but they had lost common ground. She got on his nerves and he would turn the sound up on the television when she came in the room. When for years she ceased to paint, and herself got more autocratic, she no longer in his view justified her eccentricity.

And as if there was not enough to divide them, their mother, after the war, began evincing symptoms of madness. She became even more hyperactive, showed signs of paranoia, her moods changed erratically and she stopped looking after her appearance or eating enough. When she thought no one was looking, she slipped chicken legs or buttered rolls off her plate and into her handbag to avoid eating them, and the room she lived in at the Cumberland became chaotic.

Nesta resumed her fun-filled, glitzy life. She left Britain for good and went to Hawaii in 1948. Seymour, by then in his eighties, had had a stroke and wanted to live in the sunshine. Nor did Socialist Britain hold much attraction for them. 'Big men made the world and great men inspired us, but it is the little man we fear,' wrote a Mayfair friend to Nesta in the postwar years.

All initiative is being throttled. We are being taxed, controlled, regimentated and pestered by every petty little civil servant. Through laws our financial condition is being shattered . . . So my dear Nesta, stay on your little Island in the Pacific, stay there until this mad crazy world becomes normal again – or perishes.[2]

'N. leaves for USA on Nieuw-Amsterdam train 4.35. Cannot settle to anything.' was Gluck's disconsolate diary entry for 26 August 1948. For weeks before the departure day she made a box, lined in satin, for Nesta's poodle, Mr Chips, to travel in. Nesta came to the Chantry House and said her sad goodbyes four days before she left, while Edith discreetly walked alone on the downs.

The Obermers stayed for six years in the Royal Hawaiian Hotel on the beach at Waikiki before moving into a house on Diamond Head. They mixed in a rich ex-patriate community and friends on world tours to the Far East and beyond stopped by while their aeroplanes refuelled in Hawaii. It was light years away from the small-town gentrified life of Steyning, and her letters to Gluck began to show how different their lives now were:

... the dogs whined about six and as I let them out I realised it was pure and fresh – the dawn of the world. I opened the big windows into my fen and orchid garden and heard a furious 'tr-trutting' and saw my big tame (wild) red cardinal bobbing about in a vexed way on top of my wild birds' food cage. I gave him lots of sunflower seeds, all in my nightdress which was no dress – and then walked down on the stepping stones all surrounded by violets to the beach and dug my toes into the cold sand, my head in the sun that came slanting through the palm trees. Everywhere was peace and sapphire sea.[3]

She used Hawaii as a base for travelling, and visited Britain each year. Money gave her freedom and she spent it easily on looking good, enjoying life and helping and entertaining her friends. She got her pilot's licence and took up surfing and deep-sea diving. The Duke of Buccleuch described, when passing through Hawaii with his wife on a world tour, being whisked through the mountain passes in Nesta's 'snow white open Cadillac with a pair of café au lait Weimaraners occupying the back seat, their amber eyes flashing above their diamond collars.'[4] Nesta was a tireless letter writer – she would write, and receive, twenty or so letters a day. She wrote in an uncensored rush in blue biro on blue paper. In the postwar years she took control of her life and lived it fearlessly. She had a crystal quality, a many-faceted sparkle and energy, that impressed and attracted and with her charm and talent for the art of friendship, and her wealth, she contrived, despite the distances, to keep her friends and make many more. People had fun when she was around. She never stopped hoping that Gluck would be fulfilled, successful and happy.

I do hope and pray that everything is falling into place about the picture and that your spirit is satisfied. I know it is going to be a masterpiece. Oh Tim! If you could only think out your life as you tell me to think out a picture ...

At the moment you are not loving when you think of your new life, you are threatening. 'I'm going to do this, that, etc and if they ... they can damn well ... etc.' All right, all right. Don't frown and fold!!![5]

By contrast to Nesta's free flight Gluck's life seemed all too earthbound. She absorbed into Edith's world, then resented her for the drain it made on her own resources. As ever she could not clearly define the boundaries between herself and her partner. The flip side of her dominance was her dependence. Edith was supportive, trustworthy, loyal and sympathetic, so many of the old pains of insecurity were assuaged. She did though, as the years passed, become consumed with jealousy which neither of them resolved. It became ultimately a tense and cruel relationship, though it began pragmatically enough.

One of the first trips abroad they took together as part of their new shared life was to the cemetery at the village of Roquebrune in the south of France to visit Yeats's tomb. For Edith the trip was a pilgrimage – to recapture that 'wonderful southern night of stars' when eight years previously she had kept vigil by Yeats's bedside the night he died.

When they arrived at the cemetery, on 10 June 1947, they found no trace of Yeats: no headstone, grave nor mention of him. Edith was totally disbelieving. Gluck, whose French was fluent, questioned the local priest, Abbé Biancheri, who checked the records with the Director of Funeral Services at Menton. The Abbé's findings shocked both women. With graves as with most things you get what you pay for. Yeats's widow, George, had a choice between a permanent site, a concession for ten or fifteen years or, cheapest and worst, a 'fosse commune', known colloquially as a pauper's grave. This she chose, or by mistake, got. It meant that Yeats's corpse had been put in a communal grave, along with four or five others of the newly dead. Every few years each 'fosse commune' got cleared to make way for more corpses. This happened to Yeats's site. Some bones were dug up in 1941 and then in January 1946 the whole site was cleared and all the bones put in the communal ossuary.

On the night of 10 June 1947, in the Hotel Mirabeau in Monte Carlo, Edith was inconsolable. She was crying and kept saying 'I would know his bones anywhere.' Gluck made notes for a poem, in rather blank verse, about the traumatic episode:

> *The Hotel Bedroom*
> Exhausted – Distraught – our pilgrimage in vain
> To whom to turn, to help
> To reach the Truth, so rudely shattered
> Then – Language I had – I seized
> The Telephone – I reached Authority
> I spoke of what we had found
> All through I heard her agonised crying, crouched on the ground
> 'Let me but see – I would know
> his bones anywhere' ran through my
> brain as I tried in vain to move officialdom.
> But this could not be, for

> ossuaries are not for rifling through
> as searching in a dustbin or waste
> paper basket to piece together what
> has been scattered with like matter.

An added problem was that Yeats, in one of his last poems, *Epitaph*, had expressed the wish to be buried in Drumcliff, County Sligo, Ireland, where his father had lived and his great-grandfather was once rector: 'Under bare Ben Bulben's head, In Drumcliff churchyard Yeats is laid' he wrote. Gluck checked the records, rechecked and checked again — with Abbé Biancheri, the town hall at Roquebrune, the director of 'Maison Roblot' the undertakers in Menton. The facts were beyond doubt as the Abbé wrote to her: (15 June 1947):

The registers of the Roquebrune Town Hall show that Mr Butler William Yeats [sic] *was buried on 30 January 1939 in a communal grave (square E, at the spot which is now occupied by the body of Madame Victoire Lanteri.) No permanent grave was acquired in his name. His bones were dug up in January 1946 and put in the communal ossuary.*

I questioned M. César Lautier, the official responsible for exhumations and the upkeep of the graves, at length. His recollections are vague, but he thinks that Yeats's body had a surgical truss circled with thin strips of steel. If this information is correct, one could perhaps, with a great deal of difficulty, find some remains of the hapless poet. But the already arduous task of finding the right bones in this ossuary is complicated by the fact that there are new exhumations every day.

When Edith and Gluck got home they went immediately to see Edmund Dulac and Helen Beauclerck. Dulac had been a close friend of Yeats for twenty-five years and of Edith for twenty years. He decided to cover up what seemed to him an appalling blunder on the part of Yeats's widow, George. Dulac wrote to the Abbé Biancheri accordingly (27 June 1947):

I write to implore you to ensure that this matter goes no further. *I'm asking you to say nothing to anybody and to take whatever measures are necessary to ensure that all those at Roquebrune who have some knowledge of these facts, either on account of their office, like M. Reynaut, or through rumour,* preserve absolute silence. *All it would take would be an excessively curious tourist for the Press to batten on to this with avidity and we must at all costs avoid the scandal that would arise from such a revelation and the pain it would cause those close to Yeats and to his other friends. If by some chance, which I cannot foresee, a*

*member of Yeats's family were to come to Roquebrune to visit the poet's tomb, it
would be necessary to behave with the greatest prudence and to employ as much
diplomacy as possible and the greatest delicacy – of which I'm sure you're
capable – to check their identity. As for sightseers or journalists, you could claim
that your duties do not permit you to accompany them to show where the grave is
buried.*

The Abbé gave every assurance of discretion. He had, since 1942, received
only one letter of enquiry about a Mr Yeats. As no one could give him any
information he assumed the letter was intended for another Roquebrune, in
Var, and did not answer it. With the Abbé's cooperation in cutting through
French red tape, Dulac and Edith drew up detailed plans to avert questions and
scandal and to repair the damage. They arranged for a temporary stone to be
fixed on the Roquebrune cemetery wall saying that W. B. Yeats was buried
there – without of course specifying 'though not for long'. They took out a
concession 'in perpetuity', for about 5000 francs, for the erection in the
cemetery of a permanent headstone which Dulac designed and a Sussex
sculptor, Joseph Cribb, immediately began to carve. The Abbé chose a site for it
right against the ossuary – 'in my opinion it's the natural site for the poet's
monument', he wrote to Dulac (12 August 1947).

Dulac and Edith discussed the matter of Yeats's reinterment in Ireland but
agreed that no self-respecting Irish parson would bury a box without being
certain that it contained the remains over which he performed the sacred rites,
and that the Roquebrune sexton might palm them off with any old bones.[6]
They gave no word of their manoeuvres to George Yeats. 'I entirely agree',
wrote Dulac to Edith (17 July 1947), 'that it is infinitely better if she can be kept
out of it and only told when everything is done. Even then she should be told
what I proposed to tell everybody else: "That a more lasting monument to
W.B.'s memory was erected by us etc etc . . .".'

Their plans were nearly complete when, on 6 January 1948, Dulac saw an
article in *The Times* announcing that George Yeats intended bringing her
husband's remains back to Ireland for reburial at Drumcliff. '. . . It is very
painful for me to have to write to you of this matter', wrote Dulac to her that
same day, 'and I wish I could spare you the pain of it also, but that is now
impossible.' He then outlined the whole sorry saga of Edith and Gluck's sojourn
to Roquebrune, the 'fosse commune', the heaping of Yeats's bones into the
ossuary, the attempts at reparation of the blunder.

I don't know what you propose to do in the circumstances, but if you will allow me to make a suggestion, I think you might say to the Corporation that it is not possible in present conditions to make the transfer and leave it at that. But if you were obliged to give details, I should say that it was owing to the war that, the Cemetery at Roquebrune having been seriously disturbed, W.B's remains had been dispersed. A monument could, however, always be erected in Drumcliffe and my stone could be sent there instead of to the South of France.

Again I hope you will think that we have acted as we should in the interests of all concerned and especially in that of our friend.

Dulac sent a copy of the letter to Edith with a covering note:

... If she now spreads the news about, she will undoubtedly cut a very poor figure as we have definite proof that she could have done something during all these years; the grave was not touched for eighteen months from the Liberation and she had nearly 10 years in which to extend the concession. Eire was neutral all that time. And if there is a scandal ... well! she will, as I said be in a very bad position and I think she has enough wits left not to do anything to bring it about. And remember, the Abbé has been told not to tell anybody except members of the family. However there is no use worrying until we hear from her.

George Yeats's response was blunt. The grave was for *ten* years not one. She had the receipts. There was no question of a 'fosse commune'. She had contacted the French minister in Ireland who said it would be quite easy to get the remains and bring them back.[7]

A police inspector was sent from Paris to Roquebrune and Biancheri went through his investigations again, and wrote again to Dulac (16 February 1948):

According to the register of burials in the Roquebrune Town Hall the poet Butler William Yeats [sic] was buried on 28 January 1939 in a communal grave. ... The grave was granted for five years, after which the bones were put in the ossuary. The register of funerals at Menton says the same as that at Roquebrune.

Could there be a copying error or a possible confusion between a five and ten year grant? Examination of the document Mrs Yeats has, would provide a beginning to the solution to this problem. One fact is certain: the bones of the late poet were placed in the ossuary. There is no doubt whatsoever on this subject. Is it possible to find the bones of the poet Yeats in the ossuary? Yes! If we empty the entire contents of the ossuary and if we have details of distinctive characteristics which will enable us to reconstruct the skeleton after painstaking research carried out under the direction of a medical expert. These details would

Headstone designed by Dulac for the cemetery at Roquebrune, to compensate for Yeats's missing bones.

The *SS Macha* docks in Nice, 1948, to bring Yeats home to Sligo

be based on the age of the deceased, his height, the circumference of his head, dental prosthesis, possible fractures, bones deformities, illnesses which might have affected his skeleton. The researches would be long, expensive, extremely difficult, but not impossible. The results would remain subject to the laws of probability. Absolute certainty is in my view impossible.

Skulls were in one section of the ossuary, fibulae and tibulae in another. Biancheri was reiterating the same story. None the less the reburial of bones of uncertain ownership was to go ahead.

For Gluck this was all too much. She had shown, for her, restraint in letting Edmund Dulac arrange things as he thought best. It was not in her nature to be passive while others got on with the action, nor would she stay silent while Ireland arranged a state funeral for, and a priest blessed, the bones of assorted Frenchmen. She wrote to George Yeats, against Edith's wishes, and to avoid suspicion of Edith's complicity, gave her own bank as her address:

Dear Mrs Yeats

In June 1947 I accompanied Edith Heald to the Cemetery at Roquebrune where, despite exhaustive search we were unable to find your husband's grave. As Edith does not speak French with ease I made all the enquiries, firstly with the parish priest, the Abbé Biancheri, and after with M. Pierre Reynaut, Director of the Maison Roblot, undertakers at Menton. Both these men stated that your husband had been buried in a 'fosse commune', that the remains had been removed at the end of five years, and that these remains would be almost impossible to find, and that if found identity would be open to doubt.

Naturally all this was so shocking that I made sure by reiteration and investigation that their information was correct and that no possible mistake was being made. I have since had all the details confirmed to me in writing.

You will perhaps wonder why I have not written to you sooner. I placed the matter in other and more intimate hands as far as you were concerned, and so far I have preserved the utmost secrecy, but now that it has been published in The Times *and other papers that you are contemplating exhumation and reburial in Ireland I felt I must write to you.*

I have no desire to make things worse than they are, but because of my knowledge of the exact circumstances at Roquebrune (my enquiries were the first in eight years) culminating in the terrible discovery that there was no grave, I cannot view this reburial with equanimity.

Will you please, therefore, set my mind at rest by letting me know that in view of all the uncertainty you will reconsider any scheme for reburial.[8]

Dulac, an irascible man, was furious at what he saw as Gluck's interference in matters that should not concern her. He called her threatening and high-handed and accused her of putting Edith and himself in an awkward position

I will now have to do my best to minimise the effect your letter has had upon George in order to save Edith from its possible consequences. I shall very naturally say that it is entirely your own effort and that neither Edith nor I had anything to do with its inspiration or its contents. Please let me know at once if I have Edith's approval in doing so. If by misfortune I have not, and she tells me that she on the contrary approves of what you do, it will break our hearts but I shall very regretfully have to tell G.Y. that I have nothing more to do with this painful affair and leave it to you to handle in the way your own desires dictate.[9]

He was expressing more than just exasperation at the embarrassing muddle over Yeats's bones. He was angry, like many of Edith's friends, at the way Gluck seemed to be eclipsing Edith and taking over her life. In a sense this anger was justified. Gluck opened Edith's letters, listened to her telephone calls and answered questions that were put to Edith. In a sardonic way Dulac was acknowledging that Edith's approval or otherwise would come from Gluck, that Edith's decisions would be made by Gluck. It was the 'YouWe' problem but in a different manifestation, the fusion of identity but now with a woman of unequal power. For Gluck it was a troublesome situation too. She was protective of Edith who anyway sought her help over the issue. She had been distressed by the Nora business, the splitting of the bond between the two sisters, the implacable resentment this caused among Edith's friends, which she was unable to mend. But she was also dominant and scrupulous about facts. The truth, or what she felt to be the truth, no matter how painful, embarrassing or inconvenient, was the code by which she tried to live. Were it not for her involvement with Edith, she would have told *The Times* right away about her Roquebrune sojourn, for the sake of fact, not scandal. Now she was in the complicity. But she could not let Dulac have the last word.

She wrote to him saying that he had Edith's permission to dissociate Edith from Gluck's letter to George Yeats. He replied to Edith (8 March 1948) asking why Gluck was answering for her.

It is from you that I wanted that permission, since it is you that are obviously concerned first and foremost in this affair . . . I never expected Gluck would abruptly brush everybody on one side to satisfy what can only be an irresponsible desire to interfere personally and rather crudely in an affair which does not in

*the least concern her. . . . Whatever happens you may rest assured you have all
our sympathy and can count on our help. But it is sometimes difficult to help
people against their own wishes. It is clear that if Gluck insists on being the 'I
who knows' with whom everybody has to reckon, I had better not try to cope with
this distressing business any longer.*

Helen Beauclerck added a postscript:

*My Kosh! Surely if Gluck loves you and wants you to be kept from gossip,
quarrelling, horrors of all sorts, she will promise to do nothing more about it. . . .
Surely she has her work, her talent – she need not put her energies into this sort
of thing? Sorry if I am incoherent but I do feel so deeply about it and am so
afraid . . .*

Gluck replied in a conciliatory enough tone, defending herself but saying it
was George Yeats not Edith who was vulnerable, and hoping that no
misunderstandings should occur between Edith and Dulac. He wrote to Edith
(14 March 1948) with yet another attack on Gluck and in effect threatening to
withdraw his friendship from Edith if Gluck involved herself any further in the
bones business:

*. . . as you seem unable or unwilling to restrain her from spending on threats of
useless and dangerous mischief energies she might far more profitably spend
otherwise, I can only retire before her and hope for the best. . . . I shall inform the
Abbé and anyone who may come into this affair that any further
communications must be addressed to you. Gluck can deal with them as she
thinks fit.*

But there was no way Edith would be disloyal to Gluck, nor had Gluck
threatened anyone. She had simply tried to put pressure on George Yeats not to
go ahead with all the paraphernalia of a State burial when the whereabouts of
the remains of her husband were in such doubt. Edith tried to make peace all
round: 'I am sorry that you should have thought Gluck's letter threatening,
however faintly,' she wrote to Dulac (17 March 1948),

*I do assure you that it was written with no such intention but in hope of putting
things right as she was extremely distressed that our friendship might be
shaken. . . . If you now retire as you say you will, I shall do nothing more until
George has disclosed her intentions. In any case this now seems best for us all. I
am having the stone brought here and will keep it until the position is clearer.
The Abbé can hold the money for the concession until then.*

W.B. might not have disliked his no-grave but it would have distressed him to think it might diminish our friendship – and I do not see why it should. Love from Kosch.

While these friends wrangled, the arrangements for the 'reburial' continued. It remained unclear whether Mrs Yeats had a receipt for a ten-year grave and, if she had, whose clerical error this was. It seems that neither the Abbé Biancheri nor Dulac ever saw her receipt. Nor is it clear who, if anyone, rifled through the ossuary and attempted the identification of Yeats's bones. When it came to the 'exhumation' and transportation of the poet, Abbé Biancheri kept a circumspect if unconvincing distance and wrote of this to Dulac (31 March 1948):

... about the 17th of March [1948] Monsieur Reynaut, the official in charge of undertaking at Menton, asked me to be present at the exhumation of the poet Yeats. But I had been called to the bedside of someone who was sick in a distant part of town and could not accept this invitation. The investigation and exhumation took place in the presence of the police, the Mayor of Roquebrune, a medical expert, a police inspector from Paris and Monsieur César Lautier, the official responsible for the upkeep of the graves. The bones of the poet Yeats were placed in a coffin. The coffin was placed in The Chapel of Rest. The remains of your friend will be sent to Sligo, either by the Irish government or accompanied by Mrs Yeats, his widow. No date seems to have been fixed. It is even possible that I shall not be informed of the departure date. I should not be surprised if my letter were opened before it reached its destination. In any case this is not important.

It is difficult even tentatively to believe that the coffin destined for Sligo contained the right remains. However arduous, costly, detailed and time consuming the reconstruction of a skeleton might be, given the choice of so many bones, it had all, ostensibly, taken place in four weeks. For it had been the sixteenth of February 1948 when the Abbé Biancheri wrote to Edmund Dulac about the need to empty the ossuary and start gathering detailed medical evidence if authentic bones were to be identified, and it was the seventeenth of March 1948 when 'Yeats' was exhumed, put in a coffin and placed in the Chapel of Rest in the presence of high-ranking witnesses. French bureaucracy is not renowned for its speediness. Perhaps, or perhaps not, in four weeks all Yeats's medical and dental records were assembled in Ireland, pathologists employed, the Roquebrune ossuary emptied and all findings analysed.

In August 1948 the Irish naval corvette *Macha* left Cork harbour for Dublin where she was inspected by Ireland's Minister for External Affairs, Mr Sean MacBride. She sailed to Gibraltar with an official of the Department of External Affairs on board, then on to Villefranche. The coffin lay in state in the town square of Roquebrune before being taken by road to meet the ship. Eleven days later the corvette reached Galway Bay. Mrs Yeats, her children and Jack Yeats, the poet's brother, went aboard and the coffin was piped ashore. From Galway the funeral cortège made its way by road to Sligo where a military guard of honour waited outside the town hall. The Minister of External Affairs, the Mayor and Corporation of Sligo and a crowd of people including Edith and Gluck gathered in Drumcliff churchyard to watch the coffin placed under the stone inscribed with Yeats's words 'Under bare Ben Bulben's head'.

Edmund Dulac's headstone, with an image of Pegasus ascending to the stars and inscribed simply with the words 'William Butler Yeats 1865–1939', was not sent out to Roquebrune until 1953, the year that Dulac died. The following summer Edith and Gluck again journeyed to Roquebrune, were met by the Abbé Biancheri and paid homage to the stone now resting on the ossuary wall.

For Edith's sake Gluck kept silent throughout her life on the events surrounding Yeats's burial. She remained agitated though over her notes, letters and knowledge about it all. After her death her executors asked the Irish government if they would like to accept, as a gift, the correspondence telling of the saga so that they might deal with it as they saw fit. They declined the offer.

SIXTEEN

COSMIC

INJUSTICE

The saga of Yeats's bones was only one of the moral issues that preoccupied Gluck in the postwar years. Questions of justice became all-important to her. She did a series of formal portraits of judges in their high robes of office. From February until July 1949 she worked at the painting, commissioned by Lord Goddard, of Lord Wilfrid Greene who retired that year as Master of the Rolls. For some of the sittings he went to her studio at the Chantry, for the rest she travelled up to the Royal Court of Justice in the Strand. More than with previous pictures the quality of paints and canvas distressed her. Colour seeped into the canvas and went dead, even when applied thickly. Edith said it was like painting on a sheet. And brush strokes done in the same colour but drawn in different directions left a suede effect. She found that black paint stayed tacky for three days and left a silvery sheen or a blue edge. Her paints frustrated her, they seemed unpredictable and not in her control. Her problems with this picture were to drive her into a decade of battling with the paint manufacturers over the quality of materials. Day by day, while working on it, she noted the shortcomings of her paints and canvas.

Work at shadow side of face – forehead already gone dead and edge of wig.

Dark side of face hell to do, like suede, light and dark brush strokes. Tacky too and goes dead as work. Ear awful.

Work at light side of face. Dark side dead and quite silvery and shining like a sixpence on edge of wig . . .

It was a contrast to the happy pictures of Christmas revelry and flowers done in 1936 when she was so in love with Nesta. But her technical struggles do not show in the finished work. 'Wilfrid Arthur Lord Greene, Master of the Rolls 1937–1949' as she called it, has none of the edge of caricature that stamped her thirties' portraits. She matched the seriousness of the subject. She used light and dark as a metaphor for truth and justice, and, as ever, showed her loving care for detail: the markers in the pages of the books, the manicured nails, the starched collar. Goddard had asked her not to paint Wilfrid Greene in a wig – he thought it sapped character – but she treats it as a symbol of status.

She finished the picture in June 1949, Edith gave a celebratory party and seventy-five Steyning residents called at the house to see it. Lord Goddard and Nancy and Wilfrid Greene went to lunch and declared themselves delighted with the painting. Goddard presented it to the Benchers of the Inner Temple and it was hung in their drawing room. 'I suppose that differences of opinion are inevitable about all matters artistic', wrote Lord Merriman, the Deputy Treasurer, to Lord Goddard (13 July 1949), 'but I can only say that I have never known a case in which approval of the work has been so general'. ' "Has Holbein come to life again?" ' remarked the librarian of the Bar library to Lord Greene. 'I shan't repeat any more eulogies – you will be getting too conceited. Very many thanks again and love to Miss Shackleton from both of us. Ever, Wilfrid'.[1]

The picture's good reception did little to lift Gluck's spirits. Somehow when Nesta went so too did the fun. Gluck and Edith worked out a domestic, ordered routine: roast dinner Sundays, six o'clock drinks with Steyning neighbours, trips to Glyndebourne and the Theatre Royal Brighton, touring holidays in Italy looking at frescoes, cathedrals, and Pisa in the moonlight. They gardened and cared for the house. Edith bought a Stanley Spencer painting of a winter scene and Gluck bought a Picasso sculpture of a bronze hand. They celebrated each other's birthdays with champagne and cake, and nursed each other's illnesses, aches and pains. It was orderly home life, but a frustration and boredom with it bubbled below the surface for Gluck, and Edith had cause for disappointment. The coldness from her friends and relatives towards Gluck did not thaw. Harry

Portrait of Wilfrid Arthur, Lord Greene, Master of the Rolls. Presented to the Benchers
of the Inner Temple by Lord Goddard, Lord Chief Justice, July 1949

Heald, her brother, visited one weekend and made rude remarks about Gluck's tweed suit and only reluctantly gave her a lift to the station. Nora brought presents round at Christmas, but would not come in the house. And Gluck continued her habit of sending notes to Alison Settle when she thought she was being awful to Edith. Worst of all, between Gluck and Edith there were all too often upsets over trivial things, which left them miserable and worn out.

Gluck's old Hillman, BUL 700 got towed away for good in September 1949. It had broken down on countless occasions but she was extremely attached to it. A week later she parted with her Hampstead studio which she no longer used. Dr Pollock, who bought Bolton House, wanted it but dithered over the price, so she sold it to the surrealist painter and spiritualist, Ithell Colquhoun, for £2,500. Both transactions left her feeling empty and nostalgic. She gave up smoking for the umpteenth time, which was always hard on her and Edith while it lasted. For each of them, work was their focus, but for Gluck the roots of inspiration seemed dry. For more than two years she worked at a painting of a vase of roses. Edith said it had the three essentials of beauty according to St Thomas Aquinas, wholeness, harmony and radiance, but the compliment had little practical spur as eventually Gluck discarded the canvas.

Two more judges wanted their portraits painted in the early 1950s: Sir Raymond Evershed, who succeeded Sir Wilfrid as Master of the Rolls, and Sir Reginald Croom-Johnson. Gluck usually painted largely from memory, using only a few sittings. The time-consuming part was the application of paint – a quest for perfection of line, shadow, texture and detail. 'I compare the painting of a picture to the rehearsing of an orchestra', she wrote to Lady Evershed (18 March 1952), 'so some days the drums are too loud for the strings and so on, until the day when all the instruments sing to me.'

She stayed with the Eversheds for five days in October 1951 in their Grange House farm in Norfolk. Sir Raymond went out shooting most of the time, but he posed for an hour or so each day. Gluck painted him in his Master of the Rolls Privy Council robes, lace jabot and ruffles, gold braid and wool wig. All that, and the high colour of his face, got from his outdoor sports, make it a bright if stern affair. Gluck took the robes home on the train in locked tin boxes and lodged them in the bank's strong room when not working with them. The portrait was presented by Evershed's uncle, Edward, to the family's native town, Burton-on-Trent, where Evershed was a Freeman. Gluck's picture shows him holding the Roll of the Freedom of the town, and with his own, and Burton-on-Trent's coats of arms either side of his head. Uncle Edward knew nothing about pictures but wanted this one to be a success with no expense spared. 'If

The Rt Hon. Sir Raymond Evershed, Master of the Rolls, holding the Roll of the
Freedom of Burton-on-Trent, 1951

you feel like diamonds in the frame he won't jib,' Lady Evershed wrote (17 October 1951). In fact he paid Gluck 500 guineas and all expenses and the picture was shown at the rooms of the framers James Bourlet & Sons in London before going to Burton Town Hall. A presentation ceremony on 5 December 1952, presided over by the Mayor, made the lead story in the *Burton Observer*. 'It is well known', said Sir Raymond at the ceremony, 'that Miss Gluck has an unerring eye for the truth, and what is worse, depicting it.' He said that as a result of the painting he had gained a friend in Miss Gluck, who not only as an artist of very great talent, but also as an individual, he had come greatly to admire.

As for Sir Reginald Croom-Johnson, he wanted to be painted in his summer scarlet robes with grey silk bindings and black stoles like a forebear of his, Sir John Powell, who was a Judge of the Common Pleas in 1688, and whose picture was in the National Portrait Gallery. Gluck quoted him a feet of 350 guineas which he felt was more than he ought spend, so they settled for a smaller picture, 51 × 46 cm, for 200 guineas. 'I wish I could have a much bigger work of yours,' he wrote (28 December 1951),

but before long in the way this country is going we shall have to reduce all our household goods to the very smallest proportions. What am I to do with an historical Dutch sideboard which measures over 8 feet long?

Sittings were hard to arrange, as he spent weekends at his home in Somerset, but he was brought by his chauffeur and butler to the Chantry House with his robes and white gloves in April 1952 for several sittings, on two of which he fell asleep. He kept gently chivvying Gluck to finish the picture. She worked at it on and off for two years, lamenting the state of the canvas and her paints. The finished painting was by no means the best of her legal portraits. Sir Reginald appears to be sitting uncomfortably, blanketed in scarlet.

In 1953 Gluck's brother, Louis, himself a barrister and QC, was knighted with the same pomp and circumstance as these men of the Establishment whom she painted and who so liked her company. On several occasions it was mooted that she should paint him too, but they were never at peace with each other long enough for this to come about. With his professional counterparts she achieved a friendliness that now eluded her with him. And while she worked at these formal portraits of eminent judges she was herself battling against a cosmic injustice. Her mother had lost her reason. Aged seventy-five, the Meteor was diagnosed as suffering from senile mania. Probably she had Alzheimer's Disease. She was not eating, coping, or looking after herself. Her eyes had a

The Honourable Sir Reginald Croom-Johnson, Judge of the High Court, in summer robes, 1954

fixed stare much of the time and she had bouts of confusion, purposeless activity, irrational temper loss and paranoia.

The 1950s were not enlightened times for the treatment of the mentally ill. The tendency was to institutionalize and isolate sufferers. Had the Meteor suffered a more straightforward illness, her life would have been made tolerable with all the palliatives money can buy. As it was, she was beyond the reach of help by money. Nor were Gluck or her brother temperamentally suited to cope with such a crisis. The rift between them proved tragic at this time.

Despite her parlous physical and mental state, Francesca Gluckstein was, in 1950, still living, albeit chaotically, in the Cumberland Hotel. A nurse in mufti, Miss McClennan, looked after her, but more support was needed. On 28 February the Meteor went to tea with her son in St John's Wood. She was irrational and hyper-manic. The family doctor, Dr Solomons, was there and he and Louis tried to persuade her to agree to an injection of a sedating drug. She refused. Louis' wife, Doreen, wanted the doctor to slip something in her mother-in-law's tea, so that they could get her upstairs calmly and nurse her. He refused on the grounds of professional ethics. After a ghastly afternoon of tears and failed persuasion, dominated by the Meteor's paranoia and confusion, she was driven back to the Cumberland by her chauffeur, Peter Smith. As Louis left the house with her he banged the front gate on to the road. The Meteor said 'Don't you bang the door on me,' and tried to open it and bang it herself, but was too feeble to do so. Back at the Cumberland, an electric heater was taken from her room for fear that she would set the place on fire. This mortified her and increased her paranoia as it meant she could not make herself a hot drink in the night. She was crying, rambling and ill.

Two days later Gluck and Edith stayed at the Cumberland for the weekend. Gluck found her mother tired, irritable and distraught. Her clothes were a mess and she was not eating. Gluck saw her brother who made no mention of plans – already made – for their mother to be committed to a mental hospital. On the morning Gluck was due to return to Steyning, the nurse told her that three doctors would see the Meteor that afternoon. They did so, and made out an Urgency Order. The next day Louis lunched with his mother in the Grill Room of the Trocadero, then persuaded her to go for a drive with him, ostensibly to look at houses. They went to Moorcroft Hospital in Hillingdon, where she was committed. She was terrified and uncooperative, and the nursing staff had great difficulty in getting her to have a bath. That evening Louis phoned Gluck and told her what had happened. She was shocked and felt that her mother had been tricked and abandoned to strangers. She had not known such drastic action was even being considered. He had not made Gluck privy to it, nor told the hospital of her. 'I was quite dazed', she wrote in her diary, 'by the terrible nature of what had been done and the way it had been done.' When she telephoned Moorcroft she thought the doctors uninformative and unpleasant. They advised her against visiting for at least three weeks. 'I endured the following weeks without any information except in one conversation with L. on the telephone who said she was very weak and had been diagnosed as suffering from disseminated sclerosis.'[2]

Her brother excluded her from participating in this family tragedy. He was by now chary of her *modus operandi* and disliked dealing with her on any issue. No doubt he feared she would make a fraught situation worse. He was also at that time a prospective parliamentary candidate with hectic political commitments. Neither of them easily accepted the nature of their mother's illness. Gluck's perception of it was that the Meteor was under strain and in need of rest. Louis, while realizing more clearly how drastic the situation was, felt that she was being uncooperative in refusing injections and to be cared for in his family home. Gluck noted: 'On my asking whether she would have to be at Moorcroft a long time he said, "Not while she behaves herself. If she continues to be stubborn and insist on having her own way I don't know what will happen." '[3]

Dr Solomons explained the clinical realities: her condition could not improve, there had been a definite alteration in her brain cells and she was quite likely to survive in her confused state

for some considerable time. This will mean she must be kept under proper supervision and control in some suitable place . . .

Any visits by lay persons or relatives cannot be other than painful; mental illness is always painful, and especially in one's near and dear relatives, and especially if the patient's protestations and statements are viewed on any rational basis.[4]

Gluck was wretched, angry and sleepless over it all. She felt that once again power was in the hands of her brother and denied to her. She perceived her mother as an innocent, rational victim, shanghaied by her brother, psychiatrists and the family doctor, and confined in bad quarters against her will. She reacted in her campaigning way:

May 3rd

Go to Moorcroft. Arrive unannounced at 11.45 am. Go straight to M's room. Get a terrible shock. M. alone sitting up in bed right over in one corner holding her shawl tightly around her, her back pressed hard against the wooden back of the bed. She looked like someone in a trap waiting for the next assault. She said quite sweetly and quietly 'Hallo, what made you come?' but did not move her position and looked desperate. I said, trying to be cheerful 'Hallo darling I've come to take you out for a drive, get your clothes on, I've got Knight here and the car, it will be fun.' 'Oh no,' she said, 'I'm not going, they won't let me you see.' Sister Jane came in and was positively rude saying 'No, she can't possibly go out.' I told her Dr Myers had said a drive would do her good. I then saw a Dr Gilmour who said 'I'm afraid you cannot take her out she's not well enough.' He said she had had a very restless night. I said did he not think she would be less restless if she went out a bit. He still refused and I had to accept the situation.

. . . I was alone with M. from noon until 2.35. Her room was bare of flowers, none of the magazines I sent her were there, not a single personal possession except father's photograph and a wireless she never uses. I sat beside her and she said 'What have I done that I should be punished like this?' 'I have been shut away here to be got out of the way.' 'They have been given power over me and can do as they like with me.'

She was resigned about it, quite aware of her situation, of the nature of the place and the fact that she was helpless. It was horrible and to comfort her I said 'I will get you out of here.' 'Oh no,' she said 'You can't do anything.' But I assured her I could and would. Not once in the whole time I was with her did she wander or talk inconsequentially. Her pillow was very small with the ticking showing through the thin cover. Her bolster was so small and useless that when she sat up all she had to lean against was the hard wooden bed back. Her mattress was a disgrace and hard and sagging in the middle. Her bed linen was filthy, soiled, as was her nightdress. I had lunch with her. The lunch consisted of large unappetising slabs of cold, tinned meat, greens and potatoes. I could hardly touch mine, but M. ate every scrap of hers and some of mine.

I had made an examination of her room before lunch. The cupboard was locked so I asked for the key. Inside I found her handbag. As I did not find her wedding ring in this, I asked Sister Jane for it. She said it was locked away in a cupboard in the hall. In the handbag I found M's magistrate's book, a terribly worn little purse with nothing in it, and a scrap of linen. No pen or pencil which she always had. On the linen I found some writing, done obviously in great distress. It must have been written before they took her pen away. 'All things closing. Taken away. Watch. Very badly treated, no breakfast or tea or anything . . . water or drink.' . . . It was like finding a message in a bottle in the sea. Dreadful.

. . . I then asked her if she wanted me to share the responsibility for her affairs. At first she thought I meant that I wanted to share her possessions with L. and said 'of course I want you to share equally'. I told her that was not what I meant, I had no interest in that, but did she want us to handle things for her together. She said 'Yes'. So I told her if she would write this it would help. She agreed and wrote the following and signed and dated it. 'May 3rd 1950. I want my daughter to share equally with my son any responsibility concerning my affairs. Francesca Gluckstein MBE JP.' Having written this M. then said 'I want to keep a copy of this, I won't give it to you till you give me one.' I therefore wrote a copy and when she had satisfied herself by making me read her statement while she checked it with my copy, she gave me the original. I then put the copy in her bag with a footnote to say I had the original.[5]

Gluck mounted this message behind a piece of perspex and kept it among her papers. She then started a 'campaign' to improve her mother's circumstances and establish the facts of her own rights in the matter. She wrote down everything she saw, felt and heard about it all and got Edith, as witness, to sign and date these notes. Equal to her distress at her mother's condition, was her anger with her brother. She wrote to Dr Solomons querying the committal orders. He urged her to come and talk to him. She refused, so he wrote to her with the details (12 April 1950): her mother had been seen twice by two senior physicians; she was suffering from senile mania; her physical condition was poor; she needed treatment; she had been certified 'in accordance with the normal legal requirements . . . I would only add that I myself feel perfectly sure that the right steps have been taken.'

He again urged her to come and see him, which she again refused to do. Instead she fired questions at a solicitor, a Mr Woodroffe: was it legal for her brother to commit her mother to mental hospital without consulting her? 'I am the elder of Mother's two children.' Could not her brother and the doctors be compelled to give her full information? What were her powers to appeal against the certification? What were her visiting rights? Mr Woodroffe gave her no comfort. No information was being withheld from her. The doctors wanted to see her. Everything had been done according to procedure and 'in a normal manner (apart of course from the fact that your brother has been so secretive about it)'. If Gluck felt her mother had been wrongly certified she was entitled to notify the Lord Chancellor's Visitor, who would then give another opinion.[6]

While seeking to get ammunition against Louis, Gluck was, at the same time, trying with both anger and desperation to make peace with him:

Luigi dear things cannot go on like this. You and I must be able to meet and discuss Mother's future together. Whatever grievances you may feel, real or imagined, must be forgotten now. We must really act together and make her last years decent and happy. At the moment the state of affairs is not only indecent but tragic. The only reason I am writing instead of rushing to see you is that the present situation is too serious for a meeting between us to be anything but pacific and loving and I don't want to meet you till I know that our meeting can be so. I will try and tell you as briefly as possible what I found as I hope you will want to meet me in the way I suggest and then I can tell you everything:

She then described in voluminous detail how sordid her mother's quarters seemed to her – the lack of magazines or flowers, the pathetic little bolster, the sagging mattress, the 'frightful little pillow one would not have given to a skivvy in the bad old days', the high-handedness of the nursing staff, the shocking lunch –

I could hardly bear the sight of it. Mother however wolfed it. There can only be two explanations for this, both of them horrible ... I truly cannot endure this any longer ... However ill anyone is you cannot take them suddenly from a life that included coming from an unrestricted personal room to a public restaurant with hundreds of people and a band playing and throw them into a strange place without a soul they have ever seen before and bereft of every personal contact and possession ...

Gluck did not see that, spam or no, her mother was at least eating it, whereas all the smoked salmon in the Cumberland had not tempted her. She internalized her mother's anguish and made it her own. She saw her as a victim of a vile injustice perpetrated by wrongdoers. The scribbling on the bed linen was Gluck's evidence of crime. She insisted that her mother's mind was clear: 'Not once did she say anything but wonderful and truly noble things.' This was the Meteor, whom she thought beautiful and remote, from whom she got her idealized view of women and who should have been a great opera singer. It was intolerable to Gluck to see her mother stripped of all status and so reduced. She could not accept what a leveller such illness is:

I have had sleepless nights for two months now and I can't go on ... You I am sure have done what you thought was for the best, under advice and pressure. That you have suffered much I have no doubt, but dearest Luigi do realise that for us to have done this together would have been easier and safer. No one can know her as we do. The present state of affairs is shameful and I certainly

cannot let it continue. Let us meet in amity and without anything to distract us
from the one purpose – to see that Mother is safe and allowed some sort of
comfort and peace at the end.
I am too upset to write any more
My love to you . . .[7]

In the same post Louis got a letter from Dr Solomons reiterating his clinical opinion about his mother – that she was physically much better, but mentally as confused and disorientated. He had found her conversation incessant, rambling and tangential. At one moment she said she had gone there for a rest and was well, and eating well, the next that she was in prison. She thought she had been in Court ten days recently, that Solomons was a well-known barrister and Dr Gilmour, whom she saw every day, his junior.

He reiterated that her condition was irreversible, that she would have to be 'kept in some suitable place', but that this did not have to be Moorcroft. And he again urged Louis and Gluck to come and see him '. . . while doing the right thing for your mother I want both you and her to feel that I can carry you both with me in any course of action.'[8]

Louis wrote formally to Gluck (10 May 1950), whom he was totally unprepared to meet except in the presence of a disinterested professional. He sent her a copy of Dr Solomons' letter, asked her to suggest a date for a meeting and to send, before then, 'any positive suggestions or definite proposals for dealing with this very difficult problem, so that I may have time to consider them'.

Gluck wrote back that she must see Louis alone before any meeting with Dr Solomons. Louis ignored this request and made an appointment, which he asked Gluck to confirm, for them both to see the doctor.

13th May 1950

My dear Luigi

. . . Perhaps my letter was not clear, but it is essential that I see you alone before
I see you with Dr Solomons, so will you let me know when I can do this,
preferably on Wednesday or Thursday. I have to be at Victoria by 5 pm in order
to catch my return train here. At the moment I cannot stay the night in London,
so perhaps you could give me some time in the morning or early afternoon, and
at 199 Piccadilly. We could then also arrange another appointment with Dr
Solomons

With my love

Hig

15th May 1950

My dear Hig

Your letter of the 11th was quite clear. Until we have seen Dr Solomons together I do not propose to see you alone.

As apparently you cannot keep the appointment with him on Thursday at 4.20 I am cancelling it.

When you are prepared to agree a joint interview with Dr Solomons and let me know convenient dates and times I will arrange another appointment with him.

Yours ever

Luigi

17th May 1950

My dear Luigi

... Not only have you ignored everything I told you in my letter of May 5th, but now you refuse my entirely reasonable request to see you alone before I meet you with Dr Solomons ...

I had asked to see you as my only concern is to make things better for Mother and if possible prevent you from making an irretrievable mistake.

... Your overriding desire only to see me with Dr Solomons is a little belated. It would surely have been better if this meeting, to which I have twice agreed, had taken place before you carried out your plans for Mother, of which, with ample opportunity, you gave me not the slightest hint.

... I had indicated in my letter that she was in danger in circumstances I would explain to you privately. You have chosen to ignore this, as also the evidence of something I found in her room, preferring to try to force me to speak on matters intimate to us both in front of a third person ...

Should you reconsider your decision I should still be glad to meet you, otherwise I must hold you responsible for everything that has happened, is happening, and is likely to happen to Mother

My love to you,

Hig

The 'evidence' she wished to show him was the bit of sheet with the Meteor's sad writing on it, which now seemed as significant to Gluck as did Desdemona's handkerchief to Othello. No meeting took place either with or without the doctor, as neither brother nor sister gave way. Edith had been in hospital for a fortnight for a minor operation. Between visits to her, Gluck worked at her Rose picture and prepared a list of complaints, for the Board of Control, about her mother's treatment at Moorcroft. 'Work at Roses, very tired and worried … Paint a little but worried and unhappy.' Arrangements were made to move the Meteor to another nursing home, 'The Priory' in Roehampton. Gluck heard of this 'from official sources', so went to check the place out, with her mother's car and chauffeur, and wrote again to her brother:

May 22nd 1950

My dear Luigi

I understand from official sources that Mother is to be transferred to 'Priory', Roehampton

I am most anxious that this should be done with as little distress to her as possible – avoiding at all costs any associations with her unhappy arrival at Moorcroft.

We should both be with her on the journey and see her in.

Will you therefore let me know what day and time Mother will be leaving Moorcroft for Roehampton so that I can arrange to be with her.

Yours ever,

Hig

24th May 1950

My dear Hig

Mother's transfer to the Priory is under consideration by the Board of Control. As soon as I receive the official permission for her removal I shall let you know the day on which it is to be carried out.

We shall have to be guided by our medical advisers as to the manner in which the journey from Uxbridge to Roehampton is to be made and as to who should be with Mother during that journey. You, as much as I, will have to conform to that advice and guidance.

Yours ever

Luigi

He had already asked for a nurse to accompany their mother, and had arranged about a car. He would not deal with 'this very difficult problem' on Gluck's terms, nor would either compromise one jot to spare the other's feelings. Gluck appealed to her cousin Julia to intercede, but there was little she could do:

I have tried to convey to you both that I consider you both have your mother's wellbeing at heart and that it would be much better if you could work together, but my dear I cannot make this happen if you and Louis do not. Being of my father's cast of mind I am unable ever to believe that anybody is always right or always wrong, but as I said on the telephone, I cannot do more in this problem of relationship which rests with you both. Any practical help I can give in helping to make Aunt Frances comfortable I am more than anxious to give . . .[9]

On Friday 26 May, Gluck was told that the transfer to the 'Priory' would take place the next day. She got there before her mother, who arrived at eleven in the morning. 'L. arrives 12 – I leave 12.45 L. having rushed out before. Lunch Grosvenor Hotel. Catch 2.18 home. Terrible day.' she wrote in her diary.

Gluck pursued her complaints of ill treatment and negligence of her mother at Moorcroft with the Board of Control, but they found no justification for them. Rather the reverse, they thought she had been carefully looked after and that her physical health had improved while she was there. Louis was appointed Receiver of his mother's Estate. Gluck sent her mother's chauffeur, Peter Smith, £15. 'I only done my best to someone I liked to serve', he said in his letter of thanks (19 August 1950), 'it is all very sad to think such a wonderfull woman will end her days as she will.'

The choice of the 'Priory' proved pacific, and the Meteor stayed there, in her twilight world, until her death, eight years later, on 17 May 1958. Gluck arranged for a nurse to phone twice a week with news of her mother whom she visited each month for an hour or so. But all true communication between them was now gone. Gone too was the chance of rapprochement with Louis. The 'problem of relationship' by now was deep. At pains to strike a wedge between herself and her family when young, time added savagely to the rift. She made a Will, the first of many, excluding mention of him from it. As the years passed they managed a sort of truce and cautious displays of affection. The day came, a decade later, when he offered her a cigar with her coffee and brandy after dining with her at the Trocadero – a gesture that she noted in her diary. Nor did the sense of quarrel extend to his children, with whom she was on fond terms.

But at the time it was all too much – another rift, another trauma. She could not have tried harder, in the name of love, for Nesta and that had gone. She had caused, however inadvertently, an irreconcilable split between the Heald sisters. Her mother had sunk into madness and her brother had turned away. It all affected her confidence and her ability to work. She was in a deep sense lonely. The élan, the sparkle, the sense of a charmed life were all swept away. Life was suddenly hard and unkind. She turned again and again to the painting of roses which she could not finish. The Maufes, Osbert Lancaster, Molly Mount Temple, Alfred Munnings, Ernest Thesiger – many of her friends from the old days went to see her portrait of Sir Raymond Evershed, The Master of the Rolls, at a private showing at the Bourlet Rooms. It was a bit of a splash, but not an exhibition. 'It would have been better', she wrote bitterly, 'if I had not had such an unequal struggle with my materials . . . I am not doing any more until I can work without frustration.'[10]

Her sense of so many personal injustices now merged with the sense that her paints too had betrayed her and she began her grand campaign against the colourmen. She called it her battle, fought it with anger, obsession and a great deal of personal sacrifice, put into it pains, fears and spoiled hopes that truly belonged elsewhere and turned it into a crusade.

SEVENTEEN

THE PAINT
WAR

What stopped me from painting was not the thought that my paintings were going to fall to pieces, but because I could not produce the effect I wanted with my materials. I could not say what I wanted, I was made to stutter and that is no good. It was as if, being known for your good calligraphy, you find yourself with only a crossed nib with which to write.[1]

It was not only poor quality materials that stopped Gluck painting for more than a decade. A conflation of troubles – the end of her romantic hopes following the break with Nesta, the Meteor's tragic illness, the social upheaval of the war, the decline of interest in realistic painting in the postwar years, the selling of her London home, her unhappiness at Steyning – all made her turn against the materials which were her means of self-expression. The creative block she suffered for a decade, from the mid-fifties on, had as much to do with loss of confidence and direction as with the quality of paint.

None the less her sense of being thwarted by her paints and canvases dated back to 1937 with 'Lords and Ladies', a picture of lilies. She wrote then of her problems to Nesta (January 1937):

I feel very sad about this canvas – To have waited so long to paint this picture, two years at least, and then have this . . . apart from horrible graining in the canvas, the paint sinks in and becomes what is known as 'dead' . . . and any subtle differences just get lost in a dim blur – it means many repaintings to try and get rid of it . . .

And in 1939, when staying at Chillington Hall to paint Diana Giffard's portrait, she wrote to the Meteor in some despair (11 December 1939):

I cannot tell you what a frightful time I have had struggling with this abominable canvas, it has all taken at least four times as long, and I have poured good work into it and it seems all in vain. That's one of the things I have got to settle when I get to London as I can't go on like this any longer.

By the 1950s she was criticizing the consistency of oil paints too. She found they showed a 'greasy turbidity', which she called the 'suede effect' whereby according to the direction of brush strokes she got a change of tone and colour. She maintained this was caused by mixing machine-ground, rather than hand-ground paint pigments with hot-pressed linseed oil – where the linseed is heated prior to crushing to extract a greater yield of oil from it. And she found certain colours were still tacky on the canvas weeks or even months after being applied. 'My paints now disgust me,' she wrote, 'they are soapy to use, and when to prove this I squeezed them out on my palette for an eminent paint chemist's opinion, he shuddered and said 'They look slimy – like slugs.'[2] After battling on and off for two years to produce her indifferent portrait of Sir Reginald Croom-Johnson, in 1953 she downed her brushes and for more than a decade fought to ensure that the quality of paints and canvases be improved.

In her fight for better artists' materials, Gluck saw herself as following in the shoes of Holman Hunt and George Frederic Watts who had, in the mid-nineteenth century, made public similar concerns. She thought it wrong that guaranteed materials were nowhere to be found at any price. The old masters had had apprentices to grind their paints and prepare their canvases. 'As it is impossible to put the clock back and reproduce what Giotto did, would it not be as well to see that the serious student and artist could obtain guaranteed materials if he is honest enough to want them?'[3] She saw ominous ramifications in terms of short life-span for modern paintings without such guarantees.

Gluck wanted five assurances from the Board of Trade and the colourmen:

1. That the ingredients of guaranteed paints should conform to a standard, clearly labelled specification.

2. That paints should bear the date of manufacture and shelf life.

3. That guaranteed matured canvas should be made available with some mark to distinguish it.

4. That a standard reliable priming for canvases should be specified and adhered to.

5. That the government should provide facilities for the colourmen to import best quality raw materials for the manufacture of artists' materials.

From 1913 to 1936 she had used James Newman's tubes of hand-ground oil paints which she maintained were completely reliable and free from the 'suede effect'. After the demise of Newman's firm she had trouble from the paints of the four leading artists' colourmen: Winsor & Newton, Robersons, Rowney, and Reeves. These firms had joined together as the British Artists' Colour Manufacturers' Association.

She intended to write a book on the turbulent history of artists' relationship to the colourmen. It was to be called *Pandora's Paintbox: Paints, Portents and Posterity*. She went deep into the history of artists' materials, from the time, up to the late-seventeeth century, when artists supervised the grinding of their own colours in their workshops, through to the development of commercial suppliers. She believed that the main troubles stemmed from the nineteenth century when diverse colourmen sold their wares, and names of paints did not mean the same thing from one colourman to another. 'The quality and quantity of pigment in powder, cake or tube, was as unregulated as the identity and proportion of meat in a sausage before the Lord Chief Justice's recent apportionment for this particular bag of mystery.'[4] Despite the efforts of nineteenth-century artists like Holman Hunt and Watts to get a standard to which paints must conform, she thought the situation had gone from bad to worse. 'For nearly one hundred and fifty years ... we have had secret concoctions of traditional materials; from now on we are to face an even greater menace, secrecy over unknown materials.'[5] She maintained that present-day manufacturers used all manner of unspecified, unsuitable and harmful chemicals and additives in order to increase and speed up production, reduce costs and prolong the shelf-life of tubes of paint.

Though Gluck got no further with her book than a two-page synopsis, she generated a library of correspondence with the colourmen, The British Standards Institution, the Arts Council of Great Britain, the British Colour Manufacturers Association, the British Museum, the Courtauld Institute, the Imperial Arts League, the International Institute for the Conservation of

Museums, the Ministry of Education, the Ministry of Works, the Museums Association, the National Gallery, the Oil and Colour Chemists' Association, the Royal Academy of Arts, the Royal College of Art, the Royal Institute of British Architects, the Royal Institute of Oilpainters, the Royal Institute of Painters in Watercolours, the Royal Scottish Academy, the Royal Society of British Artists, the Slade School of Fine Art, and the Society of Women Artists. She lectured and published articles including 'The Impermanence of Paintings in Relation to Artists' Materials', 'The Dilemma of the Painter and Conservator in the Synthetic Age' and 'On the Quality of Paint'. For a decade she spent a third of her annual income on the whole campaign. She broadcast, appeared on television, wrote to the papers, artists, politicians, directors of galleries, the Queen and almost everyone else as well. Nesta took up the cause in Honolulu:

Sir Colin Anderson came through here the other day, who is another director of the Tate Gallery. I asked him whether he knew you and he immediately said 'Oh – that woman who is making everyone's life hell over trying to get a paint standard?' I said, 'But don't you think there should be a paint standard?' 'Undoubtedly,' he said. 'Then don't you agree that she is doing a remarkably fine job, giving up her own work to get this through?' He said, 'Oh yes, I admit it's necessary, but I don't see why she should set everybody by the ears in the process.' I said, 'As far as I can remember that is exactly what Christ did, and it's apparently the only way as long as mankind remains in the lethargy it's in now.'

It was at the Queen of the Islands cocktail party and he moved away. Why do they have such people as trustees and who is he? At any rate you have become a household word in art circles I gather since this fight![6]

Gluck mustered support worldwide. In Calcutta, Dr Bhandari, the chief chemist at Shalimar Paints Limited, supplied her with Ivory Black made from Indian ivory flakes, rather than from charred bone used in the machine-made equivalent, mixed with cold-pressed linseed oil from the villages of Madhya Pradesh near his home town. He had already supplied Indian Yellow, for restoration work in Italy, made from the urine of an elephant fed on mango leaves and water.

In Steyning, though dinner guests, relatives and those with no interest in the technicalities of the matter got glazed with disbelief and boredom at her unceasing preoccupation with the subject and her 'monopologues' as her nephews and niece termed her dinner-table discourses, friends helped all they could. Dr Andrew Thomson, an academic chemist, took great interest in her

work, undertook experiments on her behalf into the relative viscosity of hot-
and cold-pressed oil and advised her on her own researches. Raul Casares, who
was married to a second cousin of Edith's, photographed her experiential proof
of the 'suede effect'. Edith told Gluck she was mad and that everyone was
painting more than ever. ' "What do you think you are going to get out of this?"
she asked and I said, "Paints".' Which was what, after a decade or so, she got.

At her instigation, the colourmen, Winsor & Newton and Rowneys, stepped
up their researches into the use of coarse or finely ground pigments in the
manufacture of artists' oil paints, the stability of drying rates between different
paints, the relative effect on paint quality of mixing pigments with cold- or hot-
pressed linseed oil. Methods of priming canvases, the quality and country of
origin of flax used in their making, the composition of glue size, the length of
time primer was left to mature, and treated canvases were given to dry – all were
scrutinized, researched and reassessed by the colourmen in an effort to satisfy
Gluck. 'When (and if!) we make you into a customer thoroughly satisfied with
our efforts, we'll celebrate with champagne. Here's to then!' Victor Harley,
Director of Winsor & Newton wrote to her (26 November 1951).

A decade or so later, after no champagne and an unrelenting correspondence
that hovered, on his side, between fascination, patience and total exasperation,
he won her approbation by marketing cold-pressed linseed oil. 'When the
Queen Mother was Queen,' Gluck, who was, after all, her mother's daughter,
wrote to tell him (27 September 1965),

*Her Majesty was interested in the efforts I was making with regard to artists'
materials and asked to be kept informed of my progress. I thought you might
like to know that in my recent letter to Her Majesty I reported that your Firm was
now marketing the cold-pressed linseed oil produced by Messrs Wilson & Sons
of Dundee and that you were selling this in this country and the United States. I
also mentioned that this was unique in the World today as though all the text
books recommend cold-pressed linseed oil there was none until you put it on the
market.*

Gluck's first appeal for national intervention was in 1951 to the Arts Council.
She maintained that their charter obliged them to protect the interest of the
artist and to improve the standard of execution of the fine arts. She informed
them that nearly all artists' materials currently marketed were unreliable. That
it was more or less impossible for artists to find raw materials and prepare their
own products. That pictures painted on unmatured primed canvas, which was

all that was sold, would not last. That only pressure from authoritative organizations or adverse publicity could influence the colourmen to improve their products. That the Council should demand guaranteed standards of materials – canvases that were properly matured and primed, paints that conformed to established principles tested by time. That these guaranteed materials should be appropriately marked, and could be more expensive if necessary and the colourmen could continue to sell unguaranteed, as at present, to those who did not mind.

An Art Panel sub-committee, made up of painters, academics, restorers and representatives of the British Artists' Colour Manufacturers Association, held an inquiry in November 1951. By the time they met, most of them had engaged in lengthy and often reluctant correspondence with Gluck. Sir Kenneth Clark was their Chairman. They were to refer their findings and recommendations to the Executive Committee of the Arts Council. 'This is the third time in 200 years that the quality of artists' materials is being specifically questioned,' Gluck told the Panel (1 November 1951). 'The other two investigations proved abortive, let us hope this, as the third, will be luckier.'

But the Panel decided there had been no substantial deterioration in the quality of artists' materials and that modern artists with sound technical methods need have no fear of their work disintegrating. It was agreed that canvas was not as good as it had been before the war, owing to the shortage of flax, and that linseed oil had deteriorated slightly, owing to the higher rate of extraction and because the best linseed oil came from the Baltic. It was also agreed that at the end of the war poor quality canvas was sold too soon after it had been primed. But Gluck's complaints of sharp practice by the colourmen and of untrustworthy materials were not upheld. 'In the face of this evidence we could not possibly recommend that the Arts Council institute a full inquiry . . .' Kenneth Clark told her (28 November 1951). 'I know how much this decision will distress you and I feel great personal sympathy for you; but I am afraid there is nothing more I can do.'

Gluck, too scornful immediately to reply, waited a couple of months, then sent him a six-page letter voicing her disgust and anger and calling the inquiry a charade. She was not, though, easily defeated. She collected, over the years, all the evidence she could of other artists' struggles with their materials. A good deal of it tallied with her own, but it seemed that most artists wrestled on, or found ways round their problems depending on the effect they wanted to achieve: 'There is a certain instability of oil pigment existing at the present time in both the yellows and the reds,' Laura Knight wrote to her (24 October 1960).

I have experienced a difficulty in preventing some of these colours from spreading with disastrous effect over other parts of a picture, even when this work has had at least two years to dry.

In the studio where I am now writing I have gently rubbed a yellow ochre background with a corner of a wetted handkerchief, the result was a slight staining of the white linen. This background was painted a year ago.

Laura Knight also thought it would be helpful to painters if the colourmen listed colours which, when used together, had an unsatisfactory chemical interaction. She found, for example, that French Ultramarine mixed with Alizarin Red turned a nasty brown and that Lead White mixed with any of the Cadmiums turned to dirt.

Graham Sutherland told Gluck that he disliked the mechanically-primed canvas, as bought from the shop. He usually painted on the reverse side of the canvas, after giving this three coats of size. He found that if he built a painting up slowly – forcing the first layers of paint into the grain of the canvas, then 'dragging' impasted strokes over this, he managed to obtain a surprising variety of touch and texture.

Lamorna Birch said, in 1953, that no paints were half as good as ten years before. Sir Gerald Kelly, President of the Royal Academy of Arts in 1951, offered Gluck quantitites of his own canvas, which had been kept for ten years by the firm Robersons, in north London. 'I am doing this because ... I have great sympathy for your attitude, rarer than ever in this world of shoddy productions. The pictures shown by the École de Paris are already being restored and repaired. They have but a small expectation of life.'[7] He began by being helpful and ended by groaning when he saw another of her letters.

The first meeting of the British Standards Institution Technical Committee on Artists' Materials was held on 9 March 1954. It was entirely Gluck's doing that such a committee came into being. She wanted it to compel the colourmen to stipulate exactly what was in the paints they manufactured and to discuss and research into the quality of paints and canvases. It was made up of representatives from various art bodies, individual artists and members of the British Artists' Colour Manufacturers Association. They met periodically until the 1960s.

One of the first problems discussed was the plethora of colour names used in a muddling way. Traditional names, particularly those referring to organic pigments, had been kept even when the chemical constituents were different. Colours were given more than one name, such as Cobalt Yellow and Aureolin,

French Blue and French Ultramarine. And new pigments were given different names by different firms – copper phthalocyanine was called Winsor Blue or Green by Winsor & Newton and Goya Blue or Green by Reeves. It was resolved that colour names should be classified and simplified, degrees of permanence marked and compounds from which pigments were made, clearly stipulated. So artists might then know that Ultramarine Genuine was made from the choicest extract of Lapis Lazuli, Aureolin from Potassium cobaltinitrite, Mineral Violet from manganese phosphate, Sepia from colour extracted from the ink bag of the cuttlefish.

In subsequent meetings the committee discussed the system of marking to be used on the labels of dry pigments, the use of additives and the desirability of specifying these, the necessity of giving the date of manufacture and batch type on the tube, the vexed question of the type of oil used in paint manufacture, the question of drying time of paint on the canvas and what could usefully be accepted as a maximum – 504 hours was suggested. The committee's findings and recommendations were passed to the Board of Trade and to industries and organizations concerned with paint manufacture and use.

The issue of the 'suede effect' was never really resolved at the BSI meetings. Gluck maintained of course that it was caused by mixing machine-ground pigments and additives in hot-pressed linseed oil. She hoped to show that other artists too were stymied by their materials. She sent a questionnaire, under the auspices of the British Standards Institution, to 187 artists:

1. (a)   When painting in oils, do you experience differences in effect when brushing different ways, rather like rubbing suede in different directions?

    (b)   If so, are those effects slightly greasy in character causing the painting to be seen with difficulty in certain lights?

2. Do you find artists' turpentine sticky?

3. Do you find that your painting does not dry easily and that after an appreciable lapse of time the paint can be rubbed off?

4. Do you find that the paint will 'sink' in one part of the canvas and not in another?

5. Have you given up using canvas, and if so, why?

6. Any general comment not included in above.

Only fifty-nine of the artists replied. Fifty-five said yes to the first question, but many either anticipated the effect and did not mind it, or thought it was a result of not sufficiently diluting the paint. And many artists had not experienced her problems over uneven drying rates and unpredictable absorbency of canvas. The answers to her questionnaire showed how problematic the concept of quality of materials was, when applied to artists wishing to achieve a multitude of different effects. None the less Gluck implied to the British Standards Institution that these findings substantiated her case. She did not easily submit to inconclusive evidence on this issue where her own experience told her so forcefully what was true.

The colourmen wanted an independent research laboratory to carry out a study into the effects of using hot- or cold-pressed linseed oil in paint manufacture. The Scientific Department of the National Gallery carried out a practical and technical analysis. A series of samples of pigments were ground in various types of linseed oil and four artists then evaluated their appearance and handling properties. They found

> ... neither differences in amounts of nitrogen and phosphorus, rate of drying, colour, foaming, taste or smell can be used as a basis for a distinguishing test between hot and cold-pressed linseed oil, because these differences may be masked or caused to disappear by 1) choosing different batches of seed, 2) refining, or 3) tanking.[8]

The colourmen maintained that method of application of paint led to the 'suede effect' and that it could be eliminated by adding stand oil, or sun-thickened linseed oil to alter the flow. None the less, to appease Gluck, Winsor & Newton, Rowney and Reeves all agreed to investigate further into mixing pigments of differing particle size, which had either been machine-ground or hand-ground, with different oils. All the paints ground to the consistency of artists' tube colours showed the 'suede effect':

> ... indeed it must now be clear to everyone that properly ground mixtures ... will always exhibit the 'suede effect' ... In actual practice the artist can do much to control the flow properties of his colour by making full use of painting media containing polymerized oils. The arguments that the colour manufacturers have been remiss in not producing colours that are free from the 'suede effect' fall to the ground completely.[9]

They did a few more experiments up until 1965, but in an ever more reluctant and desultory way. Gluck wanted the BSI to set a standard for the specification of cold-pressed linseed oil but the Committee saw little point, as its advantages had not been proved and there was only one supplier, Wilson's of Dundee.

She continued to correspond with Winsor & Newton over absorbency in canvases. They queried her technique. She first 'blocked out' her painting in oil colours thinned with turpentine. They suggested that an excessive amount of turpentine might soften the priming and cause the paint to sink in. She also sometimes put a freshly-painted canvas in a glass frame to stop it getting dusty. Winsor and Newton thought this might retard the drying rate and cause some colours to stay tacky. Gluck maintained that her painting technique had not changed and yet problems suddenly appeared.

She insisted that canvas be made from the best quality flax, sized with the best glue in the best conditions of temperature and humidity, and treated with the purest linseed oil. All of which Winsor & Newton tried to do. They conducted tireless experiments on her behalf. They reviewed their production schedules to give canvases a longer drying time and reintroduced an underfloor heating system to provide a more even distribution of heat.

In the early days the firm's director, Victor Harley, seemed to enjoy both her letters and the challenge she set him to improve materials. He was fond enough of her to tease her: 'Are you a good patient?' he wrote to her (23 December 1952) when she had bronchitis.

Somehow I doubt it; and I think I'd rather be your colourman than your doctor. Anyhow even if you don't do what you're told, do be sensible and take care of yourself. I can't say any more than that I hope you are very soon full of health and strength sufficient to make us unbutton the coat of turpentine from each particle of levigated powder colour.

But after seventeen years of correspondence and experimentation his patience snapped. He felt he could not satisfy her and advised her to get her materials elsewhere.

The matter might have drifted to a close, leaving Gluck disconsolate and dissatisfied, had not the two colourmen, Tom Rowney of Rowney & Son and Victor Harley of Winsor & Newton, met by chance at the opera in November 1967. A programme note on the composer Christoph Willibald Glück prompted them to talk of the 'suede effect' and their most exigent and uncompromising customer. They agreed that after years of corresponding with her on the morality of mass production, the technical composition and purity of paint, methods of research and the availability and economic considerations of raw materials, they would try to provide her with perfect paints, which were right for her and which she felt to be pure, no matter what experimentation might prove.

A month later Tom Rowney went down to the Chantry House with his chief chemist, Mr Chalk and talked to her of their plans. '... Mr Chalk is very busy indeed in the laboratory', he wrote to her (14 December 1967) after their visit. 'From all appearances he has given up everything else and is settling down almost exclusively to your work. You have certainly done something to him, I wonder what it is! I know he enjoyed his visit to you very much indeed.'

What Mr Chalk was doing was grinding pigments by hand, on a granite slab, and mixing them with Wilson's cold-pressed linseed oil to make Gluck's perfect palette. For months he experimented with relative quantities of oil and pigment and varied grinding times of different pigments. Lump yellow ochre, mixed with cold-pressed oil at a relative weight ratio of seventy to thirty, was ground for two hours. Genuine Vermilion, mixed at a ratio of eight-five grams of pigment to fifteen of oil, was left for five hours on the slab with periodical grinding. Crimson Madder was mixed with oil at a fifty to fifty ratio, ground for between one and two hours, then left overnight and a further ten parts of cold-pressed linseed oil added the next day. Lump Viridian, at a ratio of sixty to forty, was ground for three hours on the slab, left overnight and ground for a further half hour in the morning. French Ultramine turned out stringy and sticky whatever the proportions, or techniques of grinding, so Mr Chalk scouted around for Lapis Lazuli to make a few tubes for her.

Tom Rowney provided her with these specialist hand-made paints, free of charge, from 1967 until her death some ten years later. It would have been economically impossible to produce them in a commercial range. The final formulation for each colour involved variations in hand-grinding, modifications with driers, different proportions of either cold-pressed linseed oil or sun-thickened cold-pressed linseed oil, and the juggling with synthetic and traditional pigments. They were paints beyond price and hers alone.

Tom Rowney also invited her to go into Rowney's shop in Percy Street, London, and choose, without regard to cost, whatever range she wanted of their best Sable brushes. He supplied her with quantities of Special Belgium Claessens canvas No. 706 primed in the traditional way. The canvas was strained in a vertical position then a coat of glue size applied with large sponges. The next day a first coat of white lead primer was applied by brush, followed a week later by a second coat. '... It is difficult to find words in which to thank you and Mr Chalk,' she told him. '... So many lost pictures throughout these terrible wasted years, and at last a chance to make up not only some of the loss of pictures, but of health and happiness.'

She made many trips down to the firm's laboratories in Bracknell, Berkshire, and was treated like a lord. Tom Rowney and Mr Chalk lunched at the Chantry, admired her paintings, looked at her individual researches into the behaviour of paint and exchanged their personal news with her. By the end of her fight, when she was on the frail side but no less forceful about her cause, the colourmen spared neither time, money nor effort in trying to please her.

She admitted, when her battle was more or less won, that she had wasted many creative years with this fight. Nor was this the only practical issue that she turned into a grand campaign with a moral imperative to defend. She was known in Steyning for her fervent battles over local issues – against the closing of the railway station, or to preserve the rights of way of a footpath. Her sense of injustice and moral outrage and her readiness for combat, were seldom dormant for long. She never intended the paint war to consume her time, money and energy in quite the way it did. The rage she channelled into it belonged more truthfully elsewhere. It was as if, having not got her way over certain fundamental issues of the heart, she was determined to have her way over this. Or, more painfully, having felt so betrayed by her love for a woman, self-love, which was work, must betray her too.

Gluck was a traditionalist. Her experience of paints made in the old-fashioned way led her to prefer them. The old masters ground their pigments by hand and used cold-pressed linseed oil, and that was how she defined quality. But she also selected evidence to substantiate her own theories. The problems she felt so strongly had to be universal. Those who loved her regretted the time she poured into her paint war and saw it as obsessive and a distraction from her work. 'Darling Tim,' Nesta wrote when Gluck was seventy-five:

When I suggest that some of your 'ways' could be improved it meant courage on my part – It would have been far easier to be a Yes-man. But it is only for you – who else could it possibly be for – not me – not Edith!

It is to try and show you that your path could be made easier – but I suppose a Leo cannot change his spots!! You have had the same problems ever since I knew you. I must just look on with anguish because I love you.

Her friendship with the Maufes 'one of my proudest friendships and your faith in me as an artist one of my greatest comforts in times of despair' – was clouded by the campaign. 'If you have solved the difficulties, does that mean you will now paint?' Prudence wrote (20 January 1964), when Gluck lectured to the Royal Society of Arts on 'The Dilemma of the Painter and Conservator in the Synthetic Age'. 'I do so tremendously hope so ... even you will not live for ever and "that one talent which is death to hide, lodged with me useless"? Lord how I wish I could paint like you.'

The long years of not painting afflicted Gluck with a sense of self-betrayal. But though her campaign wasted her talent, it was not in itself a waste. Her persistence led to an unequalled scrutiny of artists' materials, a greater understanding of the properties of oil paints and a revision in ways of preparing canvases. As a conservationist, she challenged the paint manufacturers to account for their products at a time when there were few safeguards for consumers. The British Standards Institution formulated and published a standard for the naming and defining of pigments. And the colourmen provided her with paints which she felt to be free of the 'suede effect' – paints she was later to describe as 'a joy to use'. At too great a cost to herself she got, more or less, what she said she wanted.

EIGHTEEN

Gluck was difficult to live with during her fallow years. Edith's interest was in Art and the realm of the imagination, not campaigns about paint. And she, like Nora, before long was made to feel excluded by a triangle of relationship. For Gluck, if love had proved elusive, marriage was to become a trap.

Life at the Chantry House was companionable enough from when Nora left in 1946 until about 1954. Servants, prepared to tolerate Gluck's demands and uncompetitive rates of pay, were found. Mrs Guy, employed as a laundrymaid in 1952, stayed twenty-five years and did whatever she was asked.

I was a bit scared of her at first. The greengrocer brought the fruit and vegetables up. I had to let her know as soon as he arrived. She came straight out and weighed everything. The grapes were two ounces under. Back they had to go and I had to take them. I said to my husband, I'm not working there. He said, that's how that sort of people get on. That's how they got money, because they look after it. But she was a very good friend to me. When my first grandson, a mongol boy died, it was her that pulled me through. Her kindness.[1]

The house was run with military precision. Menus were planned, with the housekeeper Mrs Gurd, at the beginning of the week. Breakfast – China tea and toast – was taken to Gluck and Edith in their respective bedrooms. Edith then worked in her study on book reviews or her 'With Prejudice' page for *The Lady*. Gluck worked on her paint-war papers, and her various campaigns, with transient secretarial staff, in the Yeats Room. Lunch was at one, in the dining room – two courses and sometimes a bottle of wine – then coffee in the drawing room. The wines came with the compliments of J. Lyons & Co. Edith liked cooking, but was dissuaded by Gluck who regarded it as the servants' domain – though she made reference in her diaries to Edith's 'wonderful puddings'. In the afternoons Gluck went to her studio.

They shopped in Brighton, saw Greta Garbo in *Ninotchka*, Lilli Palmer in *Oh My Papa* and Grace Kelly in *Cornish Seas*. Despite Edith's indifference to opera, they went to first nights of *Alceste, Ariadne auf Naxos, Idomeneo* and *Macbeth* at Glyndebourne. They spent motoring holidays in France, weekends in the Beach Hotel, Worthing, and summers in Cornwall. On Coronation Day, in June 1953, they listened all day to the ceremony on the wireless. They went sailing in Cowes and dined with J. B. Priestley, a work colleague of Edith's from the twenties, who lived nearby. Edith went up to the annual party for *The Lady*, held at the Savoy, and stayed overnight in town. Gluck went into Brighton to search for suitable Valentine cards for Edith in the early Februaries of their life together, and on Gluck's birthday Edith always put fresh-cut roses on her breakfast tray.

They cared for each other's illnesses and frailties. Edith, who by 1953 was sixty-eight, suffered from bouts of low blood pressure, headaches and days of feeling peaky. Gluck had days of staying in bed because of arthritis, bronchitis and depression. Her friend, Hermia Priestley, attending one of her lectures on paint standards in the fifties, thought how rapidly she had aged.[2] Her panache and flair were gone. She still got her hair cut at Truefitts in Bond Street, but it was a mannish haircut, rather than a daring style. She had a navy-blue nautical suit with brass buttons made at Cowes, but it was by no stretch Stiebel or Schiaparelli. She now bought her shirts and pyjamas at Marks & Spencer in Brighton.

Nesta wrote and floated through. She broke her nose surfing in Hawaii and had a new, aquiline one constructed. She and Gluck spent brief holidays together, on the Isle of Wight and in Cornwall, but these seemed to compound Gluck's sense of domestic trap. They visited the Meteor in 'The Priory' and she recognized Nesta. Gluck no longer had the sustaining support of a relationship with either Nesta or her mother. Nesta had flown to her tropical island and the Meteor, in her madness, was beyond communication. She was being treated with Sodium Amytal and electroconvulsive therapy, but no treatment existed that could again balance her mind.

On the days she visited the Meteor, Gluck usually lunched with her brother at the Trocadero. Provided they avoided the topics of the Trust and her money, the meetings were amicable. A quiet word to him about her problematic car yielded a new one in 1954 – an MG Magnette. It seemed to Louis that she had settled down in a stable, if disappointingly unproductive way. Occasionally he visited Chantry but kept the meetings as neutral as possible:

L.H.G. and Doreen arrive 2.50 pm leave 5.10 pm. Entirely impersonal two hours. Everything 'amiable'. Felt very sad after as not one sign of real affection or interest shown.[3]

She no longer dealt directly with him about her finances. She had found, in Brighton, an accountant, David Tonkinson, who became her *homme d'affaires*. He was fond of her, respectful of her talent, tolerant of her long phone conversations at nine in the morning and diplomatic with her Trustees. He tried to dissuade her from buying hour upon hour of his time, he was a senior partner in a large firm, but it was worth it to her to be insulated from dealings she knew she could not herself conduct in any pleasant way. For financial affairs that should, in the 1950s, have cost her between twenty-five and forty pounds, she was paying up to £500 a year. By the 1970s she was paying thousands.

In 1955 Gluck chose to enter into a deal with the Fund which bound her and Edith more closely together than 'Love to all Eternity'. Both of them by that time lived off investment income and modest earnings. The Chantry House needed substantial repairs and was costly to run. The Fund agreed to buy the house and North Cottage, one of two cottages that were part of the estate, thereby giving the two women welcome capital. The Fund then let the estate to them at a rent of ninety-seven pounds and five shillings a year. Edith and Gluck were responsible for rates and maintenance. By the terms of the lease if Gluck moved out or died, Edith could be given notice. It was a standard enough lease, drawn up by solicitors, and no doubt the clause was meant as a safeguard against Gluck accruing houses in which she did not live. But it meant that Edith was now dependent on Gluck for the roof over her head. She was seventy, Gluck was sixty. To the Trustees it must have seemed simply as if they were helping two women of advancing years. But that same year the relationship between Edith and Gluck took a turn for the worse.

On 26 November 1954 a Steyning couple, David and Anne Yorke, dined at the Chantry. Gluck described it in her diary as a delightful evening. They ate pheasants, there was a great storm, the electricity went out and Gluck lent the Yorkes a torch to find their way home. 'E. and I very late to bed but feel grand and it was fun.' The Yorkes had married in 1950 and had two small sons. They lived in a manor house, Gatewick, grander than the Chantry, and themselves felt restricted by small-town life. Anne Yorke was Edward Burne-Jones's great-granddaughter, David Yorke was descended from Sir Philip Yorke, the Earl of Hardwicke, Chancellor of England in the eighteenth century. Their interests were cultural, their manner informal and friendly, their connections aristocratic and artistic of the kind the Meteor and Nesta liked. The next day they introduced Gluck to the painter Claude Harrison and she bought a painting by him of the seafront at Brighton. Meeting the Yorkes cheered her, they were her first true friends in Steyning. There was none of the reserve and implicit criticism toward her that came from Edith's camp.

On Christmas Day Gluck went to Gatewick – where there were silver-gilt table decorations – and had a 'lovely evening'. Edith dined with Nora. The Yorkes saw in the New Year at the Chantry and invited the two women to join them in Spring on a Greek cruise. They accepted. The sale of Chantry House went through in March 1955. Two months later Edith, Gluck, and David and Anne Yorke left for a holiday organized by Hellenic Tours. David Yorke found Gluck entertaining but tiresome. She had to keep out of the sun (she suffered from porphyria), was for ever trying to conjure porters that did not exist, wanted breakfast in bed at expensive rates and a cabin on a short channel crossing. More crucially on the holiday Gluck seemed to transfer, in a way that was like the shadow of an obsession, her needy, romantic feelings to Anne. After they returned she catalogued in her precise, lonely fashion the hours spent at Gatewick in 'The Tower' – Anne's private living room, Anne's visits to the studio, her phone calls, their trips together to London and Brighton. Such incidents became the emotional focus of Gluck's life. And the more she saw and heard of Anne, and they were in contact virtually every day from 1955 until the early 1960s, the more beside herself with jealousy Edith became.

Gluck monitored the tensions, scenes, recriminations and turbulent emotions that seemed more appropriate to adolescence and the opera than to gentrified English country life:

Go to Gatewick. Ouzo and sugarbush and long playing Marlene Dietrich. A. in housecoat. Leave 8 pm.

Terrible scene E. about A Y. Feel like death. Very bad night.

Go to Gatewick 5.30 to 7.30. E. furious when I return. Exhausted, frightened and unhappy. All the old accusations and troubles.

Frightful morning. Hammer and tongs till lunchtime. E. makes herself ill. Goes to bed temporarily. After dinner terrible and hope final scene with E. . . . Go down to Gatewick to see Stanley Spencer on TV. E. makes ghastly scene on my return at 10.40 pm.

A. asks us both to TV Stanley Spencer. E. refuses and is still working when I leave at 9.45 pm. Scene at 11–12 on return.

Meet A. with Charles [her son] *unexpectedly at post office 3.50 pm. She comes back to see studio with Charles. As leave, see E. who looks angrily at A. and Charles. A. upset and I too. When I speak to E. about it later she makes terrible scene. Exhausted and miserable.*

Were to go out to dinner and Renée Clair film but it was eventually abandoned. Furious, miserable and resentful at the waste of time and life by such wicked scenes.

My birthday. E. puts roses on my tray. Look lovely – a nice card too. Go to Gatewick at 2.15 pm to 3.25 to get birthday presents from Anne and David. Electric torch, socks, a nice card and cast iron Napoleon door stop [Gluck was later to drop it on her right big toe]. *Miserable scenes E. Champagne.*

Edith's 72 birthday. Calm until teatime when makes minor scene. Usual subject.

Terrible scene. E. gets letter from A. One of the worst days I have ever lived through.

Another terrible scene. E. writes to A. and gives me letter to take with me when I go at 1 pm. Go with A. to 'The King and I'. Home at 6 pm. E. calm and evening peaceful.

David writes letter to E. I give it to her. Terrible scene after she reads it. I get her to burn her copies of letters.

E. goes out handing me a note and stays out to lunch. I cannot settle to anything. I am nervous wreck.

I am desperately unhappy at silly wicked atmosphere. Entirely unjustified cruelty.

I go to Gatewick and then Brighton. Give dinner to A. & D. and Claude at Penny Farthing. Very pleasant. Drive A. there and back. Terrifying scene by E. on my return. She stands at corner by church watching.

E. makes scene on usual theme of breaking up. When I come in at 5.15 all in darkness and no tea.

Terrific scenes. A. sends letter as result of hearing E. scream abuse over telephone. Another horrible day.

Go to Milestones to lunch with E. A. & D. there. A. does not greet at all and goes out without looking. E. put out. I telephone on return and E. makes scene.

.. feel unbearably miserable . . . very uncertain about everything . . . increasingly depressed about life and work. No one understands that I must be in a vacuum if I am to find my way.[4]

Misery can be a protracted affair. Such were her jottings virtually every day for about six years. Gluck saw herself as the victim of Edith's jealousy, but she made no modification to her own behaviour which was the catalyst to all the storms. Anne Yorke was entrenched in family life which Gluck in no way threatened – there was room for her within its orbit. From her husband's point of view, his wife was providing stimulating company to an elderly, talented eccentric, who, he thought, should never have buried herself in Steyning in such dreary and provincial company. But Gluck's feelings for, and behaviour toward Anne Yorke, marginalised Edith and made her into the cuckold. As the painful years rolled on, round and round in a groove of provocation and recrimination, they damaged beyond repair their chances of a decent life together. Tension bound them together as it wore them out. Trust went, and so did ease.

Nor was there any clear way out, if that was what either of them truly wanted, as both, on occasion, said they did. Edith was stuck in what had been her home, dominated economically and emotionally by Gluck. While they battled, Gluck was having a new studio built in the Chantry grounds. As at Bolton House, this too had all the north light in the huge working area, a sleeping gallery, kitchen, bathroom and workroom, its own walled garden with fountains playing, its own entrance. The whole estate now belonged more to Gluck than to Edith. Gluck moved her paints and easels in on 13 May 1958. The same day her brother phoned to say the Meteor was dying. She died four days later.

Probably Edith felt totally bound to Gluck. Beyond that fact she did not, in her seventies, have enough capital to buy another house. Nora, retired from *The Lady* in 1953, quickly went physically and mentally downhill, and was cared for in a nursing home. She died in 1961. Their brother Harry died in 1956. Edith often spent weekends with an old friend (to whom Gluck could not be rude enough), Diana Wood, an architect living in London. They holidayed in Venice, France, Italy, Ireland. She came back rested and well but the old troubles soon resurfaced.

Edith's friends and relatives were horrified at what they saw happening to their civilized, whimsical, clever friend. Most of them resisted visiting the house when Gluck was there. Helen Beauclerck, alone after Edmund Dulac's death in 1953, stayed from time to time at the Chantry, witnessed the scenes and made no attempt to be civil to Gluck. No doubt buried within the relationship was some paradox of love and truth, but to all appearances things seemed rather shocking. Few of Gluck's friends knew what was going on. Many from the halcyon days of the thirties, she no longer saw, or were no longer alive. She heard of Constance's death on the television in 1960. 'Distracted and very shocked and unhappy about Constance ... terrible depression ... Constance's funeral early afternoon. Feel desperately sad.' Nesta, who was not afraid to confront Gluck, reprimanded her when she stayed for a week in August 1958 about the laceration of Edith's feelings:

N. starts new version (fourth) of green apple. This time with pink background. I have terrible struggle all day trying to work out Cyril's portrait. A. comes to studio 3.30–4.30. N. ticks us off in a curious way about E. and general situation. A. and I fed up.[5]

Gluck kept the Yeats Room, her study and her new studio locked when she was not working in them, which angered Edith because of its implication of lack of trust. The studio, separate from the house, could be reached either through the grounds of Chantry, or from the road:

I told A. she did not know how I suffered nervous tension owing to her refusing ever to come through to the studio by the Chantry House. Because just when I should have been quiet after lunch I was on tenterhooks that I could not get out to the studio in time to let her in. She was equally unhappy at the thought of running into E. or coming into the house at all, the amosphere of which she says she loathes. . . . I said I could not go on feeling that if the studio gate was locked, she would not come round to the Chantry House front door. I pointed out that it was, after all, half my house . . . she said of course she would come to the house if necessary only it was like Jane Eyre and Rochester.[6]

To get away from the 'general situation', Gluck went each year for a fortnight in the late 1950s to a health clinic, Enton Hall, in Sussex. A regime of fasting, enemas, colonic irrigation, steam baths, cold baths, massage and very early nights resulted in rapid weight loss. She checked in weighing around ten stone and checked out weighing nine. Breakfast was hot water and an orange, lunch tomato juice, and supper a leaf or two of lettuce and perhaps a yoghurt. From time to time she got dizzy and breathless and had to be revived with Ribena laced with 'something else'. With the help of a homeopathic doctor there, a Dr Pink, she touched on the truth of what was wrong:

He asked me innumerable questions about how much pleasure I got out of my work. Could not get him to talk diets as he came back repeatedly to this theme. In the end after telling him everything about my work, reactions to same, hours of work and what I had been doing about paints and linseed oil, he suddenly said: 'Diet is not what is wrong with you. You are suffering from frustration with your work.' And then, though of course no one could know it better than I, I realised how fearfully true this was and how I must concentrate all my forces on seeing I could get back to happy unfrustrated work with all else kept at bay. I liked him . . . I feel I have wasted my life and especially the last ten years. I must get back to what I was.[7]

The chief problem in keeping all else at bay was that she perceived herself as the victim. It would have shocked and astonished her to hear people say, as they did, that she was powerful and manipulative. She believed herself to be revolving around the needs and demands of Edith and Anne without acknowledging how she caused them to revolve around her own needs and demands. Both women phoned and wrote to Gluck at Enton, and she phoned them and wrote to them each day. They visited her and brought gifts – all in a fortnight's separation:

We lay and talked looking out of the open window. The air was keen. I said to A. 'I don't intend to revolve round anybody any more. People will have to revolve round me or I can't have any people in my life.' . . . She went at 6 pm not allowing me to see her off. She left some lovely chestnut buds and I missed her . . .[8]

A week later Edith arrived bringing a huge bunch of flowers:

blossom, giant snowdrops, grape hyacinth, blue hyacinths, narcissi, white and yellow and large and small daffodils – very sweet smelling and the epitome of Spring. Also books to read. . . . After a rest a long talk about my changed views and attitudes. At first E. was very stubborn and tried to bring out all the dreary old complaints, but I soon stopped it by saying no amount of recriminations would alter me, that the past must *be buried utterly, I would not be a battleground any more and that* everyone *without exception would have to observe this, or I would just dispense with their companionship. . . . After tea she went at 5.30 pm and I felt much more at peace. Telephoned to see if she was all right at 9.45 pm as she had seemed very tired and failing when she drove away.*[9]

From Anthony Kimmins, a client at Enton and son of the founder of Chailey Heritage School for which Nesta and Gluck had raised money before the war with their exhibition of Royal furniture, Gluck heard rumour in 1959 that Nesta, widowed two years previously, intended to remarry.

'We shall all soon be hearing of the wedding and how Honolulu blazons it forth' he said with a cheery wave. This gave me a great shock as Nesta had denied emphatically last year that there was any truth in the rumour. I said 'who is it?' and he could not recall the name but said he owned a ranch and most of the island. I said I thought it would be a good thing to happen, and he agreed, but I felt sore and angry.[10]

Gluck immediately wrote to Nesta to ask if the rumour was true. She got an unsatisfactory reply and wrote in her diary:

I answer at once . . . my only comment on her unbelievably typical evasions about marriage was 'Congratulations! as they say in "My Fair Lady".' The rest of the letter was about 'Illustrated London News' and linseed oil. Let's see what she makes of that. My relief if she marries will be great. Both for her sake and mine.

It was all something of a muddle – romantic dreams but domestic discord and unhappiness, high ambitions but the dry campaign for better paints, the pain of old wounds, the advancing years, past glory all but forgotten and a sense of self-betrayal so acute as to make her ill. She wrote a bitter little poem about Nesta's freedom and called it Zgr – her pet name for her:

Zgr
She gives everyone the slip
Stealing away silently into the black night
Steering by well-remembered stars
Round the treacherous coast
of life.
But however known the coast
The terrors lie beneath
And the stars remain aloof.

Nesta did not marry again, even if her suitor did own most of Honolulu. Nor did she withdraw her loyalty to, and affection for Gluck. A few months prior to these rumours, of what Gluck regarded as betrayal, Nesta wrote (14 July 1959):

Darling Tim

I have talked to you so much and so long lately that I woke with a start in the middle of the night and realised that perhaps after all I had not put any of it down on paper . . . I so hope you had a bit of a good Xmas . . . I had a lovely one at the Ranch and saw again a Lunar Rainbow one night. Mother of Pearl with violet and faintly touching both ends. I long for you on those occasions and think of you intensely. In fact you have no idea how just thinking of you helps me when I feel frustrated, contemptuous of myself, lonely – or a mixture of all three. I don't know why exactly, but it's true and rather interesting. Have you read Dr Zhivago *yet? . . . it is his thoughts on art and life and descriptions of moon on snow and how it glazes a goblet of wine. . . . There are many places which I just long to read aloud to you so that we can glut over them together. It strikes sparks deep down* under *the solar plexus.*

While Gluck stifled, Nesta was flying high. She adapted stylishly to rich widowhood. Her exotic travels, works for charity, and artistic and sporting successes, were written about in the Honolulu papers. She made such headlines as 'Englishwoman claims title of oldest surfer at Waikiki'. Rear Admirals, pickle farmers, industrialists, Princesses, musicians, artists, beachboys, film producers, Lords, Dukes and Marchionesses gathered at her parties. She served them caviare and hamburgers. Profits from sales of her paintings went to the blind. She recorded readings for libraries for the blind, made endowments for painting and music scholarships and gave money to striving artists. Dismissive of her own abilities, she tried to help others to achieve. She confided to Gluck that she felt she had never dug deep enough within herself to find out where her own abilities lay.

Portrait of Frau Karl,
1942

Autumn, 1955–68. The
painting Gluck worked at
for thirteen years, as she
battled with machine-
made oil paints

She was uninterested in Gluck's paint battle. She urged her to end the fight and get back to Art. Nor did Gluck stop work entirely from 1953 to 1967. But she slowed right down, painted in an unfocused way and some of what she produced was poor.

In October 1954, Edith cut from her rose garden, and put in the drawing room, a single bloom of a white, Frau Karl Drushki rose. The next day Gluck began painting on a panel the face of the rose, snipped at the stem, with a cool grey background. She called it 'Portrait of Frau Karl'. She worked for a fortnight before complaining that the background would not dry and then again getting absorbed in her campaign.

For thirteen years, on and off from 1955 to 1968, she painted a dish of fruit, walnuts and leaves with 'autumn tinged vine leaves' from Gatewick. She intended it as an academic study of the quality of paint, but it became a study of a painter's block.

Red apple tacky. Woodworm powder falls on it, but can be picked off. Work at grapes.

The most terrible scene of all. E. then goes to have a perm. I am left more dead than alive. After lunch manage to work at Group. Pear and green apple and plum.

Work til dark at foreground. Great bothers with it. Lemon yellow used first time, made freshly by Newman.

Truly horrible scenes. Shattered for day. Cannot settle to anything.

In August 1957 she accepted another commission to paint a judge, this time a relative, her second cousin Sir Cyril Salmon. A year later he made the headlines as the 'Notting Hill Race Riots Judge'. He sentenced each of nine white youths to four years' imprisonment for racial assaults and there was a furore at the severity of the sentences: 'Everyone,' he told the accused, 'irrespective of the colour of their skins, is entitled to walk through our streets in peace, with their heads erect, and free from fear. That is a right which these courts will always unfailingly uphold.'[11]

He said he could afford only half the fee Gluck proposed of 500 guineas. She visited him at the Royal College of Justice and they agreed he should sit in his blue summer robes. Gluck then had an attack of pneumonia and could not work. 'I feel very ill and breathing difficult and painful. Thought I'd reached the end.' She painted him dwarfed by heraldic trappings, taking up only a third

Portrait of the Rt Hon. Justice Lord Salmon, 1960

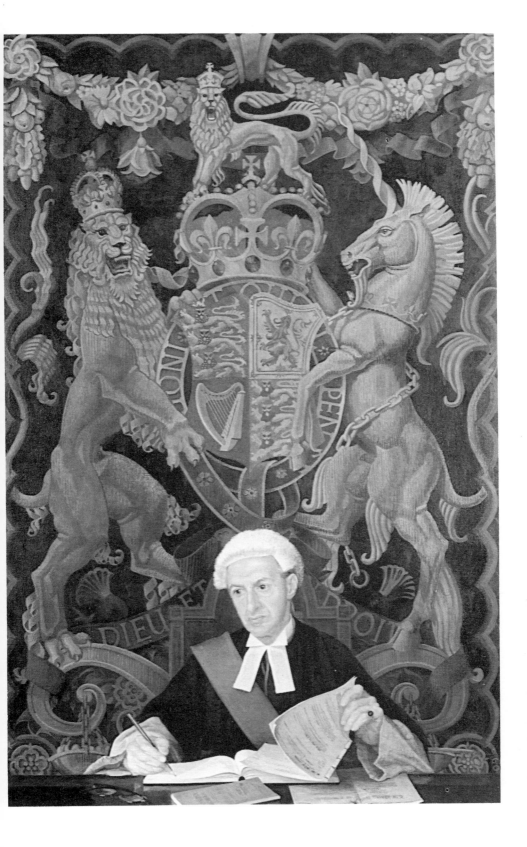

of the total space, which made him disgruntled. 'This is most disturbing for me', Gluck noted in her diary.

She put in months of work on all the heraldry. For someone disgusted with paint, it is an extremely painterly piece, crammed with detail, from the worn edges of legal documents, to the strings on the lyre, or the cameo on the signet ring. She wanted to avoid the clichés of scarlet and ermine, so used brilliant blues, reds and golds, with touches of green and cyclamen. She shows the chains, red claws and bared teeth of justice, the faces of the lions and the unicorn enraged and cold. She spent a day on the blue cover of the book in the foreground, another on one of the pink cuffs, another on the lion's crown, another on the curls on the lion's legs. 'Work morning and till 3 pm on unicorn's tail endings and border ... technical difficulties from canvas. Musgrave to dinner, saddle of lamb, marmalade pudding, E. made soup.' was her diary entry for 31 January 1959.

She went on with it all through 1959: 'work very hard all day against awful disturbances and terrible scenes ... paint green swag ribbon. ... Do not know what to do to get peace.'[12] By October Cyril Salmon was pleading with her to part with it:

Everyone who saw it was in raptures over the portrait and you know already that I think it is perfect. You can't better perfection – so isn't it time for the man with the hammer to come and release you from this particular labour? I'm longing to have it ...

But she did not let it go. '... as there is not really such a thing as perfection, she replied (31 October 1959), 'there is no reason why what passes for it should not be bettered.'

It was not cost effective work – two and a half years for 250 guineas. She became fussed and worried about dichroism, the surface of the canvas and the tuft under the unicorn's tail. She finally cleaned her palette on 20 May 1960. The next month at a party at the Chantry House, eighty people from the town came to see the portrait. She handed it over to Sir Cyril on 27 June 1960 – three years after the initial commission. 'A brilliantly original conception brought off miraculously well ...' he called it.[13]

In August 1960 Gluck went alone for a few days to Seaford. She sat huddled on the beach in a cold wind, reading the four Gospels and planning a painting of the Crucifixion, which never got done. On the way home she bought five black goldfish for the pool and some fish food, and when she got in had a row with Edith about bedrooms, because Helen Beauclerck and a new housekeeper, Miss

Burges, were both due to arrive on the same day. In autumn Nesta visited for a day and Gluck felt the strain of trying to cram a year's news into a few hours. Craig, nearly blind, went into a nursing home and Gluck dealt with the selling of her bungalow and sparse possessions. Edith holidayed in Venice and returned looking well. Miss Burges's cooking proved unsatisfactory and she left under a cloud. Gluck gave up smoking for two weeks. Anne Yorke invited Gluck and Edith for Christmas lunch at Gatewick. Edith declined the invitation and instead visited Nora. It was the last time the sisters were to spend Christmas together. Three months later Nora died and her ashes were buried in Steyning churchyard beside those of her mother.

Edith became more reserved, withdrawn and compliant, as she reached her octogenarian years. Perhaps she simply felt worn out. Gluck made all the household decisions and bossed her about, but when Edith was alone for a few days she cut back the magnolia that was making her study dark, invited friends to dinner and enjoyed cooking the meal herself.

Gluck painted a portrait of Anne Yorke in 1963. It took three months and she felt frustrated by how slowly the paint dried and by having to work some of the time with a bound right thumb. She severed the tip of it and it was sewn back on by Dr Dunce. The portrait is a tense study, the skin taut, the eyes wide and sad. The sittings inevitably led to outbursts:

Terrible scene with E. late at night which makes me feel terribly ill. She thought she heard me on the telephone. Had listened outside my door. Ghastly. Sad.[14]

Gluck's pictures began to reveal a sense of time running out, of compounded loneliness and the coming of death. To herself, she admitted her mistakes, and the waste of her talent:

I have never had a fear of death . . . when I was young I felt as if I had been thrown out to work my passage home. . . . I felt death would be the moment of release from the efforts of daily 'living' . . . I realised very young the value of lying fallow. I forced rests on myself while painting . . . then when I felt I had become sufficiently detached, I would return, suddenly. This detachment gave me a less biased eye and I could see whether I had failed or succeeded. But always this longing for a truth I could live and being as I was, this was never to be fulfilled. As life went on I spent it prodigally, unwisely. A sense of timelessness deceived me into thinking my time was limitless for creation. Only within the last tormented years have I seen how ambivalent this sense of timelessness has been. It gave eternal qualities to my work perhaps but it limited its output.

Now I find myself failing in my human strength. I see that I am swimming straight back to He who sent me out and I do want to reach that haven having a prize in my hand. Something worthy of the trust that was reposed in me when I was sent out . . . I have not done my job yet, so pray to be able to accomplish it.[15]

She painted a picture of a dead bird and called it 'Requiem'. Tybalt, the cat, caught and brought in a dead hedge sparrow. This small corpse provided the impetus Gluck needed to work fast. On the third day it started to decompose and on the fifth to smell badly. Gluck stayed up until 2.30 in the morning struggling to finish the painting. By the seventh day she was through and Lovett buried the remains. Gluck cleaned off her palette and the current cook, Mrs Gratcher, served gammon and treacle tart for supper. The picture is of a sorrowful thing – feathers bedraggled, unpreened and incapable of flight, claws useless, beak snapped shut and eyes sightless. Gluck's identification was with the fact of death – the end of all performance.

She cared for creatures. There were two huge bird tables in the gardens with hoppers and trays. She ordered twenty-eight pounds of bird seed and seven pounds of peanuts at a time. Each day in winter the baker brought a large brown loaf which was cut up into tiny squares for the birds. When the frog population became scarce, Gluck had three heated pools dug in the garden for breeding them. Mr Lovett then had to cut the grass with a handmower for fear of hurting them. They spread all round Steyning.

Gluck hoped that she would find in death the peacefulness that eluded her in life. She painted a series of tiny pictures, about thirteen by eighteen centimetres, and called them her 'Intimations', taken from Wordsworth's poem *Intimations of Immortality*. 'Cold Grey Stones' was of the tide coming in on the deserted beach at Worthing. 'Homeward' was a lone bird flying into the sunset. The sky, which figured so romantically in her early landscapes, becomes in her late paintings a cool haven. In 'Transience' a blackbird alights on a tiled roof, sings, and stays poised for flight, unconcerned by any domestic upsets beneath the eaves. Gluck felt dazzled by the sky when painting this. All her care for detail went into the lichens on the roof and the colours of the slates. Compared to the ornate portrayal of human justice in her portrait of Sir Cyril Salmon, it is a simple, calm piece.

Around her, life faded. Craig went totally blind. Each birthday Gluck sent her a parcel – a bed jacket, or a shawl, or Blue Grass perfume. Tybalt got cat flu, became limp and listless, died in October 1965 and was buried with great grief under the silver birch tree in the garden. Gluck and Edith endured the

Dialogue Crepusculaire, 1961
'Intimations': *Transience*, 1964

The Wave, 1966

Homeward, 1964

incapacities of age. Doctors were summoned at all hours – for shingles, heart pains, breathlessness and dizzy turns. Without her work Gluck suffered from frustration and despair:

I swerve between optimism and the deepest depression very easily. I do try to keep my eye on the ball – which is to get back to work, to my vision. But vision comes from a basic certainty and I am still far too easily wobbled.[16]

She needed from her work another triumph, another affirmation. Mercifully she found within herself another burst of creative energy. It earned her one last show and final accolade.

Requiem, 1964

Orchestra, 1967. 'This group of pansies never existed except in my inner vision and was built up by inner harmonies'

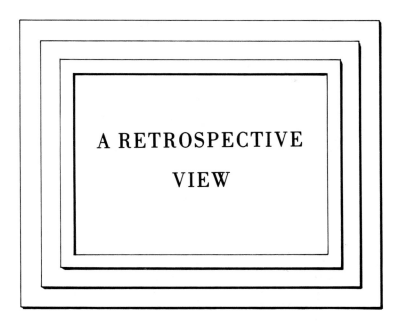

NINETEEN

A RETROSPECTIVE

VIEW

Gluck's perfect, hand-made paints were a challenge to her. She had to show her worth again. 'I cannot begin to tell you how marvellous it is to have such paints...' she wrote to Nesta (5 February 1970). 'Oh how I wish you could see them and share the thrill of genuine lapis lazuli and the feel of the paint on the brush.' In the late sixties she began to work with them, admitting to extraordinary nerves and depression at the task ahead. When, early in 1969, her friend the painter and art historian Martin Battersby spent an afternoon with her looking at her work from the thirties, she panicked at the contrast between her productivity then compared to the fallow years.

One of the first pictures of her renewed vigour, done in 1967, would have made Queen Mary drop her *lorgnette*. Called 'The Piper of the Merry Maidens', it was of a phallic standing stone near Lamorna. According to Cornish legend, The Maidens, a circle of stones near Lamorna, come alive toward midnight and sing strange songs about the sea. That summer, when staying down in the Dolphin Cottage, Gluck again painted the views she loved of Boleigh Farm and St Buryan at dawn; the same strip of land, huddled dwellings and wide sky, but more tentative than her early work and adding little.

For months she painted a jug of pansies on a marble slab. 'Feel so happy and contented,' she noted in a rare expression of joy. 'This group of pansies never existed except in my inner vision and was built up by unheard harmonies.'[1] Mr Lovett picked fresh pansies each day from the garden. In January 1967 she finished and signed it and made one of her by then infrequent visits for dinner at Gatewick. 'All out of tins and fizzy Portuguese rosé!!!'

Time was not on her side. Her hands were swollen with arthritis, she needed a hearing aid, she suffered attacks of vertigo, arthritis, asthma and bronchitis, insomnia and exhaustion. 'Feel very tired and depressed about future and my failing strength' was a typical diary jotting from 1968 on. She had a series of bad falls: in the attic at 2 a.m one morning when she hurt her ribs, in Cornwall when she hurt her knee, in her studio when she bruised her nose and sprained her wrist, on the studio path one snowy January day. In the early seventies a housekeeper, Winifred Vye, was hired to live in and look after Edith, who had become exceedingly frail. Edith tried to hide her disabilities from Gluck.

Mrs Mayer said she was horrified to see E. walking by Pecknell's. 'Had no idea she was so bad.' This was just before E. fell in yard.

Shocking report from A. about seeing E. peering in Alison's window. Used the word 'heartbreaking'.

Miss Vye scene at lunch with me re. E.[2]

The rows lessened, talk of breaking up ended and jealousy abated. Gluck's preoccupation with Anne Yorke faded, and months passed without reciprocal visits to the Chantry studio or Gatewick. Gluck watched Edith with a mixture of protectiveness, attentiveness and unconcealed impatience. Edith became forgetful and threw away the key to the wine cellar, lost her house keys, and forgot to attend to her financial affairs. Gluck took a sharp view of such absent-mindedness. Miss Vye tried to protect Edith:

I tried to shelter Edith from Gluck, but Gluck wanted no one near Edith but herself. One woman can dominate another and take over their lives. It was a love hate relationship. Edith believed in her but Gluck put her through a mangle. She wanted power and control of body and mind. She trusted nobody. Everywhere was locked. We used to do the housekeeping on Saturdays, Mrs Guy and I. One week I had the benefit of a halfpenny. Gluck said 'Go down and ask Miss Vye for the halfpenny she owes me.' . . . You can't say anything absolutely

bad about her because then she'd confound you and be nice. She was just very
difficult to live with. She didn't have a grip on her feelings . . . . Only Nesta
knew how to deal with her. It was a joy when she came to stay.[3]

Craig died in 1968 and Helen Beauclerck in 1969. The Maufes celebrated their diamond wedding in 1970 in their house, Shepherd's Hill, in Buxted, Surrey. Prudence wore a diamond tiara, and Edward sported a diamond brooch on his lapel. There were 160 guests, a choice of excellent sweet or dry champagne and 'the best fork luncheon' Gluck had ever tasted.

Only Nesta seemed eternally young. In 1968, as a very rich widow (Seymour lived until he was ninety-two), she moved from Hawaii to Switzerland and so visited Chantry more frequently. She lived in luxury in a house 'Le Tourbillon', in Vaud, not far from Lausanne, with devoted servants, a cat and a dog. She had a hide-out, a chalet in the mountains 'where the narcissi meet in great white waves in the spring'. She continued with her salon life, infinitely happier to be in Europe than Honolulu, and ever more sought after and adored. There were parties at the Villa Coward, inherited by Noel Coward's lover, Graham Payn. Ginette Spannier wrote to tell Nesta that the only nice thing about 1973 was meeting her. When Edward Heath was Prime Minister, Nesta dined on occasion at 10 Downing Street and he was a visitor at Le Tourbillon, as were Joan Sutherland, Joyce Carey, Yehudi and Diana Menuhin and a host of those with talent, rank or money. When Gluck and Edith were her house guests, Nesta insisted on paying Edith's fare, arranged for her to have a private sitting room and ensured that Monica Sterling, whose books Edith had years previously favourably reviewed, was among the guests.

Only Nesta could go on telling Gluck, right into old age, about her impossible behaviour:

. . . You interfere FAR too much in other people's business and none of your
arguments are anything but specious really. You mind your OWN business and
if small unpleasantnesses happen and people forget to do what you want, weigh
them against world importance AND GET ON WITH GIVING THE REAL
YOU A CHANCE.

. . . I wish I could forget, but I can't, that awful morning when some man
came and wanted to see Edith, and you stood at the garden door and angrily
screamed so that the whole neighbourhood could hear you. You were angry
because she 'hadn't told you where she was going!' Good God! What price
freedom? It was NOT YOUR BUSINESS to do anything but say quietly, 'I
think she may be in the garden. She probably won't be long. I'm afraid I must

*get on with my work.' NO ONE would have thought that rude. But your way
must have made the wretched man even more uncomfortable than it did me . . .*[4]

*I love you so very much and I can't bear to see you wasting so much of your
energy on useless fears, for you have so little time to spare! – hence my
abominable exasperation. Now. Do not waste your time writing or dictating
pages. Don't write anything. I understand all without any more word-flowing.*[5]

Gluck could not discard her imperfect feelings along with the machine-made
paints. The hardest cut of all was for her to see herself clearly. Among her
jottings about the Aga, the housekeeping, her medication, the frogs and the fish
in the ponds, paints, Steyning affairs and work in hand, she noted her state of
mind:

That cell of most terrible solitary confinement – my brain.

*We always know deep inside us what is right and if we go against this we
always pay for it, maybe years later.*

She went on campaigning, knowing how wasteful it was. In 1970 in the sub-
post-office in Steyning she saw a greetings' card of an ill-drawn girl with orange
hair and frilly knickers. It was designed by one Gluck for Royle Publications. 'I
can only tell you with absolute truth,' the true Gluck wrote to the solicitor,
Michael Rubinstein, 'that after first seeing this card I felt I would never be able
to sign my own pictures Gluck again, which of course I am now determined to
maintain my right to do after fifty years of use.' She had already written a
furious letter to the card's creator – a Mr Dickens of Acacia Gardens, Kent, who
had haplessly settled on the monosyllable as his nom de plume. 'I must', she
wrote, 'receive your immediate reply to this letter with your agreement that as
from its receipt you will:

1 *Cease using the nom-de-plume Gluck or Glück* in any circumstances.
2 *Notify Messrs Royle Publications Ltd to this effect.*
3 *Substitute another nom-de-plume for any of your work Messrs Royle
Publications Ltd may already have in hand for publication, signed either Gluck
or Glück, at the same time giving them a new nom-de-plume in substitution.'*

Mr Dickens answered in bewildered tone, calling her variously Gluck
Esquire and Mr Gluck, saying he thought that as his (her) style of work must
differ from his own he doubted there would be confusion, but that he was quite
prepared to make a feature of the umlaut, presenting it as two quite big little
circles.

Gluck bundled the correspondence off to Mr Rubinstein. He drafted a temperate and conciliatory response telling Mr Dickens that enormous confusion and damage had occurred and asking him to drop, once and for ever, the use of Gluck or Glück. Royle Publications agreed to stop using the name 'so long as it is quite clear that we are not admitting that you are legally entitled to claim this ... Mr Dickens proposes to use the name "Gluckli" on any new work which he does for us and perhaps you will let us know that what we have said in this letter is acceptable.' Unluckily for Gluckli it was not quite. Gluck wanted, and got, an assurance that the 'u' should have an umlaut, leaving Mr Dickens with the glottal stopper Glückli – an impediment almost as ugly as his cards. Mr Rubinstein told her firmly that he proposed to close his file and winged in a bill, ruefully acknowledging a considerable undercharge.

Despite such diversions Gluck achieved, in old age, two paintings which redeemed her years of battling over paints and showed that her talent was intact. These she called 'The Path to the Lough' and 'Rage, rage against the Dying of the Light'. The inspiration for 'The Path' was a landscape in Rosapenna, near Ballyclare, Northern Ireland, where Edith's cousin Dido lived: 'I owe you so much – you made it all possible.' Gluck wrote to Dido in 1969:

From when you first drove us to Rosapenna and gave me such a warm welcome at Fairview, everything I have dreamed of painting in landscape became released and I therefore owe you a great debt ...

She called the picture an allegory. The path is misty, winding, circuitous and uncertain, but leads ultimately to still water, calm mountains and light sky. 'I was for the first time utterly relaxed and peaceful when it was finished', she wrote to Nesta (14 August 1970), 'and felt it was the first picture I had ever painted that told *all* of my innermost thoughts and feelings – I can die happy if that picture survives.'

The picture was 51×76 cm inches and she enjoyed working with her new brushes on a larger surface. She signed it in 1969. She had promised it to the Bougheys, but had difficulty in parting with it and kept it for another year. Eventually Richard Boughey, whose brother, John, Gluck had painted shortly before he was killed in 1940, collected it at 11.30 on 8 August 1970. It fitted with difficulty into the boot of his car. 'Very sad about it going,' Gluck noted in her diary (8 August 1970). 'I mourned loss of picture by evening.'

Worthing Beach was the inspiration for the other outstanding picture of her old age. She and Edith used to take weekend breaks at the Beach Hotel. Room 88 on the third floor was their favourite, with its adjoining bathroom and view of the sea. Gluck spent days walking on the beach, talking to the bait diggers or sitting in the beach shelter taking notes and drawing. One cold evening in 1969, the beach was deserted.

Not only were there no people but the beach seemed scoured clean – no sea wrack, no rubbish, nothing. Then I saw in the distance this small patch of something light coloured, and when I went to look there was this dead fish's head lying just at the edge of the sea in a small depression with the tide coming in. I couldn't get it out of my head. The next evening – two tides later don't forget – I went back. And the head was still there, a little more stripped and skeletal and in a hollow a little deeper; and I knew I must paint it. For me, what had seemed a symbol of decay and death had become an emblem of resurrection.[6]

Its eyes were eaten away and it was surrounded by lug worm casts. She took photographs and notes, had the head posted to the Chantry and began painting it with its nose pointing toward the ocean. For a title she took the recurring line from Dylan Thomas's poem written to his dying father: 'Rage, rage against the dying of the light'.

It is a severed head with dark sightless chasms where its eyes had been. She was painting her death, the end of her vision as an artist, the loss of love, the wasted years: '...now that I am old and nearing the end of this life my homeland comes clear and it comforts me'. Her theory was that this beached creature was trying to get back to the sea. Into the worm casts, the scales and torn tendons of the fish and froth of the water, she put the same delicacy of texture and detail as in her flower paintings. Nesta thought she was sick and recommended a psychiatrist. Gluck worked at the picture from 1970 until 1973:

Very depressed about the picture and how long it is taking and whether I am achieving what I want or spoiling it.

Very worried *by outgoing sea bit and scrape it out. Cannot find what I want.*

Again tackle sea and again fail. Vote before starting work. Stay up till 4am because of election. Wash brushes at 3am with tv in bedroom.[7]

Again and again she wiped out and repainted the small stretch of sea to the left of the picture. As ever she could not leave it be and declare it finished. Edith thought it a masterpiece – the best she had ever done. Gluck asked Lovett how much he thought it was worth. He said £4000, and she agreed. Miss Vye admired it as a painting, but saw cruelty and loneliness in it and hated it for the

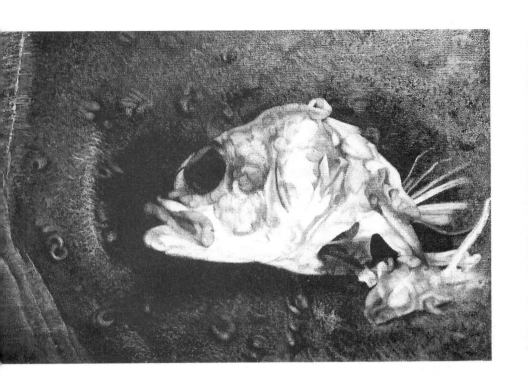

'*Rage, rage against the dying of the light*', 1970–3

cost to domestic harmony its creation seemed to exact. It was to be Gluck's last major picture, original, unexpected, technically superb, and with all her old flair of composition and verve.

In 1970 she repeatedly wrote to Nesta of her desire to have another exhibition and to 'come back just sufficiently as a painter before my demise'. She made a few tentative enquiries but found herself more or less forgotten by The Fine Art Society and other London galleries and she did not get very far.

I think really because I haven't got my Zgr to bite them all in the calf as of yore – I do so need someone to chat them up . . . I am certain the show would not only be

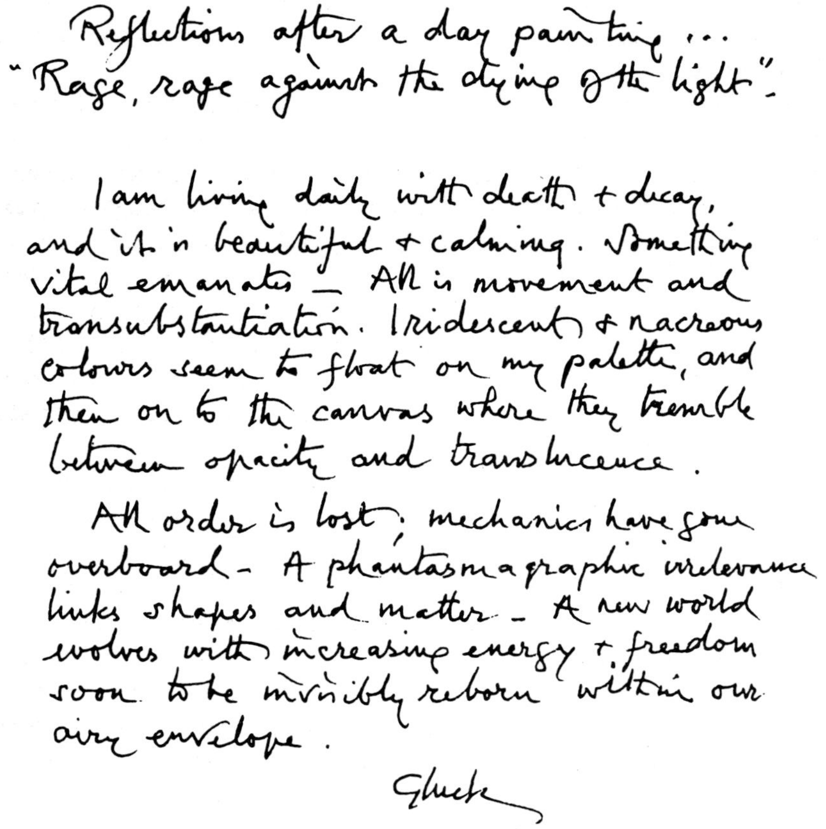

Reflections after a day painting . . .
"Rage, rage against the dying of the light".

I am living daily with death + decay, and it is beautiful + calming. Something vital emanates — All is movement and transubstantiation. Iridescent + nacreous colours seem to float on my palette, and then on to the canvas where they tremble between opacity and translucence.

All order is lost; mechanics have gone overboard – A phantasmagraphic irrelevance links shapes and matter — A new world evolves with increasing energy + freedom soon to be invisibly reborn within our airy envelope.

Gluck

Gluck's 'Credo'

a sell-out but give me some consolation before I die for all the years of frustration.[8]

She wondered if Nesta might help find a suitable room in a grand private house where she might show her pictures. She thought this would be away from 'the scrabble of normal exhibition stomping grounds' and 'almost Garboish'.

Nesta did not come up with anything specific, so Gluck went again to The Fine Art Society in 1972. 'As my last show was here in 1937, I think it is time we considered another', she told the gallery directors, Andrew McIntosh Patrick and Tony Carroll: They got out photographic records of her exhibitions in the 1930s and went down to the Chantry House for Sunday lunch on 14 May 1972. They saw that Gluck had managed to reacquire much of her best work and they offered her an exhibition then and there. They thought 'The Dying of the Light' a stunning picture.

For Gluck this was her resurrection, and the happiness of her declining years. She called the directors 'the boys'. They took her from the obscurity into which she had allowed herself to fade. 'This', she told them, 'will after all be my last one-man show and I would like to go out with a bang!'[9] Though she plagued them with her obsessions and demands, preparations for the exhibition, which was to be held in May 1973, were exciting and happy. The two men treated her with straightforwardness and affection. 'Very respectful reception', she noted of her next meeting with them in June, 'lunch in Andrew's flat 12–3.15.' Her brother Louis, delighted at this renaissance, arranged for cars to chauffeur her to and fro from Steyning to London and his children and grandchildren convened for a celebratory dinner at his house.

In June 1972 Gluck and Edith, who was getting ever more frail, spent three weeks in Switzerland as Nesta's guests. On her return to Steyning, Edith began evincing signs of extreme forgetfulness and confusion, and increasing loss of motor control. On a walk with Miss Vye her legs gave way and from then on she had to rely on a walking frame. It was difficult for Gluck too. She wanted to produce more pictures for her show and to involve herself in all preparations for it, but she could not put such acute domestic problems from her mind. Her anxiety and preoccupations made her, if anything, even more short-tempered with Edith. She finished a painting of a spray of myrtle and a shell, but it seemed to have no special significance, beyond the fact of buds bursting to reveal strange effervescent flowers. She was devastated when Tony Carroll did not want to include it in the show. Diplomatically, he told her she must keep some back for her next exhibition.

In November 1972, preparations began in earnest for the show the following Spring. Nesta called at The Fine Art Society, impressed them with her charm, told them she was 'whirling with contacts' and began putting the word about to her numerous influential friends. Gluck signed all pictures in her possession, advertised in *The Times* and *The Telegraph* to trace the whereabouts of those sold long ago, negotiated with a framemaker, worried about the lettering of the flag to be hung outside the gallery, the quality of photography in the catalogue, the design of the room, the publicity, and whether champagne or sparkling wine would be drunk at the party. She allowed no one to get on with their job without intervention from her.

She could not bring herself to say that 'The Dying of the Light' was finished, and she went on and on working at it. Worry took its toll and on a day in December, ten days before Christmas, when a batch of frames arrived all marginally the wrong size, when she felt 'hysterically overtired and strained' and the water tanks overflowed in the roof, she had a heart attack and was carried up to bed in a chair. Fearful of alarming 'the boys', she phoned and told them she felt 'as bright as a button'. She phoned David Tonkinson, too, and added a codicil to her Will asking for the exhibition to go ahead even if she died. Christmas – upon which, as with all feast days and holidays, Gluck set great store – was 'rather grim' that year. Edith and Miss Vye went to neighbours and Gluck stayed at home alone.

As the deadline drew near, Gluck became impossible. She drove 'the boys' to distraction. Publicity, she felt, was inadequate, the walls of the gallery and her frames were not going to match, the wrong picture was to be on the catalogue cover, some of her best pictures were not being given a showing, everything was under-insured, the exhibition was not running long enough, important decisions were being made without proper consultation with her, the invitation cards were too big for their envelopes. 'Go to London with Nesta. Go to gallery and make mayhem,' she noted on 26 March.

'Dear Gluck,' Andrew McIntosh Patrick wrote to her (9 April 1973),

time is getting short and we feel that the arrangements we have made with great care and professional judgement must not be confused at this stage. I would be much relieved to hear from you that you will leave it to us to look after our part of the arrangement – that is to handle promotion etc. – and you continue to paint your beautiful pictures. We have already talked about a second exhibition but quite honestly if we feel we do not have your confidence and consideration and if our way of working distresses you so frequently the whole matter becomes

much too difficult.
With the fondest and most respectful greetings – and to Miss Heald ...

They wanted her to feel happy and well-served, but not at the price of their own sanity. Nor did she risk sacrificing so valuable a relationship. She wrote screeds of critical memoranda which she had the good sense not to send.

A few weeks before the exhibition opened, Tony Carroll went down to Steyning and insisted on collecting 'The Dying of the Light'. Fifty-two of the best of her pictures were included in the show – a display that encapsulated her life and work: the portrait of grandfather Hallé, done in an hour, the drawings of Craig in Lamorna, the Cornish skyscapes, raindrops on the window panes of her studio in Earls Court, her self-portrait with cigarette, braces and quizzical sidelong glance, the old pony-stable studio at Bolton House, Sybil Cookson's daughter, the Cochran reviews, Constance's flowers, the Meteor in widow's weeds, Nesta's profile merged with Gluck's, the punt on the lake at the Mill House, the village hall at Plumpton, Edith doing her stint as a firewarden, the grand legal portraits, a bird flying into the sunset, a wave breaking on a deserted beach, the fish's head.

Her brother booked her a suite of rooms for a month at the Westbury Hotel, opposite the gallery. Banished by 'the boys' during the setting up of the exhibition, she peered at their activities from her hotel window and phoned through her criticism to them. Nesta arrived two days before the private view and stayed in a room adjacent to hers. She had sent more than thirty invitation cards to her friends. Queen Elizabeth The Queen Mother regretted not being able to see the show as she was off to Balmoral and would not be back until all was over. She said she well remembered Miss Gluck from when she called at Buckingham Palace in 1950 'to explain her anxieties about paint.'[10] A 'very private view' was arranged by the gallery for Sir Louis and his family, the day before the exhibition opened. He was appreciative of the invitation and unequivocally delighted at this late splash for his sister. She made it clear to the gallery that there were to be no special prices for him.

The private view was on Monday 30 April with a champagne party in the evening. The red leather visitors' book was out again. There were not many of her smart friends from the thirties – time had had its way – and no Queens, but still the showing was good. The Yorkes, the Simons, Salmons, Glucksteins and Neaves duly signed their names. And of course Nesta, delighted to see Gluck again in the swing. David Tonkinson, Gluck's accountant, for whom the show generated a great deal of more or less unnecessary work, said he had never seen

Gluck happier, in her suit, cravat and with walking cane, surrounded by people who admired her paintings. It was thought Edith would not be able to stand the strain of the party so after Nesta returned to Switzerland she came up with Miss Vye and both stayed a night at the Westbury. Prudence Maufe wrote that she and Edward were 'too old for any parties now, though we do hope very much to make an effort to see the show as we both enormously believe in Gluck – indeed I think that she has real genius and will live.'[11] In the event they put in an appearance: Prudence in a long black thirties dress, shuffling with a walking frame, Edward in a black cloak and having somehow lost an ear. Gluck was overwhelmed to see them there. 'Sometimes God can be so kind,' she said as they came through the door.

A newspaper strike, the day after the private view, delayed reviews. When they came they were full of praise. 'Gluck is a remarkable personality and her paintings are remarkable too,' wrote Marina Vaizey in a long and glowing article in the *Financial Times*.

At her best she is superb – exquisite flower paintings . . . small landscapes that are exquisitely stylised orchestrations of colour, kindly amusing little paintings of domestic scenes in the second world war, and above all else, portraits. . . . She combines a formidable sense of composition with a subtle use of colour to make paintings that are replete with vivid and living presences. . . . Based on observation of objective reality, linked to inner feeling, Gluck's work combines the highest professional skill and an indelible emotional quality that makes her work outstanding.

Gluck's fear of inadequate publicity proved groundless. There was a buzz of interest in her. Roy Strong, then Director of the National Portrait Gallery, came with two curators and bought the self-portrait she had painted in Plumpton when the YouWe love had failed. Virginia Ironside interviewed her for the *Sunday Telegraph* and Bevis Hillier for the *Connoisseur*. The *Illustrated London News* gave her a three-page splash and she got coverage in most of the daily papers. The *Paris Herald Tribune* called her a 'transcendentally gifted painter' who produced works of 'beauty and magnificence'. More soberly, *Architectural Design* wrote of how naturally, unselfconsciously and purely her sense of form captured the spirit of modernity of the twenties, thirties and forties – the 'Odeon style' of the 'Nifty Nats', the atmosphere of utility furniture and army canteens of her wartime pieces.

Gluck rejuvenated. Each day when the gallery opened she came over from her hotel, sat with her paintings and talked to all who called. Within days most of the pictures were sold. Katharine Hepburn spent a long time looking at the show and was impressed to see Gluck there. Friends called in and took Gluck off to lunch. Val Spry, who as Val Pirie had arranged the flowers for the white group 'Chromatic' and subsequently married Constance's widower, Shav, went to the exhibition, waited for Gluck and was warmly greeted by this now tiny, bent figure. 'We've some wonderful memories, haven't we,' Gluck said to her of those far-off thirties days. Edith wrote each day – droll, self-deprecating letters from stiff, arthritic fingers:

May 20th, 1973

Dearest Grub

Why did we suddenly stop writing to one another? My guess is that you were too busy and I was too dull. Here's wishing a good recovery to both of us.
This is an arthritic day, so my writing is bad as ever – and I have only small beer chronicles to report. We have a sunny day here – too bright to be ideally Aprilish. I can get no gardening done but Mrs Guy and Mrs Gurd went out on their own accord this morning and trimmed and tied up the rose that was flapping on the flower room wall.
Miss Vye conducted me to the bank in my horrid pulpit affair [her walking frame]. *She is feeding the fishes but will post this afterwards when she goes out with the dog.*
I would have liked to celebrate your return by hanging out flags and letting off fireworks, but suppose I must restrain myself.
I wish you could be keeping your suite at the Westbury. It would certainly make the Steyning dullness easier to endure.

Love as always darling Grub

from your Grub

Prices for the pictures ranged from around £300 to £4000 for 'The Dying of the Light'. 'Bettina' went for £1300, 'The Three Nifty Nats' for £1400, 'Pleiades' for £1000. Both Yvonne Mitchell and Patrick Gibson, Chairman of The Arts Council, wanted to buy 'The Dying of the Light', but Gluck would not part with it. After the gallery took its 33.3 per cent commission and settled her share of expenses, she received a cheque for £10,747 and four pence. As ever, she did not think money a fair exchange for her pictures. She would have preferred them to be in public galleries or in her studio.

A few days after the finish of the show, and before returning to 'the Steyning dullness', Gluck slipped in her hotel room alone at night and broke her right wrist. She suffered the pain until morning, then was taken to hospital. The next day she went home with her arm in plaster. It was a symbolic return, for her painting days were done and her broken wrist and swollen hand were the literal expression of this finish. Trivialities she professed to abhor consumed her attention again. Something was wrong with the Aga and Miss Vye was off on holiday. Gluck and Edith packed to spend the month of July with Nesta, the travel arrangements all seen to by Louis. It was to be Edith's last holiday. Nesta arranged for a physiotherapist to treat Gluck's hand three times a week: 'I am very upset to think that I shall perhaps be a nuisance over this but it is apparently crucial to my recovery for painting or even perhaps living', Gluck forlornly told her (11 June 1973). She still had the same unwavering desire to create, but the blaze of glory was over, though the longing for a truth she could live and the desire to reach the haven of death with a prize in her hand stayed with her until the end.

TWENTY

THE DYING OF THE

LIGHT

Romantic optimist that she was, Gluck hoped for new glory after the triumph of her 1973 show, as she hoped that after death would come redemption in the sky. The Fine Art Society directors were diplomatic about her future. They knew she was old, frail, inordinately ambitious and painted slowly. They also knew that hope about her work was her one antidote to depression. Realistically, a follow-up exhibition, though much discussed, was unlikely. She was nearing eighty, frail, arthritic, with a weak chest and troublesome heart. A number of unexhibited pictures, retained at the gallery, deserved a viewing, but there were not enough to match her comprehensive retrospective show. The mooted plan was for a new exhibition called 'Summing Up', based on a group of new paintings to do with the law. These would form the caucus backed up by existing pictures.

Gluck made a few visits to the Law Courts and took notes, but not much came from them. There were problems about organizing cars, arranging lunch, leaving Edith, and the exhaustion and disruption of it all. Her spirits plummeted when she realized how remote new achievement was. The 1973 exhibition was her swansong. It highlighted her talent, popularity and limitations – she had not and could not produce enough new good work to satisfy her public.

Her relationship with The Fine Art Society was though successfully re-established. She called it her second home. Andrew McIntosh Patrick and Tony Carroll visited Chantry, were liked by Edith and Miss Vye, sent large bouquets of flowers on Gluck's and Edith's birthdays and gave Gluck the warmest of receptions when she visited them in town. Her pictures were included in subsequent mixed exhibitions: 'Ernest Thesiger' and 'Mrs Sawyer' in a Christmas show along with works by Whistler, Turner, Lady Butler, Augustus John and Henry Lamb, and, in the gallery's centenary exhibition in 1976, Gluck's early drawings of Craig, 'Bettina' and 'Rage, rage. . . .' She wrote the catalogue note to an exhibition of Dod and Ernest Procter's work – her personal memories of them from her Lamorna days – and in 1976, an exhibition of Romaine Brooks's work included the portrait of Gluck 'Peter, a young English girl'. 'Have terrific reception', Gluck noted of her welcome to the party for this show. She sat beside her portrait, which intrigued visitors to the gallery.

Through The Fine Art Society, too, she met Keith Lichtenstein, an art collector and admirer of her work. He had bought many of the best of her paintings and invited her to see them in his home. 'How happy I felt', she wrote to him (4 April 1974),

when I saw my pictures looking so 'right' and at ease – I could not wish for a better home for them and it gives me a sense of peace to visualize them with you. How difficult it is to express such complicated emotions as are aroused by seeing, what is after all a part of one's self, in new surroundings, being understood and liked for all the right reasons which you have so sincerely expressed.

To Steyning friends she confided her sorrow at having parted with her pictures and her anxiety that, as so many of them were under one roof, some catastrophe might overwhelm them all.

He became a good friend and she referred to him as her patron. He talked to her on the phone almost every day, encouraged her all he could, sent roses on her birthday and on a weekend when Nesta was staying at the Chantry, invited her, Gluck, Edith and Miss Vye to lunch. Gluck intended to paint his portrait, but somehow no time was found. He urged her to shape her notes on painting, paints and the Gluck frame into publishable form and introduced her to a prospective biographer, Susan Loppert.

Gluck wanted her life in print, as she wanted her pictures in public galleries and her immortality assured. But she was too egotistical and authoritative for co-authorship. If anyone was doing the writing, she felt it should be she. For eight months in 1975 Susan Loppert drove to Steyning once a week to interview her. The meetings were amicable, if emotionally unrevealing. Problems arose over the drawing up of an agreement. They disagreed over the time needed to complete the book and over the division of anticipated profits. But the most serious stumbling block was the question of Gluck's editorial control. She wanted a clause stipulating that the manuscript be submitted to her for approval which would not be 'unreasonably withheld'. Susan Loppert feared such a clause might mean the right to bowdlerize whatever she wrote. Both negotiated through agents, but the differences proved irreconcilable and the project foundered.

Such continuing interest in her and her work shored up Gluck's spirits while homelife got ever more dismal. Edith had a series of bad falls and needed constant care. As with the Meteor's illness, Gluck again coped badly with a medical problem:

Feel might go mad or have coronary. . . . Bad day as usual. Try to get some work done but very nearly impossible. Feel very ill and desperate.

E. difficult beyond words ending with bad crash in bathroom which overthrew the mangle.

E. in serious condition. A total collapse. Dr Frank visits.

My birthday starts with terrible depression. E. has v. bad fall in her bedroom just before lunch. Is shaken all day.

E. behaves horribly all day.

After Miss Vye left to rest, E made to get up and lift clock off mantelpiece. Nerves gave way and I went to studio till teatime.

E. has several falls. Very wilful. Very bad night – stormy weather.

E. unmanageable. *Monstrous.*[1]

Gluck was unable to accept that Edith, who was embarrassed by her own frailty, could not overcome it. She was angry with her for it. She watched her every move and reprimanded her constantly – for trying to put a log on the fire, for not wearing her shawl, for spilling her tea. No doubt she watched because she cared, but it cannot always have felt like that to Edith. When Tony Carroll visited Chantry, on a bad day for Edith, alone with him she said of her painting by Stanley Spencer, 'Apple Tree in Snow', 'Do you think if I sold that I'd have enough to get out?' Gluck was unable to accept that time can wipe away a distinguished career and make a very clever woman very helpless. Nor would she leave the running of the house to those whom she had employed to do the work: Miss Vye, Mrs Gurd, Mrs Guy, Mr Lovett. As ever, she became consumed with all the material domestic matters she professed to hate.

Gluck's brother arranged for the installation of central heating and of a chair-lift up the stairs. A neighbour, Clare Griffin, came to work as a personal assistant, advising Gluck, listening to her, chauffeuring her, helping in the house, going to the bank to get her money – Gluck insisted on single pound notes, which she then put in drawers and forgot about. Gluck wanted to complete another rose picture and start the new law pictures, but she spent little time in her studio.

And Edith was fading. She became incontinent. Gluck, at her wits' end, responded without mercy. The doctor, seeing how badly they were managing, suggested Edith go into a nursing home. Edith heard of the plan and felt betrayed. Her confusion was intermittent, her problems those of mobility and motor control. Before leaving Chantry, her home for more than forty years, she systematically destroyed all the records of her life – her letters, diaries, writings. She tore up or burned basketful after basketful of papers. But the letters from Yeats she saved. On the red Charles Jourdan shoebox, containing Gluck's love letters to Nesta written in the 1930s, she left a note 'All lies'.

Nesta, eternally crystal, strong and uncomplaining, offered the promise of a kind of haven from such facts of life. 'It is not believable that Edith should have been so afflicted,' she wrote to Gluck in 1975.

You have been plunged most cruelly into Hell. When you can you must come to me and stay as long as you can. Any time. Suddenly – if you see an opening. There will always be room. . . . Darling Tim . . . I want you to feel you are not alone and if there's anything I can do, please, please tell me. . . . This letter is full of more than words.

Gluck agreed to the nursing home, but the decision filled her with ambivalence and guilt. As ever, the sacrifice was to the merciless and demanding god of Art: 'I do not know how her condition can be treated here safely . . .' she wrote to Nesta.

If she came back . . . I could never leave the house without fears and certainly it would finish any possibility of painting or creating any more . . . I was only just beginning to come back to some sort of feeling out of a suicidal numbness . . .

The nursing home, 'Homelands' was about eleven miles away at Cowfield. Edith was admitted there on 20 January 1975. It was well run, but she felt abandoned and lonely and in 'prison and pain' from having to use a catheter. Gluck found driving a strain, so Clare Griffin chauffeured her to the home – usually twice a week. In April Gluck was herself ill with a chest infection: 'Went to see E. first time for a month. A very worthwhile but heartbreaking meeting. She did not look well and had tears in her eyes when she saw me.'[2] On subsequent visits Edith seemed sad and forlorn: 'She called me back for the first time to say goodnight. This finally broke me.'[3]

Alone in the house, she said its upkeep was killing her, that it was dead to her without Edith, and she talked of moving permanently to the studio. She wrote one of her pithy, bitter little poems:

> I've had 'em large
> I've had 'em small
> I've had 'em short
> I've had 'em tall
> They're all the same
> What e'er the frame
> The first and last
> Are most steadfast

Steadfast Edith certainly was. And the last.

It was all too late to make amends. There were too many wrongs to right. It was not Edith's infirmity but her own that stopped Gluck from painting now. She had the place to herself, her perfect oils, her first-rate canvases. The Fine Art Society wanted any work of quality she cared to produce. The critics were as gracious about her work as in her heyday. She had shown, with the technical excellence of 'The Path' and 'Rage, rage . . .', that none of her ability had waned. Her staff saw to the cooking, the shopping, the cleaning. Her accountant managed her business affairs and negotiated on her behalf with her nephew, Roy, who had succeeded his father as Steward of the Fund. Money was there as needed. Her doctor, Richard Boger, the last in a succession of practitioners who tried to treat her, gave a great deal of his time. She still had, above everything, the ambition to paint good and lovely pictures. That was the altar on which so much else was sacrificed. But ever more by the day the pains of age prevented her from working.

In autumn 1975 she went for the last time to her cottage at St Buryan. 'Edith very sweet and glad I was going to Cornwall to create'[4] No creation came – she had an attack of emphysema and spent most of the time in bed. The rose, her favourite flower, that she was going to paint 'as perhaps no one has ever painted it before', wilted in her studio. And, to her dismay, she and Nesta suffered some kind of quarrel, which led to a coolness Gluck could not endure:

Whatever you do would never alter what has kept our friendship alive for over 40 years and so many thousands of miles apart. During the whole of that brief telephone call I was in tears. . . . Dearest Zgr can we not now return to the precious lien that binds our friendship and forget all the trivial misunderstandings that have, and are, causing me great unhappiness. I have as you know a heavy and increasing burden of responsibility to see that Edith does not die miserable and feeling, as she does, that everyone has forgotten and deserted her.[5]

In September 1976 Clare Griffin told Gluck that she was going to have a baby the following April. 'You've got one child, why do you want another?' was Gluck's unenthusiastic response. 'My sole means of transport was removed at a stroke,' she wrote to Martin Battersby. The following week Miss Vye said she would be leaving at Christmas. Her name had been on a council housing list since 1950 and now she had the chance of a flat in the nearby town of Storrington. Gluck panicked and saw herself without support. She immediately made arrangements to move Edith to a nursing home close by Chantry House in Steyning. 'We are not telling her anything in order to avoid upsetting her, but fear from something she said at our last meeting that she has an inkling but no details', Gluck wrote to the matron of the new home. Edith had been at Homelands for nearly two years. The staff knew her and were kind to her, the place was pleasant and efficiently run. The only virtue of Carisbrook Nursing Home was that it was close to Chantry. Edith was moved there on 11 October and died, in unfamiliar surroundings, a few weeks later, on 5 November.

Gluck had spent the previous couple of days in London. She had stayed at the Westbury and seen *Chorus Line* with Nesta and they had dinner together. On the way home Gluck visited Edith:

Leave Nursing Home approximately 5.45. Home by 6 pm. Lovett sees to luggage. . . . Miss Vye had supper downstairs and my drink was left in my

bedroom. I said I would put tray on landing. All this took place before 10.30.
Then I mucked about and at last exhausted got into bed but before lying down
telephone rang. Boger spoke. It was 11.15 pm. Rang for Miss Vye who helped
me put on some warm clothes over pyjamas and then waited for Dr B to fetch me.
We left Chantry House at 11.25 to go back to the Nursing Home.[6]

Gluck went into shock. For days she told no one of Edith's death. In the small hours of the night that Edith died, Miss Vye, on her way to her bathroom, heard Gluck crying and saying aloud, 'O Edith I'm so sorry. Forgive me.' The funeral was at Worthing Crematorium on Friday 12 November, a laurel wreath with no inscription or identification the sole adornment on the coffin. Gluck seemed not to recognize anyone at the funeral and spoke to no one. Edith's obituary in *The Times* referred to her friendship with Yeats, and spoke of her as one of the principal women journalists of her period. Her ashes were buried in Steyning churchyard alongside those of her mother and Nora.

Two weeks after the funeral Gluck suffered another heart attack. On Christmas Eve she felt 'unspeakably sad' as she stayed up late wrapping her presents and getting in a mess with the paper, labels and cards. On Christmas Day she lunched alone with Miss Vye who left for good the following week. Gluck bore no rancour and they stayed on visiting terms. After Miss Vye, there followed a succession of temporary housekeepers and after the housekeepers a succession of state-registered day and night nurses.

There was no more talk of painting now. Bow-chested with asthma, her heart none too certain, Gluck got through the days. On many occasions Lovett carried her to her bed, she grew so frail. The world was out of reach. She lay, sideways, across her huge four-poster so as to watch from her window the changing sky and the view of Chanctonbury Ring, the clump of beech trees on the South Downs that, in 1939, she and Nesta called 'YourOur downs'. 'Out of reach.' she wrote. 'One might as well expect to reach Katmandu or the top of Everest as the end of this bed.' She listened to Chopin and Debussy, ran the house from her room, and wanted to be gone. She likened herself to a tattered sail, shredded by the gales of life 'A blinding glimpse of sun, but promise there was none.' Along with jotted instructions about servicing the Aga, oiling the door locks, calling the piano tuner, planting the lobelias and feeding the fish, she asked for the end. 'My pain within', she wrote.

> Why could I not join the rout
> of wind and rain and sky and sun
> and tattered finally beyond repair
> cease to despair.

Again, and yet again, and then again – a pressing occupation for the last ten years of her life – she added codicils to her Will. When the codicils became too numerous, David Tonkinson began afresh and another Will was drafted. It became a document of assertion and, in its omissions, of vendetta. Her miniature silver paintbox, on a silver necklace, given to her as a child by Sir Joseph Lyons, was to go to the Victoria and Albert Museum; her easels and painting materials and bottles and tubes to do with her experiments on paint to the Artists' General Benevolent Institution; her books to the London Library; her Picasso bronze hand to the National Gallery of Scotland; her Kemmler grand piano and Amati violin to the Royal College of Music; her diamond horseshoe tiepin and coral bull's head tiepin to Anne Yorke's sons; her silver and jewellery to her nephews and niece; the drawings Munnings did of her down in Lamorna, in those heady years when she first realized she was an artist, the drawing Arthur Watts gave to her when they were neighbours in Hampstead, the Redouté watercolour of pansies and the Dürer engravings bought when she moved to Chantry; the drawings by Cocteau, Beerbohm and Leslie Blanch – all she carefully distributed, then redistributed, to her friends and relatives.

Only the young were to receive material reminders of her – there was nothing for Louis or Nesta. As for her money, there was no question of it reverting to The Fund. 'They don't need it,' she remarked. What she felt to be the injustice of her economic dependency, of being bound by her father's terms, of having to defer to her brother, had kept her simmering throughout all her years. She used her Will to settle a score. She wanted her much-loved cousin, Julia Samson, her great nieces and nephew and her faithful staff all to receive token amounts. The bulk of her money – and she had accrued some £90,000 – she was to assign, in equal divisions, to the Donkey Club, Wivelsfield Green; the Artists' General Benevolent Institution; The Royal Society for the Prevention of Cruelty to Animals; and the National Society for the Prevention of Cruelty to Children.

At Christmas 1977, Gluck endured a stroke which ravaged her physically, but left her mind unimpaired. She was dying and she knew it. Her brother, none too well himself, and his wife had booked to go to Switzerland for their winter holiday. Lady Gluckstein suggested they either cancel or go on the understanding that they would miss Gluck's funeral. They went on the trip. Gluck's cousin, Julia Samson, drove through the January fog from London to Steyning to see Gluck one last time:

We talked and had tea. She thought of me as young and her sensibility

wouldn't have let her make a young person sad. I said I'll come and see you next
week. She didn't say anything, just looked at me and her eyes were very very sad.
There was a passion there inside. Perpetual liveliness.[7]

There was no next week. Gluck died the next day on 10 January 1978. She
was eighty two. In her Will she stipulated that she wished to be cremated and to
have a non-denominational service. With religion, as with gender, she wanted
something singular. For her, God was the divine judge, Love the eternal goal,
Art, at its best, a linking of the two, and her own individual light the only clue to
follow.

To her nephew Roy fell the task of trying to organize a service she might have
wanted. He took her request for a non-denominational service to mean no
reference to God and no presence of clergymen. As a procedural guide, he
loosely followed the Liberal Jewish Synagogue form of burial. Those who knew
her, gave readings of passages and poems. She had asked in particular for a
reading of the words of Christian at the end of Bunyan's *Pilgrim's Progress*: 'I
leave my sword to him who can wield it. My scars I can take with me.'

Her brother, despite bad weather, ill health and his assurance to his wife that
they would keep to their holiday plans, cut short their trip to Switzerland to
attend the funeral. He took no part in the service, though his youngest son for
the first time ever saw him cry. Whether the tears were of grief or anger, who
knows. He was offended by her obituary in *The Times* which spoke of her
running away to become an artist, with half a crown. Nor did he realize, when he
saw her Will, which excluded all mention of him from it, that The Donkey Club,
Wivelsfield Green – one of the main beneficiaries of her fortune – was a hospice
for the incurably ill. To him it seemed like a scornful rebuff, the squandering of
funds, for what, he wondered, had she ever cared about donkeys. He spoke of
her stabbing him even from beyond the grave. He attended the gathering after
the funeral at the Chantry House then he and his wife tried to fly back to
Switzerland. All planes were grounded because of snow, and they were forced to
spend the night at Heathrow.

As for Nesta, Andrew McIntosh Patrick had told her of Gluck's death:

January 11th, 1978

Andrew, dear Andrew

How kind you were to tell me. I can never be grateful enough.
   It was a great shock.
   I'd had a long letter only about 3 days before . . . I'm not quite sure still

exactly when she died. Louis said it was easy, but I wonder –

She was so special wasn't she? – absolutely maddening – but so loveable! –

What will happen to all the pictures she left? I hope you get them. You and Tony made the whole difference to her life. It was a happy ending really – and it could have been, without you – such a sad one.

I'll see you when I come over –

Love and deep thanks

Nesta

Asked if there was anything of Gluck's she would like, Nesta replied, 'Oh, a few of her fine-haired brushes.'

Gluck's ashes were scattered in her studio garden. As requested in her Will, a thesis was commissioned on her battle to improve artists' materials and all her papers on it sent to Harvard University. At her request, The Fine Art Society staged a memorial exhibition. It ran for six weeks over the Christmas season in 1980. Again there was a splash of intrigued interest in her life and work. The *Sunday Times* colour supplement ran a six-page feature on her. The commercial value of her pictures began to rise.

'I have never yet been able to get from anyone a satisfactory answer to my constant question –' she wrote to Tony Carroll two years before she died:

What is the link? By what content would one recognise a picture was mine? I, of course am the last person to be able to answer such a question. So?? It will be too late for me when posterity decides.

In her oratorical style she spoke often of the exacting standards she set herself and of the heights to which as an artist she aspired:

. . . Feel that every work is your last and must say all you can of your feelings whatever your stage of development. . . . Just as no man shares his finger prints, so no man shares his heart or soul. All men are original if they are truthful, even though in that truth we must discern the common root of mankind . . .

That instant of Vision. That moment when you saw. Even as you look again, it is no more, no, nor ever will be. So it is you who by your emotional awareness and concentration can live for all eternity in a second of time.[8]

Behind the portentous tone was such a desire to do some 'good and lovely work' before she died. The best of her pictures have a simplicity and directness, a pure sense of harmony and form, a perfectionist use of colour and brushwork.

But aspiration and analysis aside, the cool, calm pleasure of her work, all that she left, as proof of having lived – Craig, perched on the rocks in Cornwall, Bettina, adjusting her hat, the gaiety of the Cochran reviews, Constance's white flowers, Nesta's face merged with her own at the opera, a patch of convolvulus with a grasshopper perched on it in the garden at Millers Mead, the punt on the lake at the Mill House, the turning tide in Poole Harbour, the sun rising at St Buryan, Edith dozing in the fire warden's office at one o'clock in the morning – all those moments and more, distilled from her life, have survived her, her proof of having been, the prizes she left behind, as fresh as the moment she perceived them, as undeniably her as the cadence of her voice, her demeanour or her smile.

Photograph of Gluck in 1973 by J. S. Lewinski

NOTES

BIBLIOGRAPHY

WORKS

INDEX

NOTES

'GLUCK: NO PREFIX, NO QUOTES'

1. Sheila Graeme, *Things Have Gone to Pieces*, Weidenfeld & Nicolson, London, 1970.
2. Gluck, Biographical Notes (undated).
3. Ibid.
4. Gluck, 'Credo', The Fine Art Society exhibition catalogue, London, 1973.
5. Gluck, Notes on the Philosophy of Painting, 1940.
6. Ibid.
7. Diary entry, 31 March 1957.
8. Gluck, 'On the Quality of Paint', *Tempera*, Society of Painters, 1969.
9. Gluck to Nesta Obermer, October 1936.
10. Gluck to Andrew McIntosh Patrick, 24 May 1972.
11. Gluck to Nesta Obermer, 22 January 1937.
12. Gluck, Notes (undated).

'THE FAMILY'

1. Yvonne Mitchell, *The Family*, Heinemann, London, 1969, p. 138–9.
2. Joseph Gluckstein to Mr and Mrs Louis Hallé, 8 August 1894.
3. Louis Hallé Gluckstein, Biographical Notes (undated).
4. Francesca Gluckstein, Biographical Notes (undated).
5. Joseph Gluckstein to Mr and Mrs Louis Hallé, 8 August 1894.
6. Francesca Gluckstein, Biographical Notes (undated).
7. Sir Harry Verney to Francesca Gluckstein, 11 October 1921.
8. Francesca Gluckstein, Biographical Notes (undated).
9. Ibid.
10. Louis Hallé Gluckstein, Biographical Notes (undated).
11. Gluck to her brother (undated, 1918).
12. Gluck, Biographical Notes (undated).

13. Ibid.
14. Ibid.
15. Laura Knight, *The Magic of a Line*, William Kimber, London, 1965.
16. Gluck, Biographical Notes (undated).

STAGE AND COUNTRY

1. Gluck, Notes on Landscape Painting (undated, 1940).
2. Ibid.
3. Gluck to her brother Louis (undated, 1918).
4. Ibid., 29 August 1918.
5. Ibid. (undated, 1918).
6. Gluck, Notes on Landscape Painting (undated, 1940).
7. Laura Knight, *Oil Paint and Grease Paint*, Nicholson & Watson, London, 1936.
8. Gluck to her brother Louis (undated, 1918).
9. Joseph Gluckstein to Louis, 12 October 1918.
10. Ibid.
11. Ibid., 8 July 1918.
12. Francesca Gluckstein to Louis, 8 December 1917.
13. Gluck to Louis (undated, 1918).
14. Ibid.
15. Ibid., 7 October 1918.
16. Francesca Gluckstein to Louis, 30 November 1918.
17. Gluck to Louis, 7 October 1918.
18. Evelyn Waugh, *Vile Bodies*, Chapman & Hall, London, 1930.
19. Gluck, Notes on Portrait Painting (undated, 1940).
20. Conversation with Tony Carroll, 15 January 1988.
21. Gluck, Notes on the back of a photograph of her painting of Romaine Brooks.
22. C. B. Cochran, *Cock-A-Doodle-Do*, London, J. M. Dent & Sons, 1941.
23. Ibid.
24. Ibid.

BOLTON HOUSE

1. Sir James Crichton-Browne, 'Reminiscences' (unpublished), 1932.
2. Crichton-Browne to Gluck, 30 November 1934.
3. By 1926 *Eve* was edited by Madge Garland, who subsequently became a close friend of Ivy Compton-Burnett.
4. Joseph Gluckstein to his wife, Francesca, February 1930.
5. Joseph Gluckstein to his son, Louis Hallé, 6 February 1930.
6. Gluck to her mother, 1931–6.
7. Motley, a team of three women costume designers, Elizabeth Montgomery, Margaret 'Percy' Hains and her sister Sophie, were, by the late thirties, the principal designers for John Gielgud, Laurence Olivier, George Devine and Michel St Denis.
8. Georgina Cookson to author, 6 April 1988.

WHITE FLOWERS

1. Elizabeth Coxhead, *Constance Spry*, London, William Luscombe, 1975.
2. Martin Battersby, *The Decorative Thirties*, Studio Vista, London, 1969.
3. Constance Spry, *Flower Decoration*, London, Dent, 1934.
4. Conversation with Val Spry, 16 March 1987.
5. Constance Spry, *Flower Decoration*, p. 3.
6. Gluck, Notes on Flower Painting, 1940.
7. Constance Spry, *Flower Decoration*, p. 7.
8. Lord Vernon to Gluck, 27 June 1933.
9. Gluck to Nesta Obermer (undated, probably January 1937).
10. Conversation with Val Spry, 16 March 1987.
11. Gluck to her mother, 11 July 1936.
12. Gluck to Nesta Obermer, July 1936.
13. Ibid.
14. Ibid.
15. Ibid.
16. Ibid.

THE GLUCK FRAME

1. Gluck, Notes on 'The Gluck Frame', undated.
2. Letters from Francesca Gluckstein and Sir Harry Verney, September and October 1932.

'YOUWE'

1. Gluck to Nesta Obermer (undated, autumn 1936).
2. Nesta Obermer to Liz Drury, 26 May 1981.
3. Conversation with Diana Menuhin, 10 January 1987.
4. Gluck to Nesta (undated, 1937)
5. Ibid., 15 January 1937.
6. Conversation with Tony Carroll, 6 January 1987.
7. Conversation with Liz Drury, 12 May 1987.
8. Gluck to Nesta, undated (1936 and 1937).
9. Ibid. (undated, 1936).
10. Ibid. (undated, 1937).
11. Gluck to Nesta, 9 January 1937.

ROOTS AND BRAMBLES

1. Gluck to Nesta Obermer, January 1937.
2. Ibid., 12 December 1936.

BLAZE WITH A FIRE

1. Gluck to Nesta Obermer (undated, 1936).
2. Ibid.
3. Ibid.
4. Ibid.
5. Ibid.
6. Ibid.
7. Ibid.
8. David Hicks to The Fine Art Society, 8 February 1973.
9. Conversation with Tom Parrington, 16 March 1987.

THE QUEEN WORE PEACOCK BLUE

1. Lady Clare Brooke to Francesca Gluckstein, 2 October 1937.
2. Sir Harry Verney to Francesca Gluckstein, 25 October 1937.

3. Lawrence Haward to Ernest Dawbarn, 17 December 1937.
4. Lady Helen Graham to Francesca Gluckstein, 4 January 1938.
5. Francesca Gluckstein to Lady Helen Graham, 7 January 1938.

'THE BRIND AND THE WHEEZE'

1. Conversations with David Yorke and Winifred Vye, January 1987.
2. Nesta Obermer to Francesca Gluckstein (undated, Spring 1939).
3. Airey Neave, who was murdered by the IRA at the House of Commons in 1979, was the architect of Margaret Thatcher's takeover of the Conservative Party from Edward Heath.

THE WAR EFFORT

1. Gluck to Nesta Obermer (undated, 1937).
2. Gluck to her mother, 16 August 1942.
3. Gluck, *The Petition* (undated).
4. Gluck to Mrs Bromley-Martin, 22 May 1943.
5. Virginia Woolf, *A Writer's Diary* (11 September 1940), Hogarth Press, 1954.

THE WAR WITHIN

1. Gluck to her mother, 16 January 1942.
2. Conversation with Liz Drury, 22 December 1986.
3. Clifford Musgrave to Gluck, 31 August 1944.
4. Wilfrid Greene to Gluck, 31 August 1944.

THE ETERNAL TRIANGLE

1. Edith Shackleton Heald, 'Women in Fleet Street', in Thomas Michael Pope (ed.), *The Book of Fleet Street*, Cassell, London, 1930.
2. Edith Heald, *Sunday Express*, 8 October 1925.
3. Ibid.
4. ESH, *Sunday Express*, 27 September 1925.
5. Sidney Dark, *Ivan Heald, Hero and Humorist*, London, 1917.

6. Conversation with June Casares, 26 November 1986.
7. Yeats to ESH, 18 May 1937.
8. Ibid., 4 September 1938.
9. Ibid., 2 August 1937.
10. George Yeats to ESH, 6 and 12 May 1938.
11. ESH to Mr Price, 24 August 1968.
12. James Agate, *Ego*, London, Hamish Hamilton, 1935.
13. James Agate, *Ego 3*, London, George Harrap, 1938.
14. Gluck to Bertram Nicholls, 10 January 1944.
15. Nesta to Gluck, September 1945.
16. Conversation with Marjorie Watts, 5 May 1987.
17. Gluck, diary entries, 1946.

YEATS'S BONES

1. Gluck, Notes for a book, 1940.
2. 'Alan' to Nesta Obermer, 30 August 1939.
3. Nesta to Gluck, 2 February 1959.
4. Duke of Buccleuch to author, 21 February 1987.
5. Nesta to Gluck, 4 August 1958.
6. Dulac to ESH, 27 June 1947.
7. George Yeats to Edmund Dulac, 9 January 1948, and transcription of phone call from him to ESH and Gluck, 12 January 1948.
8. Gluck to George Yeats (copy undated, but probably 2 March 1948).
9. Dulac to Gluck, 5 March 1948.

COSMIC INJUSTICE

1. Wilfrid Greene to Gluck, 7 August 1949.
2. Gluck, Notes on her mother's illness (undated).
3. Ibid.
4. Dr Barnet Solomons to Louis Hallé Gluckstein, 5 May 1950.
5. Gluck, Notes on her mother's illness (undated).
6. G. E. Woodroffe to Gluck, 21 April 1950.
7. Gluck to her brother, 5 May 1950.
8. Dr Solomons to Louis Gluckstein, 5 May 1950.

9. Julia Samson to Gluck, 24 May 1950.
10. Gluck to Pierre Jeannerat, *The Daily Mail*, 2 December 1942.

THE PAINT WAR

1. Gluck, 'The Impermanence of Paintings in Relation to Artists' Materials', Royal Society of Arts Lecture, 1964.
2. Gluck, 'The Dilemma of the Painter and Conservator in the Synthetic Age', Museum Associations Conference, 21 July 1954.
3. Ibid.
4. Ibid.
5. Ibid.
6. Nesta Obermer to Gluck, 14 June 1954.
7. Sir Gerald Kelly to Gluck, 30 January 1951.
8. Christine Leback Sitwell, 'The Dilemma of the Painter and Conservator in the Synthetic Age: the Paintings and Correspondence of the Artist, Gluck', Grant Thornton, Brighton, 1987.
9. Ibid.

LACUNA

1. Conversation with Mrs Guy, 26 November 1986.
2. Conversation with Hermia Priestley, 18 February 1987.
3. Diary entry, 5 September 1957.
4. Diary entries, 1955 to 1961.
5. Diary entry, 1 August 1958.
6. Diary entry, 26 March 1959.
7. Diary entries, 24 and 30 March 1959.
8. Diary entry, 25 March 1959.
9. Diary entry, 2 April 1959.
10. Diary entry, 19 March 1959.

11. Sir Cyril Salmon at the Old Bailey, 15 September 1958.
12. Diary entry, 12 August 1959.
13. Cyril Salmon to Gluck, 28 June 1960.
14. Diary entry, 10 June 1963.
15. Gluck, Notes (undated).
16. Ibid.

A RETROSPECTIVE VIEW

1. Gluck, Notes (undated).
2. Diary entries, August 1972.
3. Conversation with Winifred Vye, 7 January 1987.
4. Nesta Obermer to Gluck, 3 August 1973.
5. Nesta Obermer to Gluck, July 1973.
6. Ursula Robertshaw, interview with Gluck, *Illustrated London News*, May 1973.
7. Diary entries, 28 May, 17 and 18 June 1970.
8. Gluck to Nesta, 19 April 1970.
9. Gluck to Andrew McIntosh Patrick, 24 May 1972.
10. Lady Jean Rankin to Nesta, 7 May 1973.
11. Prudence Maufe to Tony Carroll, 21 February 1973.

THE DYING OF THE LIGHT

1. Diary entries, August and September 1974.
2. Diary entry, 4 May 1975.
3. Diary entry, 5 June 1975.
4. Diary entry, 23 September 1975.
5. Gluck to Nesta Obermer (undated, April 1976).
6. Diary entry, 5 November 1976.
7. Conversation with Julia Samson, 24 February 1947.
8. Gluck, Notes on painting (undated).

BIBLIOGRAPHY

Agate, James, *Ego 2*, Gollancz, London, 1936.

Agate, James, *Ego 3*, Harrap, London, 1938.

Battersby, Martin, *The Decorative Twenties*, Studio Vista, London, 1969.

Battersby, Martin, *The Decorative Thirties*, Studio Vista, London, 1969.

Cartland, Barbara, *We Danced All Night*, Hutchinson, London, 1970.

Cochran, C. B., *Cock-A-Doodle-Do*, Dent, London, 1941.

Compton, Susan (ed.), *British Art in the Twentieth Century*, Royal Academy of Arts, London, 1987.

Cooper, Emmanuel, *The Sexual Perspective*, Routledge, London, 1986.

Coxhead, Elizabeth, *Constance Spry*, William Luscombe, London, 1975.

Dark, Sidney, *Ivan Heald, Hero and Humorist*, Pearson, London, 1917.

Delafield, E. M., *Diary of a Provincial Lady*, Macmillan, London, 1930.

Fisher, Richard, B., *Syrie Maugham*, Duckworth, London, 1978.

Fox, Caroline and Greenacre, Francis, *Painting in Newlyn, 1800–1930*, Barbican Art Gallery, London, 1985.

Gluck, 'The Dilemma of the Painter and Conservator in the Synthetic Age', Museum Associations Conference, London, 21 July 1954.

Gluck, 'The Impermanence of Paintings in Relation to Artists' Materials', Royal Society of Arts Lecture, London, 1964.

Gluck, 'On the Quality of Paint', *Tempera*, Society of Painters, London, 1969.

Heller, Nancy G., *Women Artists: An Illustrated History*, Virago, London, 1987.

Hone, Joseph, *W. B. Yeats 1865–1939*, Macmillan, London, 1962.

Knight, Laura, *Oil Paint and Grease Paint*, Nicholson & Watson, London, 1936.

Knight, Laura, *The Magic of a Line*, William Kimber, London, 1965.

Mitchell, Yvonne, *The Family*, Heinemann, London, 1967.

Orioli, G., *Adventures of a Bookseller*, Florence, 1937.

Pope, Thomas Michael, *The Book of Fleet Street*, Cassell, London, 1930.

Secrest, Meryle, *Between Me and Life: A Biography of Romaine Brooks*, Macdonald & Jane's, London, 1976.

Spry, Constance, *Flower Decoration*, Dent, London, 1934.

Spry, Constance, *Flowers in House and Garden*, Dent, London, 1937.

Tuohy, Frank, *Yeats*, Macmillan, London, 1976.

Waugh, Evelyn, *Vile Bodies*, Chapman & Hall, London, 1930.

White, Colin, *Edmund Dulac*, Studio Vista, London, 1976.

Woolf, Virginia, *A Writer's Diary*, Hogarth Press, London, 1954.

WORKS ILLUSTRATED

Most of Gluck's paintings are in private collections. Dates and sizes are given where known. Measurement is in centimetres and height precedes width. Unless otherwise stated, the works are oil on canvas.

Black and white:

INDEX

References to illustrations are in bold type.